Joyce Cary:
Liberal Principles

JOYCE CARY:
LIBERAL PRINCIPLES

by
Cornelia Cook

VISION
and
BARNES & NOBLE

Vision Press Limited
11-14 Stanhope Mews West
London SW7 5RD

and

Barnes & Noble Books
81 Adams Drive
Totowa, NJ 07512

ISBN (UK) 0 85478 414 4
ISBN (US) 0 389 20201 0

To George C. Clark

Printed and bound by
Mansell Bookbinders Ltd.,
Witham, Essex.
Typeset by Chromoset Ltd.,
Shepperton, Middlesex.
MCMLXXXI

Contents

Preface

In preparing this book I have made extensive use of the Collection of the Papers of Joyce Cary and the Cary Collection of Printed Books in the Bodleian Library, Oxford. The large and invaluable Collection of the Papers of Joyce Cary contains all extant draft material for Cary's published and unpublished fiction and non-fiction, as well as personal notes and letters. Much of the material was the gift of Dr. James M. Osborn. References to material in the Cary Collection are accompanied by the classification number. Barbara Fisher's Handlist to "Files and Notebooks in the Manuscript Collection of Joyce Cary: a classification and analysis", of 1965, remains the basis of the notebook classifications, and a great aid to those who use the collection.

The Cary Collection of Printed Books contains Cary's own library. It is divided into three sections. Section A contains works by Cary and works or items about Cary. Section B contains books presented by their authors and books annotated by Cary. Section C contains the residua of Cary's library.

In quoting from Cary's holograph drafts, notes and letters, I have not altered spelling or punctuation. In such quotations, empty square brackets indicate an illegible word, and double square brackets indicate a doubtful word. I have not reproduced cancellations within quoted passages. Cary's hastily written "and" often resembles "d". I have rendered this "and" throughout.

In quoting from Cary's typescript drafts, notes and letters, I have corrected obvious typographical errors, to prevent annoyance. I have retained aberrations such as abbreviations, incorrect spelling and unusual punctuation which are more likely to express the man than the machine.

References to the novels are to the Carfax edition, with two exceptions. *Except the Lord* was not issued in the Carfax edition. References to *The Horse's Mouth* are to the authorised text, edited by Andrew Wright and published by George Rainbird in association with Michael Joseph.

I have chosen to offer a selected bibliography. A bibliography of Cary's published works has been compiled by Barbara Fisher and published in *The Bodleian Record,* VIII, no.4 (April 1970), pp. 213-28, and in *Joyce Cary: The Writers and His Theme* (Colin Smythe, 1980). I have therefore listed only works of Cary's cited. Novels are listed chronologically. I have listed those other works consulted in Cary's library and at large which have directly contributed facts or understanding.

Acknowledgements

I thank Mrs. Winifred Davin, Cary's literary execturix, for her generous help, encouragement, and time. And for their kind assistance and goodwill I thank Professor Dame Helen Gardner, Dr. J. I. M. Stewart, Professor A. G. Bishop, the late Professor Norman Callan, my colleagues at Queen Mary College, Mr. Philip Bull and the staff of the Bodleian Library, particularly Mr. D. S. Porter. The oldest debt is to Ben Reid. I gratefully acknowledge the financial support and confidence of the Danforth Foundation. And I thank P.R. Cook.

1

Introduction

> The grand, leading principle, towards which every argument unfolded in these pages directly converges, is the absolute and essential importance of human development in its richest diversity — Wilhelm von Humboldt, *Sphere and Duties of Government*
>
> Epigraph to J.S. Mill, *On Liberty*

With clarity and forcefulness Joyce Cary's novels explore the themes of creativeness, power, freedom and their manifestations in the world. Recurring character types, plots involving the problems of historical change or of a character's displacement in society, and the fascinating milieux of art, politics or religion give form in his novels to Cary's carefully developed ideas which find exposition or explanation elsewhere, in such non-fiction works as *Power in Men* and *Art and Reality*.

These ideas began to assume coherence in the years of varied activity and education and in the vast quantities of unpublished, destroyed, or rejected work which preceded the publication of Cary's first novel in 1932. When he wrote *Aissa Saved*, according to his own accounts, Cary had confronted a significant problem of man's relationship to his world. "I had realised the fundamental injustice of the world. It had 'come home' to me".[1] This realisation was instrumental in shaping Cary's view of the world's character as "free and therefore diverse and unpredictable".[2] Its implications, widened or clarified by further periods of study and self examination, provided Cary with a theme and plots for all his future works of

11

fiction.

A world free and harbouring injustice, diverse and unpredictable, sounds like a dangerously disordered world. But Cary's notion of an active Bergsonian world of incessant creation or ever-present change is qualified throughout his writings by a set of principles which bring to it the order of purpose and optimism. These principles put a positive construction on freedom, regard injustice as an intimation of a necessity which — though inevitable — allows of tranformation, and regard diversity as a source of enrichment. Seeking to extricate the predictable from the unpredictable in the world's character, these principles make the latter the grounds for hope in progress and the former the agent of progress itself. The principles according to which Cary translates a theoretical idea of man into practical modes of conduct to promote the happiness of individuals and the betterment of their world are those of liberalism.

Cary's liberalism is both philosophical and political. Although he did not become a Liberal Party member, and declined an invitation from the Liberals to contest a Parliamentary seat, Cary contributed to the literature of Liberal opinion in his essays and several longer volumes, including one written for the Liberal Book Club. The themes of his novels present a sustained effort to convey and criticise the principles of liberalism, and reflect a continuing and increasingly focussed interest in the history of the Liberal Party in Britain.

To call attention to this bias is not merely to highlight an aspect of Cary's fiction, but to name the primary thematic principles of that fiction and to assert that Cary's major achievement as a writer — an achievement which should designate him a major figure among modern writers — is the realisation of a lively, significant fiction with a serious liberal bias.

Cary may be compared as a liberal to other writers of the age. In his display of the elements of comedy, realism and humanism which Malcolm Bradbury finds in "liberal" writers of the fifties,[3] Cary is akin to this generation which read him at the height of his popularity. On the other hand, Cary's Edwardian and Colonial settings remind us that he belongs to the generation of the major liberal novelist of the early years of the century, E. M. Forster. But while Forster's fiction speaks from an earlier age, idealising a liberalism that is past, or passing — or seemingly not to come, Cary discovers and urges a liberalism of the present and future. Where the Forsterian idealism quails before a humanity seemingly *doomed* to imperfection and compromise, and consequently distorts reality by envisaging improbable characters or implying inevitable failure, Cary's books derive vitality and optimism from a sense of *discovery* of the resourcefulness of human nature in its dealings with a fickle reality, and from a spontaneous, hearty delight in human character.

The marks of Cary's fiction and of his position as a liberal novelist are his emphasis on character (especially self-revealing character), which displays and affirms a potent individualism, and a commitment to the free expression of conflicting opinions, which challenges the reader's judgement while widening his experience. Cary learned not to make his characters "illustrations of general laws",[4] but to let them live in the unpredictable world of real experience, enacting the multiform nature and needs of that world, read — in a *tour de force* of liberal method — in a context of conflicting desires and opinions through uncensorious liberal eyes. Only in the whole composition of each fictional experience does the author's commitment to individualism, self-fulfillment, freedom and progress manifest itself as the shaping ideology of the art. Further, Cary's novels yield, along with an expression of liberal principles, a fascinating picture of Liberal politics in late nineteenth and early twentieth century Britain and at large in a changing British Empire.

Cary called himself a liberal and in doing so allied himself with a tradition the origins of which he traced to "the Protestant tradition, and the Whig revolution of 1688 with its [Lockean] ideals of toleration and individual right", and which, he said in 1955, had characterised the "dominating mind" of Britain "for more than a century".[5]

The liberalism that came to dominance in the nineteenth century was eclectic but critical in its relationship to its philosophical and religious progenitors, undogmatic but passionate in its commitment to liberty and human dignity, and alive to contemporary material and cultural changes in Western society which called for reassessment of traditional modes of government. The evolution of a heterogeneous community of republicans, radicals, and reformers into a Parliamentary Party pledged to the independence and betterment of individuals and communities, which called itself Liberal, was the major political development in Victorian Britain.

The philosophy of British Liberalism — and the basis of Cary's liberalism — is pre-eminently that enshrined in the writings of John Stuart Mill in the mid-1800s. Mill's theory derived from Protestant and Humanist beliefs in progress on earth, from the empiricist and individualist theories of John Locke and the related schemes of the Utilitarians, coloured with idealist shades from continental thinkers and romantic revolutionaries. Mill named the individual the most important element in society — more important than the state which properly existed only to ensure the individual the greatest possible opportunity for self-fulfillment. Human nature, Mill said, after Locke and Bentham, is essentially reasonable; individuals allowed to express this nature fully would inevitably act wisely to improve themselves and achieve the common personal and social aim of general happiness. It was no accident that Cary's first serious attempt to portray the history and thought of liberalism in fiction was a projected trilogy to be entitled "They Want to be Happy".

Conscience, not authority, was the source of the wisdom which guided the pursuit of happiness. Conscience and reason would see that an individual best safeguards his own happiness by insuring the happiness of others. Education was essential to the cultivation of these faculties. Law and government Mill deemed necessary to effect the aim of happiness. Government must actively secure freedom of thought and expression and provide opportunity for growth, without dictating the direction of that growth.

In Mill's view, reason was not man's only gift. From his own experience of the importance of feeling and from romantic writers, he had gained a regard for individual creative power— "imagination". The Utilitarian aim of general happiness had, in his view, to incorporate this irrational power and the varieties

14

of its expression. Hand in hand with wisdom—capable of blending the lessons of experience with a thirst for greater fulfilment—such creative power was the source of constructive progress.

Education was for Mill—as for all liberal thinkers—the key to uniting imagination, achievement, and happiness. This belief is fundamental to Cary's liberalism and central to his fiction. In *Castle Corner* his liberal spokesman calls education "the only real revolution anywhere" (*CC*, p. 111).

Mills' emphases on freedom of expression and development, individualism, happiness and justice, and indeed elements of his rhetoric, were retained in the comments of liberal thinkers and politicians throughout the remainder of the nineteenth century and into the twentieth. In 1877 a commentator on "Liberal Principles" named the principles which all liberals—however divergent their practice—shared: Progress, love of Freedom, Self-government, Equality before the law, respect for human nature, Political Justice, and preference of national interests over minor interests.[6] Writing on the New Liberalism in 1920, C.F.G. Masterman qualified Mill's thought only by his more pragmatic emphasis, calling Liberty the fundamental principle and "human betterment" the aim of the New Liberalism, and naming as its guiding activities the strife against the poverty and narrow national interests which thwart the growth of men and nations, the encouragement of right choice through freedom of experience, and the active belief in "a manifest progress" fostered in the climate of "an educated and enlightened Democracy".[7] In 1927 Walter Runciman headed a list of the theoretical and practical bases of Liberalism with "Individual freedom, Social Loyalty, Education . . . ."[8] And Cary's own critical treatise on the nature of freedom, *Power in Men*, reveals by the emphasis of its three organising headings—"Power in Men, as Liberty . . . Democracy . . . Education"—its adherence to traditional liberal principles even while it criticises or qualifies their interpretation.

Mill's writings gave liberalism a method for seeking truth and a rhetoric as well as a statement of principles. These, too, are germane to Joyce Cary's fiction. Truth had to be drawn with an open mind from a welter of opinions and an ambience of shifting historical conditions—through experience and

15

argument. The principle of freedom of expression had descended to Mill through Milton and Locke with, as John Morley pointed out,[9] ever expanding scope. Mill's statement of the principle is worth quoting, for Cary annotated it in his copy of *On Liberty* and one can descry in it the basis of Cary's method in fiction.

> He who knows only his own side of the case knows little of that. His reasons may be good, and no one may have been able to refute them. But if he is equally unable to refute the reasons on the opposite side; if he does not so much as know what they are, he has no ground for preferring either opinion . . . Nor is it enough that he should hear the arguments of adversaries from his own teachers, presented as they state them, and accompanied by what they offer as refutations. That is not the way to do justice to the arguments, or bring them into real contact with his own mind. He must be able to hear them from persons who actually believe them . . . He must know them in their most plausible and persuasive form, he must feel the whole force of the difficulty which the true view of the subject has to encounter and dispose of; else he will never really possess himself of the portion of the truth which meets and removes that difficulty. . . .[10]

Again Cary annotated Mill's reason for so championing free expression:

> The peculiar evil of silencing the expression of an opinion is, that it is robbing the human race; posterity as well as the existing generation . . . If the opinion is right, they are deprived of the opportunity of exchanging error for truth; if wrong, they lose, what is almost as great a benefit, the clearer perception and livelier possession of truth, produced by its collision with error.
>
> (*On Liberty*, p. 79)

How provocative must Mill's remarks have been to the novelist; how fertile their implications for Cary's fiction. Mill lamented that the majority of educated men "have never thrown themselves into the mental position of those who think differently from them, and considered what such persons may have to say" (*On Liberty*, p. 97). Cary's method finds its blueprint in the words of the political theorist:

> . . . any person whose judgment is really deserving of confidence . . . has felt, that the only way in which a human being can make

16

some approach to knowing the whole of a subject, is by hearing what can be said about it by persons of every variety of opinion, and studying all modes in which it can be looked at by every character of mind.

(*On Liberty*, p.82)

To pursue truth through the penetration of varying characters is Cary's method—developed through the single character focus in *Mister Johnson* and *Charley is My Darling*, the juxtaposition of antagonistic or complementary pairs of characters in the African novels, *Castle Corner*, *A House of Children* and *The Moonlight*, and triumphantly realised in the first person narratives of the first and second trilogies.

Chester Nimmo's experience in *Except the Lord* is a religious and political pilgrimage to that reverence for truth and that understanding of the complexity of truth which were the fruits of Mill's philosophical searchings. Nimmo's evangelistic rhetoric recalls that of Mill's disciple L.T. Hobhouse, as Hobhouse's own echoes Mill in its tone of fluently persuasive argument.

> Liberalism applies the wisdom of Gamaliel in no spirit of indifference, but in the full conviction of the potency of truth. If this thing be of man, i.e. if it is not rooted in actual verity, it will come to nought. If it be of God, let us take care that we be not found fighting against God.[11]

Joyce Cary's sensitive ear and his immersion in the literature of liberalism often bring to his novels such genuine tones of liberal rhetoric. Mill borrowed the metaphor of organic growth and cultivation from the romantics and Carlyle (and uses it pre-eminently when speaking of development of the sympathetic feelings and imaginative or artistic perception). "The cultivation of the feelings became one of the cardinal points in my ethical and philosophical creed", he reports in his *Autobiography*,[12] and in *On Liberty* he asserts that

> Human nature is not a machine to be built after a model, and set to do the work prescribed for it, but a tree, which requires to grow and develop itself on all sides, according to the tendency of inward forces which make it a living thing.

(p. 117)

Such a metaphor is integral to the language of his followers. Masterman refers to the era of Mill and Gladstone as the days in which "were sowed the seeds of the emancipating and reforming processes"[13] of liberation, and in the desperate days of liberal eclipse, Lloyd George makes liberalism itself—as representative of the best of human impulse and political practice—the object of cultivation: "Liberalism is a cultivated plant. If you leave the ground without being ploughed, fertilized, weeded, or sown it will become the battleground of anarchy and sterility."[14] Chester Nimmo, recounting the struggle to wholeness of his own soul, makes his central Liberal principle "freedom which is room to grow".[15]

Although he characterised his age as one of faith undermined, Mill was confident of the human capacity for growth, confident in an expanding human possession of truth, and in progress in well-being. He derived an optimism from his faith in human perfectability, ". . . a quality of the human mind, the source of everything respectable in man either as an intellectual or as a moral being, namely that his errors are corrigible" (*On Liberty*, p. 82), from his belief in individual liberty as "the chief ingredient of individual and social progress", and from his confidence in the liberal-utilitarian theory itself as an improving set of principles:

> The corollaries from the principle of utility, like the precepts of every practical art, admit of indefinite improvement, and, in a progressive state of the human mind, their improvement is perpetually going on.
>
> (*Utilitarianism*, p. 22)

Later liberals shared his faith in progress and saw Liberalism itself as its guide. Thus Masterman calls Liberalism "a broad road of travel along which may walk honest pilgrims through the confusion of life",[16] and Hobhouse, remarking that "Every constructive social doctrine rests on the conception of human progress", too, sees that progress as the product of the intellectual and spiritual elements in human nature acknowledged by a romantic liberal individualism: "The heart of Liberalism is the understanding that progress is not a matter of mechanical contrivance but of the liberation of living spiritual energy".[17]

Cary's fiction repeatedly asserts this faith in progress: in Sara Monday's life of recurrent amendment and renewal; in Gulley's Jimson's artistic "liberation of living spiritual energy" and his love of starting again; in Thomas Wilcher's impulsive recognition that "We must renew ourselves or die"; in *A Fearful Joy's* enactment of the spirit and manifestations of Edwardian progress; and in Chester Nimmo's realisation—the realisation that makes him loyal to the Liberalism he served and fills him with "faith" and "hope"—that "man is a mystery and his destiny is hidden in a depth of time beyond imagination", but that "the conscience of a nation"—that is, the common conscience of its individual members—can bring about social justice.

Nimmo's remarks, referring to a specific political incident, and the importance Cary attached to the actual political scene in the second trilogy, remind us that British Liberalism is not solely a matter of theory. It has evolved from the interaction of formulated ideals with personalities and with practical responses to immediate problems. After the reforming Whig aristocrats and Protestant individualists came wealthy industrialists seeking material progress and Nonconformists seeking liberty under its countenance. The former of these coloured liberalism with altruism; the latter, with radicalism. The presence of these forces within liberalism often distorted Mill's theory—retaining religious belief along with his humanism; swamping his anti-authoritarian and gradualist stances in waves of Imperialist fervour and popular reform. Mill's insistence on minimum government, at first adduced—with Benthamite notions of freedom as absence of restraint—as a basis for the principle of *laissez faire*, ultimately gave way to the New Liberalism, with an emphasis on constructive restraint, of the twentieth century.

The Liberal Party, officially designated as such in the 1830s was a growing, changing phenomenon throughout the nineteenth century. As Mill was its evangel, Gladstone was its presiding figure, and deserved this representative title, for it was he, pre-eminently, who translated the principle which Mill had enunciated,

> A being of higher faculties requires more to make him happy
> . . .he can never really wish to sink into what he feels to be a lower

19

grade of existence. We may give what explanation we please to
this unwillingness . . . but its most appropriate apellation is a
sense of dignity, which all human beings possess. . . .

(*Utilitarianism*, p. 8)

into the practical promotion of individual power and liberty in
the areas of work and earnings, education, religion and politics.

Gladstone was not the initiator of a Parliamentary liberalism
with a broad popular base; his effectivness was in consolidating
the influences, practical, theoretical and Parliamentary, of such
figures as Cobden, Bright, Mill, Palmerstone and Russell, and
in acquiring an increasing degree of popularity with the varied
sections of the community which formed the local sources of
Liberal support. Gladstone became representative of an
individualistic moral earnestness which more than any
coherent theory united Liberalism's supporters. He preserved
the Christian element in liberalism and, through his own
idiosyncratic affiiliations with its patrician past, its progressive
enthusiasms, and its popular libertarianism, seemed himself to
embody an ongoing tradition. Committed to Liberalism's ideal
of full humanity, Gladstone presided over a period when the
ideal seemed accessible, compassing, as the mid-nineteenth
century did, the most striking growth in political education and
popular articulateness the English people at large has known.
Gladstone, by his wide popularity and his party's emphasis on
responsibility and participation, was instrumental in lifting the
basis of political Liberalism from local interests to a national
consciousness, of whose emphasis on freedom, wisdom and
diplomacy he appeared the epitome.

A recent commentator has observed that "between 1860 and
1920 it was generally accepted that, whatever actually
happened in politics, the 'principles of Liberalism' were a
miscellany of vague humanitarian enthusiasms chiefly for the
relief of the individual from metaphysical rather than material
distress", that "the national party, as it began in the 1860s, was
not an organisation, but a habit of co-operation and a
community of sentiment."[18] Collected statements of Liberal
supporters throughout the period certainly support this
judgment.[19] But Liberal legislative policy and practice in the
Gladstone era is recognizably the offshoot of its traditional
theoretical bases, emphasising education, toleration, increased

enfranchisement, land and tax reform, free trade, and—until perverted by runaway Imperialism—commitment to the integrity of nations and their freedom of self-development.

Liberty, erected by Mill as the central Liberal principle and the continuing aim of Liberal political endeavour, proved the concept towards which the greatest shift in post-Gladstonian Liberal thought occurred. Freedom as absence of restraint revealed itself in times of economic stringency as inadequate to the cultivation of "full humanity" and the achievement of social justice. Cary's *Power in Men* is a late echo of the criticism of *laissez-faire* which issued from Edwardian liberals and guided the steps of practical politicians at the dawn of the twentieth century.

The Edwardian years brought to birth the New Liberalism— with a social democratic rather than a *laissez-faire* orientation. At their commencement the party was divided and embittered. Rosebery, grown too conservative for the majority of Liberals, had resigned the party leadership in 1896, and in 1898 Gladstone had died. Liberals split over the Boer War and the nation viewed their discomfiture in disunion. But 1902 brought the end of the war, and Liberals regrouped in opposition to Balfour's Education Act of 1902 and current legislative treatment of unions, while disunion—precipitated, ironically, by Chamberlain's "Tarrif Reform" campaign against Free Trade—tore through the Conservative government in its turn. At this time the composition of the Parliamentary Liberal Party had gained in Nonconformist, anti-property strength. Education and enfranchisement had widened the party's lower-middle class support base as the Parliamentary stipend drew the people and their representatives closer in character. Social welfare and education were uppermost among the aims of such members. The Liberal landslide of 1906, therefore, which brought the Campbell-Bannerman Government to power, precipitated a period of momentous change in the thought and social architecture of Britain.

C.F.G. Masterman describes the difference between the Old and New Liberalisms, emphasising both continuity of aim from the achievements of the Old to the objects of the New and the contrast in means advocated.

The older Liberalism was, perhaps, too much wedded to a

21

theory. That theory was that the betterment of mankind would be best attained by freedom of opportunity, freedom of trade, freedom of competition, the removal of all artificial bonds of exaction and enslavement which man had laid upon man. They believed in this enfranchisement as "progress"—that any other way meant disaster in which the poor themselves would be the greatest sufferers ... When Gladstone, as Chancellor of the Exchequer was tearing down tariffs, taxes on light, taxes on knowledge (despite the opposition of the House of Lords), or as Prime Minister constructing a national education system, or extending factory law and measures for the protection of women and children, he and his followers were concerned with but one object only—the warfare against conditions of material disablement which pressed so cruelly on the masses of mankind . . .

And if the New Liberalism is driven now to demand a supplementing of that work by a more direct and State-organised attack on poverty, it is not with condemnation of the marvellous results already attained.

The Platform of the New Liberalism Masterman described as based "on four strong pillars".

It is proposed to ensure for all men and women: (1) Wages adequate to the maintenance of efficient life in modest comfort, with the decent upbringing of children; (2) hours of work so limited that time is provided outside this period of drudgery for happiness, self-improvement, and the free existence of a human being with all human beings need; (3) a decent house and, where possible, a piece of ground as a garden with it ... and (4) provision against those periods of unemployment which are produced by fluctuations of the world market. . . .[20]

Old age pensions, National Insurance, Lloyd George's land campaign, the acceptance, growth and politicization of trade unions, and the widening of educational opportunity were signs of the influence of the New Liberalism in the Edwardian years. Ultimately, Liberal achievements in social reform were small, but the concepts which motivated them destroyed the assumptions which fixed the British social hierarchy.

Ironically, Liberalism suffered in the change. The alliance of altruistic intellectuals, workers demanding power, education and increased sustenance, and passionate religious individualists was a tense one. Fears of moving too far too fast conflicted with frustration at the failure of progress to realise a new world. The freedom sacred to individualists clashed with the justice demanded by social planners. The Liberal party was ultimately brought to disarray before the organised ideological challenge of the post-war socialists.

These events fascinated Joyce Cary. Again and again he turns in his novels to the events of these changeful years. Nearly all Cary's novels from *Castle Corner* to the Nimmo trilogy are set in the period between 1880 and the 1930s. All fit into a distinctive pattern, linked not only by the romantic-humanist theme of the individual as creator and the utilitarian theme of individual desire as the foundation of social progress, but also by an effort to identify and characterise the nature of the time itself. Cary memorably registers the drama of the transition from the world of the Old Liberalism to that of the New and the succeeding drama of the decline of Liberalism from the moment of its Edwardian acme. The political interest is clear in *Castle Corner* and the Nimmo trilogy; a special group, *A House of Children*, *To Be a Pilgrim*, *A Fearful Joy* and *The Moonlight* composes a fascinating study of Edwardian society at large.

To focus Cary's interest in this era of change and his relationship to liberalism, it is helpful to understand something of his experience as a child of the Edwardian era and something of that phase of history itself.

The Edwardian era may be described broadly as the years 1900 to 1914.[21] This brief but coherent era significantly shaped the ideas and conduct of the novelist whose works were written twenty to forty years after its passage. Cary was born in 1888 in Londonderry. He spent his childhood at his father's residence in London, close to the home of his sporting uncle Tristram, and among his relatives in Ireland. Both homes provided characters for *Castle Corner* and *A House of Children*. Politics was a subject of debate and of real experience in the Irish households. Cary's family suffered the blows dealt the unwary resident landlords by the Irish Land Acts, and Cary himself witnessed the physical violence which accompanied the collapse of the home rule movement in 1899.[22]

The year Edward VII ascended to the throne Cary became a schoolboy. Two years' later, in 1903, he entered public school.

Upon leaving Clifton in 1906 Cary visited Paris, and from 1907 to 1908 he studied art in Edinburgh. In the latter year his ambitions shifted from painting to literature. He published privately a collection of poems entitled *Verses*, and shortly afterwards announced his desire for a university education. Cary went up to Oxford in 1909 to read law[23] and in his second year returned to bohemian Paris in the Christmas vacation with John Middleton Murry, the future editor, novelist and critic, with whom Cary shared rooms in Oxford. Cary's next step was to London where he attempted unsuccessfully to launch his writing career. In 1912 the desire for experience and adventure took him to the Balkan War where he served with the British Red Cross in Montenegro. In 1913 Cary joined the Nigerian Political Service and served there until 1919, when he returned to Oxford, to the home and writing career that were to be his for the rest of his life.

Throughout this period which effected the transition from Victorian to modern Britain, Cary's character and outlook were being moulded. The adventures of the early years, extensive reading during the African period, and the continuing attempts at artistic expression all formed part of the novelist's training. Further, Cary's vantage point was one offering broad scope. Because Irish political development lagged behind the English, Cary as a boy saw Victorian conceptions and habits of life dislodged in Ireland and watched the fitful progress of revolution there. His entry into the African service occurred at a time when the agents of Imperial government were evolving the principles of indirect rule which Cary was later to criticise and defend in *Britain and West Africa, The Case for African Freedom* and elsewhere. Away from the shock of violent change experienced by those who fought the Great War in Europe, engaged in absorbing and implementing the new methods of colonial government, Cary was again at liberty to appreciate the nature as well as the force and importance of transition.

Afterwards, Cary's ideas remained largely those formed during this period. George Orwell, in 1941, described Cary as "a man who has thought deeply over the problems of our time, and has been above current political movements and their characteristic jargon".[24]. Cary's social position as a member of the patrician class made him an uninvolved onlooker at the arrival in 1906 of the "cloth caps" in Parliament. His absence from England during the war distanced that event from Cary's experience.[25] But his books are evidence that the implications of these revolutions lodged in his thought and stirred there long afterwards.

The Edwardian experience, culturally alive and culturally disturbed throughout the British realm, is framed by two Imperialist conflicts which vastly altered the British Imperial idea: the embarrassment of the Boer War and the horror of World War I. At the opening of the era which witnessed the most striking Liberal victory of all time, a Conservative Government was in power; at its close the Liberals were implementing their policies only with the support of the Parliamentary Labour Party, itself a birth of Edward's reign.

The Boer War and its aftermath shocked and split the nation as a whole. Imperialists had to answer for a conflict both degrading and cruel. Military unfitness caused panic among those who saw Britain's martial supremacy threatened; it awoke deep social concern in those appalled by the ill-health of a populace revealed as up to sixty per cent unfit for service. Fears of national degradation beset the majority and spawned war on decadence in art and morals. The minority, more apt in recognising the real causes of the embarrassment, attacked poverty. As the Establishment attempted to shore up traditional British virtue through patriotic propaganda, censorship, and condemnation of a degenerate urban working class, the middle class through its Liberal Government attacked the Establishment itself by subduing the House of Lords and attempting to redistribute wealth through taxation and land reform. Masterman named the very bases of traditional British culture, the Landed System, the Established Church, the Popular Religion as "In Peril of Change".

A veneer of tradition, embodied nowhere more completely than in the cosmopolitan, but recognisably Victorian figure of Edward VII himself, covered the unrest, but no mind doubted that under it all the ground was shifting. Samuel Hynes, in *The Edwardian Turn of Mind*, reveals the presence of momentous change by simply listing significant contributions of these years: aircraft, radio-telegraphy, psychoanalysis, Post-Impressionism, motion picture palaces, the Labour party.

Lulled by its own sense that this was "a time of waiting rather than a time of action", Britain moved by myriad means steadily and unwittingly towards a shock more sudden than the dreaded evolutionary degeneration, more effective than political radicalism in arousing national reform—the war. "By coming to pass—" Hynes writes,

> almost, as it seemed, accidentally—it contradicted and destroyed the benevolent assumptions of the Edwardian Age, denied liberalism and progress and the goodness of the human heart, and left men with no cause but war itself.[26]

The keynotes of Edwardian social change sound in the biographies of the Wilcher children of Cary's *To Be a Pilgrim*. Edward Wilcher's participation in a radical Government provokes his estrangement from his father, the traditional Whig. His decadent behaviour offends the puritanism of his mother, despite her devotion to him. His foresight in art and politics perplexes Wilcher. Lucy Wilcher's religious radicalism deals a mortal blow to family happiness which is predicated on pride of station and its attendant duty to dignity. Thomas Wilcher assumes responsibility for Tolbrook and family affairs because Edward prefers politics to his hereditary role as master of the estate, and because the second son, Bill, has been rendered, by his upbringing and service in a dated military tradition, unfit to cope with financial exigencies in a changing social order. The character of the Edwardian era thus forms the historical generalisation under which this varied group of individual personalities finds its meaning and collective identity. In turn, Wilcher's struggle to comprehend this identity and his relationship to it provides Cary's most revealing portrayal of this significant and fascinating era.

Cary was always at pains to clarify the relationship between his own life and the significant events of his lifetime. Wilcher's dilemma in *To Be a Pilgrim*—whether to move backwards with his upbringing or forward with the times—was Cary's. His own decision to remain an Edwardian and a liberal afforded him a consistent pattern of action and formed the basis for his novels' emphasis on individual liberty and creativeness as the sources of progress in a world where injustice and beauty are facts of life.

Although Cary's philosophy of life, his idea of his place in society and his religious faith were established by the time he wrote his first published novel, he never ceased to ponder the nature of his own experience and the complex social developments of his age, and to grapple with the peculiar problems of the relationship between form and meaning in art. The result was increasing clarification of his own "notions of the world" and a corresponding growth in the sureness and skill with which he embodied these notions in fiction.

The eclectic nature of Cary's philosophy and its relation to his art are both implicit in the signal term in his discussions of the world and its inhabitants: "character". The term, recalling Mill's insistence on the uniqueness of the individual and the wisdom of studying "every character of mind" implies the empiricist and individualist bent of Cary's though. But it is also importantly related to Bergson's idea of the whole personality or fundamental self which alone is productive of existence and capable of the free act.

Cary elucidated his own use of the term "character" when in 1941-42 he plunged into a revision of the philosophical influences which had shaped his outlook, so that "if I should ever attempt to set down my own notions of the world, I should explain how I came by them" (Ms. Cary 272, P. 52). Out of this study (in which criticisms of Bergson and Kant figure largely) emerged Cary's statement that "the world is a work of imagination, always in being, a mind with its necessary character". In this formulation two of Cary's central preoccupations emerge; the importance of "imagination" or creative power as a source of existence, and the importance of "character", the "necessary form" of existence—whether of a mind, a life, or the world itself. The formulation is Bergsonian or Blakean, but Cary's resistance to idealism leads him, like Blake, to relate it to the social, political and religious contexts in which individuals lead their lives.

What Cary called "character" had a twofold source: form and activity. To be perceived, the world—or anything in it— had to have a form; that form Cary saw, with a vision akin to Blake's, as evolved and maintained through an incessant struggle against limiting necessity. That continual struggle against a complex necessity gave the world its vitality and unpredictability. It therefore accounted for both injustice and

27

the seemingly irrational aspects of the human character—emotion, desire—and produced perceptible discrepancy between intent and consequence. Activity, that is, created possibility, which defines both freedom and the aesthetic experience.

The sustaining tension between form and activity Cary viewed as part even of the divine character. God was credible to Cary only as a "character" embracing these limitations. God, like man, could will good and hate evil; he could create novelty. But he could not alter his own nature or do away with the past; to do so would be to deny his own formal existence. Aesthetic intuition and religious belief thus gelled for Cary in a vision of God "as the soul of the world. . . . as the active will incessantly urging us to love, to create beauty, to seek truth, to will happiness to all people"—the source, that is, of morality and fulfilment in men—whose nature, like beauty, "we know by intuition, whose activity we see every day" (Ms. Cary 293, S.22.K).

In the social context form and activity are linked in Cary's vision of progress. Government is the created social limitation ensuring the full development of individuals. Progress in society composes personal expression of character into social forms—fashions, arts and ultimately government itself. Society, therefore, evolves the forms suitable to the pursuit of its characteristic activity, which in turn promote that very evolution. Political experience thus mirrors in its own way the creative tension of change inherent in all existence.

In the light of his abiding interest in change it is worth noting that Cary's writings in many ways register the influence of the age's pre-eminent philosophy of radical change—Marxism—while constituting a rejection of it. When Cary speaks approvingly, as he often does, of "revolution", he invariably alludes to a minor but influential push in the gradual evolutionary progress he advocates. He speaks enthusiastically of "revolutions" in the arts, in areas of social reform, or international relations, and in education ("the only real revolution"). Cary fears the Marxist revolution not only because of its violent potential but because, while he accepted social democracy, an orthodox Socialist society with an emphasis on planning and justice seemed to him an enemy to individual liberty and to progress. He urges constructive struggle, but, regarding economics as subject to chance and accident, he cannot envisage a planned economic revolution, and viewing society as a natural growth, he cannot envisage a profound shift of the balance of power within it.

Cary therefore, while criticising the existing socio-political "system" does not fundamentally oppose it. He demands development along the lines of traditional liberalism, a strengthening of the virtues of the established system and the elimination of its faults or inadequacies. It is significant that social criticism in his novels is made not from the point of view of liberal orthodoxy, but through figures essentially outside the "system", which survives this challenge even while its faults are revealed. Gulley Jimson (like Edward Wilcher) criticises the system but opts out of it; Sara Monday cannot understand it; Lucy Wilcher flees from it in a resort to a conservative anarchism. On the other hand, in *The Moonlight*, Amanda's rejection of Harry and Robin—both, in their ways, outside bourgeois ethic or convention—leaves her a firm embodiment of bourgeois values, and in the second trilogy the liberal values of gradualism, constructive compromise, and the rights of life and liberty are given their most deliberate support.

Cary's novels from the start draw a picture of a necessity compounded of chance, physical and economic law, and human desire which, in constant interaction, call forth innovative triumphs and produce continual change. This picture is invariably embodied in the settings of the novels and focussed in their characters. Cary's central characters are usually isolated by age, ignorance, or quirks of temperament from the community surrounding them. That community itself is often one undergoing transition—Ireland of the rebellion, Africa in the days of colonial development, England in times of war or internal social crisis. These problematical situations are exploited by an increasing authorial control which brings to focus, by way of individuals' responses to historical or cultural necessity, Cary's insistence on those liberal principles—individualism, free expression, education—which could, in his view, lend order and purpose to a world "free and therefore diverse and unpredictable".

Cary's first three novels, *Aissa Saved*, *The American Vistor* and *The African Witch*, are set in Africa; the action of his fourth novel,

Castle Corner, moves from Ireland to England and Africa. Their concerns evoke Cary's own experience or observation and his characteristic preoccupations. We find explorations of primitive faith and superstition in the contexts of African natives and Irish peasants. We see the desire for self-fulfilment producing confusion in individuals reaching out for the benefits of more advanced civilization, while remaining ambivalent towards the master-civilization which holds these benefits. We see the disillusionment or defeat of political and religious idealists, and we see the self-defeat of stubborn individualists who isolate themselves in a social world where personal relationships and community progress require flexibility and compromise.

I shall not discuss the first three "African" novels which have been carefully examined by Professor Mahood in *Joyce Cary's Africa*. The themes of these novels are explored with greater understanding and clarity in Cary's later work. Cary himself accurately named the weakness of these early books in the simple statement, "the better I drew my characters, the more they would fail as illustrations of general laws" (*CC*, p. 8). The novels are undermined by Cary's tendency to include all relevant experience and to expose the crucial "question" in each novel through a proliferation of characters representative of "different aspects of the question" (*Aissa*, p. 10). Such weak characters—included for purposes of explanation—weakened his fiction, while strong characters unbalanced the novels by becoming more real—that is, more complex and individual—than the ideas they represented. I shall discuss this problem with reference to *Castle Corner* in Chapter Two. To extricate himself from this uncomfortable position which reached its climax in the failure of *Castle Corner*, Cary "turned to write about the simplest of characters in a simple background, with the simplest of themes, Mister Johnson, the artist of his own joyful tale" (*CC*, p. 8).

Mister Johnson, published in 1939, marks a significant alteration in Cary's method; locating his interest firmly in the central character, Cary established the pattern through which he was to realise a powerful defense of individualism in all his future novels.

Cary's tendency to pursue wholeness through multiplicity is

also evident in the structural development of his fiction. Characteristic of his espousal of Mill's principle that "the only way in which a human being can make some approach to knowing the whole of a subject is by hearing what can be said about it by persons of every variety of opinion", are his habit of lodging in diverse characters opposing attitudes to a question, and his disposition to write trilogies. His desire to capture the randomness of a free world made the construction of a plot uncongenial to Cary, an attitude overcome only when he became fully aware of the relationship between limitation and verisimilitude in art.

The idea of necessary activity had presented Cary with a Bergsonian vision of a world in flux. The impossibility of reproducing this activity in a contrived work of art emerged to Cary as the ultimate limitation on the artist, already limited by his materials and his own physical and intellectual character. Instead of attempting to capture an infinite multiplicity, the artist, Cary learned, must himself become God-like, operating within the character of his work, supplying the "givens" of his situation—the forms, conflicts, causes and effects of a created fate. Limitation in fiction—the shape afforded by plot, balance of characters, handling of time—Cary grew to see as no falsification, but an extension of reality.

The harnessing of multiplicity was, however, the result of considerable trial and error in Cary's work. The use of antithetic characters is to be found throughout Cary's fiction but the instinct which led him to offset Mister Johnson against Assistant District Officer Rudbeck or Clerk Benjamin or dictated the obvious opposition of the conservative, instinctive John Chass Corner and his liberal intellectual brother Felix became the principle of organisation and a vehicle for Cary's view of human nature in the complex antitheses of the trilogies. Greater maturity, too, enabled Cary to anatomise the typical character of an historical moment or a phase of human development in individual characters displaying its constituent elements. Thus he splits the childish character in *A House of Children* into the pragmatic Harry and the imaginative Evelyn, and represents the paradoxical Edwardian character in the fearful Thomas and the progressive Edward Wilcher of *To Be a Pilgrim*. Here, and again in *The Moonlight* when he juxtaposes

31

Ella and Rose to illuminate a Victorian strife between impulse or feeling and duty or morality, it is ultimately to discover a battle waged not between individuals, but in the heart of all human nature.

Cary sketched his first multiple novel, a series called "Tod" in the early 1930s.[27] This work unfolded Cary's multiple view through an historical plot and theme, tracing the dissipation, after 1885, of the Victorian confidence in automatic material progress. Its organization around three major characters (like the love triangle of the unfinished *Cock Jarvis* which he was writing simultaneously), forecast Cary's method in the published trilogies. The "Tod" series clearly influenced his next attempt, another historical saga in three books entitled "They Want to be Happy", of which *Castle Corner* was the first and the only one completed. The effort to realise and invest with significance a great diversity of human character and a large crisis-filled historical span defeated Cary. Later, in *Herself Surprised*, *To Be a Pilgrim* and *The Horse's Mouth*, Cary channelled his multiple view of humanity into three major (but not mutually exclusive) types, the creator, the conservative, and the woman. History remained in the background of these novels, contributing to the definition of these types, taking its character from their experiences.

Another projected trilogy, tentatively entitled "The Captive and the Free", was begun and abandoned between the writing of the two published trilogies.[28] Its plan presaged the Nimmo trilogy in the narratives of Major Gye, his wife, and Lord Drummer. Its theme—recalling that of "Tod"—was the influence on individuals of economic alterations in the world between 1890 and 1940. It is interesting to note that, paradoxically, the series which Cary abandoned were those originally conceived as multiple novels with collective titles, "They Want to be Happy", "The Captive and the Free".[29] His successful trilogies have no such titles and, indeed, assumed the trilogy form during their development.

Cary admitted in his preface to *Castle Corner* that he wondered if anyone would notice the "meaning" of his book, or whether "the contrast of different characters, though all making their lives, seeking fulfilment of one kind or another, did not result in that very neutral tint which we find in the events of real life"

32

(*CC*, p. 7). the neutral—or, more precisely, inconclusive—aspect of *Castle Corner* results from Cary's *laissez-faire* attitude to form in the novel. When writing "Tod" in 1933 Cary noted, "General theory of *rambling story* is *the details* by the way . . . *whole point of book is* to avoid composition of plot . . . *Anything may happen at any time* as in life" (Ms. Cary 259, N. 44). Even as late as 1950 Cary clung to this attitude to plot, commenting "A plot is the last thing I think about . . . The right and significant form of any work of art is not in any plot, but in a final character of being".[30] The *laissez-faire* method failed to secure "a final character of being", to sustain verisimilitude or to illuminate a theme.

Fourteen years after *Castle Corner*, when Cary wrote *Prisoner of Grace*, he had rid himself of the idea that episodes in a novel must occur with the randomness of life. His notes explain that the extraordinary plot of that novel with its complicated domestic and political intrigues, was constructed to sustain the novel's theme.

> Note. Only point of *strange plot* to shew NATURE of REAL GRASP of position which continually FADES. UNLESS RENEWED by grace of imaginative love, and sympathy . . . Only EXCUSE of plot is to bring home nature of *ideal faith*, not only in family but in *politics*.
>
> (Ms. Cary 288, S.20.C)

An appreciation of the need for limitation in art freed Cary to exploit those formal devices by which he subsequently makes each novel a complete reflection of its central character's nature and experience. Liberated from the fallacy of randomness Cary's art grew in technical sophistication and in realism.

Exemplary of this growth was his choice of the narrative technique of reminiscence to explore—in his favourite context, the Edwardian age—the way history and character impinge on one another in *A House of Children*, published early in 1941 and *To Be a Pilgrim*, of 1942. *A House of Children* is a reminiscence of an Irish childhood, based on Cary's own. The consciousness of the child eclipses that of the adult narrator. The book focusses on Evelyn Corner's growing awareness of his creative nature and its relationship to those of his brother Harry and his Irish cousins. The children dwell amidst fantasies and discoveries more real to them than the emotional conflicts of the surrounding adult world and the political unrest in Ireland at the urn of the century.

Thomas Wilcher's story in *To Be a Pilgrium* emerges from the involuntary reminiscences of an old man nearing death. Wilcher's thought travels ever backwards through the tumultuous Edwardian years to his childhood in the Victorian twilight. The man becomes the child as these years take on a reality more immediate than the modern world in which he dwells. The niece and nephew who represent this world are as strange foreigners to his understanding. This regression measured against the forward progress of Wilcher's remembered lifetime reveals a panorama of personal evolution and historical change.

Various explanations can be educed for Cary's adoption of the reminiscence and his focus on the Edwardian world at this time. All his previous novels had drawn to some extent on his personal experience. From Cary's family experience presented objectively in the context of historical change in *Castle Corner* to *A House of Children*'s subjective presentation of real characters under a fictional guise, Cary moved logically to *To Be a Pilgrim*'s wholly fictional reminiscence of family life and personal crises in the Edwardian transitional era. Each step in this evolution demonstrates technical innovations which enliven character and strengthen Cary's themes.

A further felicitous accident no doubt contributed to Cary's selection of the reminiscence for these two novels. In 1940 and 1941 Cary read Proust in the English translation, noting this master's technique.[31] Annotations in his personal copies of the volumes deal with Proust's method, its occasional lapses, and the techniques used to convey character.[32] Cary did not fail to note the problems associated with the first person narrative. But he recognised its effectiveness in enabling one character to organise a novel whose total statement derives from the ramifications of thought and actions in other characters.

Finally, the reminiscence proved an apt mode of expression to link the perplexing historical phenomenon of the Edwardian personality to the personal self-portrait of the conservative in *To Be a Pilgrim*. The technique which follows the vagaries of one

34

mind, implicitly embodying doubt, irresolution, or excessive emotion, was excellently suited to capture the character of that transitional age.

The fulfilment of Cary's desire to unite character and historical event in such a way as to affirm their mutual influence and to capture the values and the fate of British liberalism in fiction came with his last completed work, the second trilogy. The work was also the fulfilment of his exploitation of divergent character types and of the trilogy form as an integral part of the work's meaning.

Cary had long ago, like his nineteenth -century predecessors, recognised that a belief in individualism, as well as challenging the absoluteness of truth in the world, posed problems for the artist as to the location of "truth" in fiction. The three mutually revealing first person narratives of the Nimmo trilogy offer three individual versions of "the truth", crucial to the significant problems of private and political morality posed in the work. The novels, which have as their centre a Liberal politician and portray the flourishing and decline of the Liberal Party between 1880 and 1926, are themselves a demonstration of the relative nature of truth and an exercise in the liberal method of permitting truth to emerge through a conflict of attitudes in an actual situation. The truth that emerges, against a background demonstrating that "politics is the art of human relations, an aspect of all life",[33] is that respect for human liberty, for the freedom of humans to fulfil themselves emotionally, intellectually and physically, is grounded in the most precious human right of all, the secure possession of life itself.

The development of Cary's art itself might be said to mirror the evolution of political liberalism from laissez-faire to purposeful restraint, growing more controlled, self-aware, and clearly focussed. Liberalism gained its strength and incurred its setbacks by making conscience—invested in the principles of personal liberty and human dignity—the final arbiter in the shaping of policy and the exercise of power. By embodying these principles in the aims and careers of his varied characters—both those who innovate and those who conserve—Cary reveals liberalism as an enduring force in the government, conduct and conscience of the British people. The respect for a varied and valuable human life which is the premise and the enduring attraction of his fiction measures the forcefulness and generosity of Joyce Cary's liberal conscience.

NOTES

1. Joyce Cary, *Aissa Saved*, Carfax ed. (Michael Joseph, 1952), p. 9. Hereafter abbreviated *Aissa* and cited in the test.
2. Cary Collection, Ms. Cary 272, p. 52. Hereafter references to the Cary Collection will be designated by catalogue number and cited in the text.
3. Malcolm Bradbury, *Eating People is Wrong*, re-issued with new Introduction (Secker and Warburg, 1976), pp. 1-8.
4. Joyce Cary, *Castle Corner*, Carfax ed. (Michael Joseph, 1952), p. 8. Hereafter abbreviated *CC* and cited in the text.
5. Joyce Cary, "Britain's Liberal Influence", *Selected Essays*, ed. A.G. Bishop (Michael Joseph, 1976), p. 210.
6. The Hon. George C. Brodrick, *Liberal Principles* (The Liberal Central Association, 1877), pp. 8-21.
7. C.F.G. Masterman, *The New Liberalism* (Leonard Parsons, 1920), pp. 26, 212, 213.
8. Walter Runciman, *Liberalism as I See It* (Ernest Benn, 1927), pp. 15-30.
9. John Morley, *On Compromise*, new ed. (Macmillan, 1923), pp. 218-25.
10. John Stuart Mill, *Utilitarianism, On Liberty*, and *Considerations of Representative Government* (Everyman, 1910), p. 97. Subsequent references designated by title, are to this edition and are cited in the text. For Cary's annotations, see Cary Collection of Printed Books, B. 401 and B. 402.
11. L.T. Hobhouse, *Liberalism* (Williams and Norgate, 1911), p. 118. Hereafter cited in the text.
12. John Stuart Mill, *Autobiography*, ed. J. Stillinger (Oxford University Press, 1971) p. 86.
13. *The New Liberalism*, p. 24.
14. David Lloyd George, "Liberalism and Liberty", a speech to the London Liberal Federation of the National Liberal Club, London, 12 May 1924, Liberal Publication Department, p. 9.
15. Joyce Cary, *Except the Lord* (Michael Joseph, 1953), p. 266. Hereafter abbreviated *ETL* and cited in the text. Cary frequently echoes Mill's language in *Power in Men*.
16. *The New Liberalism*, p. 211.
17. *Liberalism*, p. 137.
18. J.R. Vincent, *The Formation of the British Liberal Party 1857-1868*, 2nd ed. (Hassocks, The Harvester Press, 1976), pp. 30, 257.
19. See, for example, *Why I am a Liberal*, ed. Andrew Reid (Cassel, 1885), or publications of the Liberal Central Assocation and the Liberal Publication Department.
20. *The New Liberalism*, pp. 133-34, 138.

21. Edward VII reigned from 1901 to 1910.
22. Malcolm Foster, *Joyce Cary: A Biography* (Boston, Houghton Mifflin, 1968), p. 24.
23. Cary's was an undistinguished university career, but that the seeds of later thought were sown in an atmosphere of conversation and debate at Oxford is remarked by Cary in "A Slight Case of Demolition", *Selected Essays*, pp. 66-70 and "Religious History," Ms. Cary 293, S.22.K.
24. Foreword to Joyce Cary, *The Case for African Freedom* (Secker and Warburg, 1941), p. 6.
25. Cary fought in the Cameroons campaign and was wounded at Mount Mora. But those in Africa saw the war in Europe only as it was sketched in Reuters' dispatches. Cary Collection, Letters, 1916-18.
26. Samuel Hynes, *The Edwardian Turn of Mind* (Princeton, Princeton University Press, 1968), p. 358.
27. Ms. Cary 178, 179, 251, 259, 260.
28. Ms. Cary 156-59, 272, 277, 281, 282, 286.
29. In a draft letter to the publisher of *Aissa Saved*, Cary discussed this novel and several unpublished works, too, in terms of a multiple novel, "I meant at one time to call this series of books, of which several are in construction, 'There's a War On', as a general title. . . ." Ms. Cary 258, S.5.E.
30. Joyce Cary, "The Way a Novel Gets Written", *Selected Essays*, pp. 127-28.
31. The Cary Collection of Printed Books contains the following volumes: Marcel Proust, *Swann's Way*, trans. C.K. Scott Moncrieff, Phoenix Library ed., II (Chatto and Windus, 1929), Cary C. 964; *Within a Budding Grove*, trans. C.K. Scott Moncrieff, 2 vols., I (Chatto and Windus, 1924), II, Phoenix Library ed. (Chatto and Windus, 1929), Cary C. 965, C. 966, signed "Joyce Cary from Trudy, Christmas 1940" in Cary's hand; *The Guermantes Way*, trans. C.K. Scott Moncrieff, Phoenix Library ed., 2 vols. (Chatto and Windus, 1930), Cary B. 240, B. 241, signed "Joyce Cary from G.M.C." in Cary's hand and annotated; *Cities of the Plain*, trans. C.K. Scott Moncrieff, Phoenix Library ed., 2 vols. (Chatto and Windus, 1936), Cary B. 238, B. 239, signed "Joyce Cary from Trudy Dec. 7 '40" in Cary's hand and annotated; *The Captive*, trans. C.K. Scott Moncrieff, Uniform ed., 2 vols. (Chatto and Windus, 1941), Cary B. 242, B. 243, signed "Joyce Cary Dec. 7 1941 from G.M.C." in Cary's hand and annotated; *The Sweet Cheat Gone*, trans., C.K. Scott Moncrieff, Uniform ed. (Chatto and Windus, 1941), Cary B. 244, signed "Joyce Cary" and annotated; *Time Regained*, trans. Stephen Hudson, Phoenix Library ed. (Chatto and Windus, 1941), Cary B. 245, signed "Joyce Cary" and annotated; *Du Côté de Chez Swann*, 2 vols. (Paris, Editions de la Nouvelle Revue Française, 1922), Cary C. 961, C. 962; *A la Recherche du Temps Perdu*, 15 vols., *Le Temps Retrouvé*, XIV-XV (Paris, Editions de la Nouvelle Revue Francaise, 1941), Cary C. 953, C. 954.
32. See annotations in Proust, *The Guermantes Way*, I; *Cities of the Plain*, I and II; *The Captive*, II; *The Sweet Cheat Gone*; and *Time Regained*, Cary Collection of Printed Books.

33. Joyce Cary, *Prisoner of Grace*, Carfax ed. (Michael Joseph, 1954), p. 5. Hereafter abbreviated *PG* and cited in the text.

2

"They Want to be Happy"

According to the Greatest Happiness Principle . . . the ultimate end, with reference to and for the sake of which all other things are desirable . . . is an existence exempt as far as possible from pain, and as rich as possible in enjoyments, both in point of quantity and quality; the test of quality, and the rule for measuring it against quantity, being the preference felt by those who in their opportunities of experience, to which must be added their habits of self-consciousness and self-observation, are best furnished with the means of comparison.

                                                    J.S. Mill, *Utilitarianism*

"They Want to be Happy" was the title Cary gave to the massive historical fiction, undertaken in 1935, which was to examine the viability of liberal principles in concrete social contexts by making real the particular contexts which challenged British liberalism in the late nineteenth and early twentieth centuries. The title reflects the liberal-utilitarian view underlying the work, that the search for happiness primarily motivates men towards knowledge and freedom and hence stimulates the valuable creative achievements of individuals and societies. The work was conceived as three volumes, exploring the fortunes of a family and the history of three nations over three generations, between 1890 and 1931. The three novels were to be called "Castle Corner", "Over the Top" and "Green Jerusalem".

In portraying the search for happiness throughout society the novels would show people seeking material benefits,

39

intellectual development, and national dignity. Cary aimed to relate this search to the hopes and disappointments of political liberalism. "They Want to be Happy" would reveal how the misuse of creative energy and misunderstanding of freedom brought about the destruction of an an historical age.

The project failed. Only the first volume of the trilogy, *Castle Corner*, was completed and published. The cause for failure, Cary noted, was an incompatibility between a general historical picture exposing "universal values" and his own deep interest in the very particular nature of individual characters. Years later Cary remarked, "I still regret the loss of my characters in *Castle Corner*, and their adventures . . ." (*CC*, p. 8).

To discuss an unfinished, unpublished work is to impose on the reader, but I should like to share an acquaintance with the evolution and content of "They Want to be Happy" which offers striking insight into the development of Cary's themes and his art. It is not necessary to detail the plots of the projected volumes, but a discussion of the series as a whole is essential to demonstrate that here, twenty years before the Nimmo trilogy, Cary was fascinated by the relationship of liberal theory to Liberal politics and by the relationship of British liberalism to events in the world at large.

"They Want to be Happy" originated in the late stages of composition of the abandoned *Cock Jarvis*.[1] *Cock Jarvis* is the story of a District Officer in the Nigerian Political Service—a former soldier, quixotic and self-reliant, hated for his sharp temper, his evangelism, inefficiency and his partiality to his natives. The novel's plot—prefiguring Cary's trilogies—forms around the middle-aged Jarvis, his young bride, and her lover, Jarvis's assistant.

Cock Jarvis presents a sustained view of injustice in human experience, unrelieved by the comedy which informs *Mister Johnson*, *Charley is My Darling*, or *The Horse's Mouth*. Jarvis's sense of justice puts him at odds with authority; his personal code of integrity makes those he loves his torturers. The intensity with which this character and his tragedy are realised points to Cary's powerful identification with this less liberal, less good-humoured fellow to himself. Ultimately Cary's intense sympathy for Jarvis robbed him of control over his character. To avoid a falsifying resolution of an impossible dilemma, Cary had to permit Jarvis to destroy himself steadily, painfully, absolutely. In the later stages of composition Cary tried to regain control over the novel, by introducing into the plot various members of the Corner family, and eventually the evolution of *Castle Corner* occurred.

It is somewhat surprising that Cary, having "lost control" of a story with one central character and the two main thematic movements which Professor Bishop labels the "revenge" and "reduction" tales, should attempt next to cope with the fortunes of a large family and three nations. But he probably approached the new series with the naive belief that its historical events would impose the organisation which Jarvis's personal and internal struggles had defied.[2]

To trace the "revolutions of history" through which Britain and its Empire were carried out of the nineteenth century and into the twentieth, away from Victoria's reign towards Ramsay MacDonald's national government, Cary chose the form of the historical saga or family chronicle. He was following a nineteenth-century European tradition embracing such giants as Tolstoy, Balzac and George Eliot which had itself made the transition in the hands of varied talents from Thomas Mann to James Galsworthy.

Cary had criticised John Stuart Mill because he conceived of his political subject in terms of "an abstract state . . . an abstract liberty . . . an abstract rule", instead of beginning "with a real individual, Brown or Smith".[3] Cary felt compelled to put his own liberal views, recently enunciated in *Power in Men*, to the test in a fictional situation containing as much as he could give it of the variety, contingency, injustice and individual idiosyncrasy of reality.

Castle Corner, on the northern coast of Ireland, is the seat of the Corner family, Anglo-Irish landowners who send their sons to Oxford, the army, and the Empire. Castle Corner opens there in the year 1897. Old John Corner is executing an eviction order he might have withheld in the days before the Land League drove him to bitterness, and the child Bridget Foy is discovering the castle almost on the day she loses the roof over her head. The novel closes in 1901, the heavily-mortgaged castle enjoying an Indian summer of prosperity derived from the soon-to-be-eclipsed sun of African gold. At this time we find

Bridget Foy waiting patiently in the castle kitchen for her son, a Corner, to fulfil the promise of his heritage and her dream.

Castle Corner was to show the weakness of what Cary called the Victorian faith in providence, a faith which assumed that the conduct of one's personal life was to be shaped by instinct and trust in God, and that the English were destined to rule in glory. John Chass Corner is the exemplar of this faith, "His voice conveyed perfectly the rich and sanguine character of the man, his instinctive confidence in the rightness of things, as established by natural providence . . ." (*CC*, p. 208). The irresponsibility of this confidence is exposed by the precariousness of John Chass's own position as a landlord surrounded by a peasant community starved of intellectual and physical sustenance and reacting with increasing impatience to the inequities perpetuated by the Imperialist ruling class in the interest of "peace". John Chass's faith is conservative and consistent, and he practises a dignified, if inadequate paternalism towards his tenants.

The kind of complacency Cary criticises was not reserved to Tories. Nineteenth century Liberalism, he felt, was guilty of a similar complacency which couched itself in the principles of *laissez-faire* and faith in human reason. Non-interference was as thwarting as oppression to the victims of poverty and ignorance. This complacency had crept into liberalism as a compromise between its primary ideals—Mill's confidence in reason and respect for liberty—and the disposition of a public with a tradition of faith and a faith in tradition, which was willing to envisage but not to provoke change.

Gladstone himself—a former Conservative, a religious man, a reactor to change more than an innovator—was more truly representative of the state of liberalism in the late 1800s than was John Stuart Mill on the one hand, or John Bright on the other. Similarly representative was the poet Browning who quickly translated doubt into faith and denied the tormenting uncertainty of relativism by celebrating individualism. Proclaiming that others should enjoy the same right as he to be "God-guided" and uninterfered with, Browning echoed sentiments very popular with the Liberal Party to which he proudly allied himself.[4]

Perhaps no issue challenged the Liberal complacency at the

time as strongly as did Home Rule for Ireland. Liberals who preached freedom throughout the world were seen to deny it to their nearest neighbours. The party which professed to believe in men's ability to reason out their own best interests, and to govern themselves wisely, failed to extend this confidence to Irish men. The party was not unified in this matter. Home Rule called forth Gladstone's courage as a Liberal as did almost no other issue; and those Liberals who supported Irish self government constituted a small and isolated band of warriors.

The Home Rule movement is not the subject of *Castle Corner*, but it echoes through countless conversations in the novel—in condemnation or reverence for Gladstone, in Felix's motives for selling Castle Corner, in Cocky Jarvis who risks his army career to defend his nationalism, in the disillusionment of the Parnellite youth. Like many crises in the Corner household, the issue is, at the moment of the book's action, shelved, but this lends no peace to the world of *Castle Corner*. The deep changes shaking the world of the Anglo-Irish are felt as a vital current in the Irish sections of the novel, and John Chass's reactionary dignity is near-tragic when he is seen as the victim of the Irish Land Acts, world economic revolution, and his own improvidence.

Felix Corner, a liberal, stands at the opposite pole to John Chass in all but his irresponsibility; he counters faith in providence with confidence in human reason. Felix, from his early failures in philosophy, has learned the danger of dwelling on abstractions rather than the realities of a situation. He distrusts all forms of "juju", whether the superstition of the priests in Ireland, the sentimental traditionalism of his father, or his son's idealistic anti-materialism. Felix is alive to the tensions within the general quest for happiness and to the need in government for enlightened control as a means to ultimate freedom of opportunity.

But Felix is a victim of the inner tensions which beset many Liberals in that time of change; the intellectual with the courage to applaud change often lacked the emotional strength to embrace it. Unable to reconcile his commitment to reform with his love for home, Felix abandons the conflict and his integrity by "going native" in Africa.

Other historical events which tested the strength and will of liberalism and altered its character at the turn of the century enter *Castle Corner* through the characters of the succeeding generation. The nineteenth century faith in providence, peace, and Empire had two ideological outgrowths: Imperialism was one and *laissez-faire* liberalism the other. Harry Jarvis is associated with the first in the novel, and Cleeve Corner, less clearly, with the second.

Imperialism held that Britain had not only a right, owing to her economic and military strength, but a moral duty to impose her enlightened rule on other nations. Here Cary examines one of the ideas, derived from events, which wove itself through practice into the fabric of Liberalism. Imperialism Cary sees as self-generating: "a feeling of grandeur . . . from the possession of an empire by means of violence", which justified itself by other ideas wrenched to its service from their original contexts. "The men who believed in the struggle for existence were right as far as they went", he observed; "and so were those who believed that Christianity was better than paganism" (Ms. Cary 28). *Castle Corner's* Harry Jarvis, the conqueror of Daji, and young imperialists like him acted in accordance with a concept which mesmerised the whole British nation, and which even the Liberal Gladstone was powerless to resist. Cary observes with irony, that

> Gladstone, even if he had not been compelled, by his own inherited religious idea, to refuse all accommodation with the scientists, could not in the eighties and nineties, have stopped the enormous rush and force of millions of imperial idealists, released suddenly by popular education from the status of the bees and ants, and the restraints of the old morality.

"The only way to conquer an idea", Cary commented in this digression which was eliminated from the novel, "is to draw the truth of it into a truer and grander idea; an idea containing at once more facts of science and experience, and more absolute value; more goodness, more logic" (Ms. Cary 28). Liberalism, the novel suggests, is the advocate of the grander idea. But Cary ends *Castle Corner* before his portrait of twentieth-century liberalism takes shape. He skilfully uses the Boer war as the issue around which Cocky's imperialism and Cleeve's radical liberalism define themselves as opposing attitudes representative of a national split and pointing to a new direction in Liberal policy. But Cleeve Corner, who was to be Cary's vehicle for exploring twentieth-century liberalism in the succeeding book, is here seen merely as an irresponsible boy whose interest in politics develops only at the last when, more through adolescent pique than political thought, he espouses a radical pacifism— ready to "smash the Liberal Imperialists". A third youth, the lower-middle-class radical Porfitt is seen embarked on a demagogic career destined to great success.

Cary's point that the search for happiness can become a political reality only when the complexity of its human reality is understood, is only effectively realised in the world of the castle itself, which Cary conjures for a last time in the Irish scenes of the book's closing. He sees in Sukey's kitchen the intransigence and unpredictability of human feeling and the diversity of human desire which always thwart the efforts of the theorist and mock the politician's task, while offering an irresistible challenge to both.

In the world of the second novel, "Over the Top", the two strands of Imperialism and liberalism undergo transformation. The former gives way to nationalism as a driving force in world politics; the latter retreats into idealism. "Over the Top", set in the years 1901 to 1916, was to show nationalism growing in Ireland and in Africa where Cocky Jarvis becomes an African nationalist and ironically instigates a sentimental programme of protective measures in Laka which ruins the native markets, the Mosi Company, and all the Corners. Cary attributed the rise of nationalism to "basic creative power inventing a dream world". "Over the Top" was also to show how this new illusion provoked the violent collapse of European stability. Drafts call the world at this time "A dream building world which doesn't perceive its own nature or human nature as dream building" (Ms. Cary 266, S.9.0). Liberalism, lost in its own dream of human goodness overlooked the implications of conflicting assertions of national will.

Cary's aim was to show that over-idealistic Liberals made of their political beliefs a religion as irresponsible as—indeed, similar to—the blind faith in providence criticised in the first volume. In "Over the Top" Delia Baskett, a religious woman, is made representative of liberalism in general. She conceives her liberalism as a necessary discipline, with "freedom" the guiding abstraction. Cary notes "She wants a rule—she wants to give herself up to this rule, which is part of the liberal view of the time" (Ms. Cary 265, N.61).

Cary thus highlights one of the important strains in the politics of liberalism at the time: its actual association in the minds and aims of its adherents with religion. Not only did Liberalism derive strength and character from the Non-conformists who sought liberty under its policy of toleration; it was also shaped by hosts of radical Anglicans who felt that such toleration and the growing social-welfare orientation of the Liberal movement were more in touch with fundamental Christianity than were the pomp and pedantry of the High Church. Remote from Mill's agnostic humanism, these liberal Christians were the descendants of earlier humanisms—those of More and Milton—and their political utterances were often more eloquent of Christianity and of liberty than of reason. In the novel, Delia Baskett, treating liberalism as a personal, quasi-religious, ideal, fails to make it a constructive social force.[5]

Cleeve Corner, who is carried to a Liberal parliamentary seat in the landslide of 1906, fails to make his liberalism constructive because he, too, substitutes a blind idealism for a practical response to political and personal problems. Because Cleeve is committed to individual freedom, he demands a sexual freedom in his private life which moral critics view as license. His public position fails to survive censure of his private life. Aspiring to open-mindedness, Cleeve adopts a *laissez-faire* attitude to the education of his children. His failure to exercise responsible guidance leaves them disillusioned and defeated by the challenge of a violently changing world.

In Cleeve's too extensive tolerance—a kind of anarchism—Cary sees merely another version of faith in providence, which he caricatures in a draft passage, "Nature and God, you know, are both good Gladstonian Liberals. They say Be free, my dears—trust to the great heart of humanity and down with government and let who will be clever" (Ms. Cary 26). Cleeve's idealism defeats him. The egoism he calls individual freedom alienates him from the wife he loves. Porfitt, whom he supported, betrays Cleeve's principles. (This about-face, on the issue of naval estimates, is the first of a series of expedient shifts which take Porfitt into the War Cabinet as Minister of Transport.) Finally Cleeve's pacifist conviction that the German people want peace shatters before the Kaiser's armies. The First World War, which broke the liberal revolution, brings this volume to a close.

Of the movement towards social democracy which gave strength to the Liberal party between 1901 and 1914, Cary shows little in the drafts for "Over the Top". This important side of Liberalism was reserved for the third volume of the series. "Green Jerusalem" was to reveal Cary's pattern for happiness in the replacement of "dream" with purposeful action: "General theme. Free planning necessary, and the lines of it to be freedom for all" (Ms. Cary 37).

By the time the notions of freedom and guidance derived from Mill and the utilitarians had acquired an increasingly practical—or social democratic—aspect in the policies of the twentieth-century New Liberalism, they were merging with—and being pushed aside by—the rising Socialist emphasis on planning. The background of "Green Jerusalem", which opens in 1916, is a world awakening to the need for planning in government. The League of Nations offers hope of international order and the Russian revolution represents an attempt to plan for national happiness scientifically, albeit crudely.

The focusses of the series' tripartite setting measure the passing of the old liberalism. In Ireland of the Easter Rising and the 1920-22 "troubles" active power defeats the old order with its reliance on providence. Some notes indicate that the events of the Irish story were to culminate in the burning to the ground of Castle Corner itself. Kay brings the African progress full circle, for unlike Jarvis who fought both exploitation and progress, Kay recognises the need to exploit Africa for the profit of its inhabitants and to promote their education and development. In England the small revolution of the General Strike ends in disaster and the hopes of the Labour Party founder in the economic crisis of 1931.

The significant events of this sketched volume continue to illustrate the recurring truth of Cary's note, "anyone can make a utopia on paper. The problem is how to secure it in fact" (Ms. Cary 31). The very complexity of ambition in individuals which generates progress obscures the movement towards happiness. Happiness is indeed remote from the events which were to bring Castle Corner and its story to an end. Yet Cary's position— already evident in *Castle Corner*—is not negative. Cary's nearest spokesman in the work is Felix Corner. Like Felix, Cary asserts the need for a degree of control which will permit variety of character and motive to issue in fruitful complement—Blake's progression through contraries—rather than in destructive opposition. In a draft of *Castle Corner* Felix's pamphlet began "Government is in the first place the management of people",and went on to explain:

> All men want to be happy. All governments offer or pretend to offer happiness of some kind . . . The root fact of human nature is that its passions can equally be satisfied by good things and bad things. The joys of revenge and self-sacrifice are equally satisfactory to the nerves, and a scientist who conquers and possesses his subject, a farmer who overcomes a sullen piece of clay, a revivalist who fills the Albert Hall and a Napoleon who devastates Europe have exactly the same personal triumph. It is only the consequences to others which are different.
>
> (Ms. Cary 24)

For Cary the balance between control and liberty could only be struck through education. The antidote to misuse of the human creative power was to cultivate the habit of reasoned assessment of the widest possible range of information. Education was necessary to enable ignorant or backward peoples to find opportunity for material and spiritual fulfilment and to promote everywhere in society the triumph of constructive over destructive ideas.

In a draft version of *Castle Corner*, Felix Corner observes of the Irish peasants, "I don't suppose any of these men could read, or they wouldn't be so contented" (Ms. Cary 28). Yet the novel reveals that this contentment is illusory. Shared misery, as much as what Cary called "the joys of joy and friendship", unites the Irish community. Bridget's dream of escape into Cleeve's world and Con Foy's bitterness towards the landowners reveal the frustrations of the ignorant. The education offered this class is inadequate and productive of further unhappiness, as Cary noted, "in bad idea of justice and superstition". The education in half-truths which Father MacFee offers Manus Foy defeats itself, equipping the boy only to substitute one blind loyalty for another. In "Green Jerusalem" Manus, who had seemed to Father MacFee an "angel" in his innocent faith in the Church, was to murder for the cause of Parnell. In the opposite direction, Cleeve Corner's refusal to direct his children's education—a personal libertarian impulse—issues in their lives as irresponsibility, promiscuity, confusion, and despair.

The antidote to such waste of human potential, Cary's notes repeatedly emphasised, "is *education* of a *certain kind. Plan education too*" (Ms. Cary 31). Echoing throughout *Castle Corner*, particularly in the words of Felix Corner, is Cary's own awareness that education is an agonizingly slow process, "it's the only real revolution anywhere. But it takes a long time". Nevertheless, the whole series was to show that education, by giving power, and politics, by using power, could together provide the means for happiness. This conclusion is summed up in a sentence from *Power in Men* which Cary wrote for the Liberal Book Club in the year *Castle Corner* was published: "Education gives liberty the full use of its reason by which to realise its desires".[6]

Castle Corner

In 1952, while writing *Prisoner of Grace*, Cary wrote to Elizabeth Lawrence at Harper and Brothers that he intended next to write a flawless novel.

> Which could be perfect? One is usually tempted to choose the slightest—the least advanced because it isn't old enough to have got the measles or the small pox or to have had an unfortunate love affair—it still has a nice complexion and most of its nose.[7]

Here, and in a subsequent letter looking forward to *Except the Lord*, Cary's attitude towards his own involvement in his creations gives insight into the failure of *Castle Corner*. "I am very keen to get about my new book for which the schemes (or rather attachments) are already forming".[8] When Cary began *Castle Corner*, even before the scheme had solidified, the attachments were well formed and likely to intrude on his

49

objectivity and selectivity. Africa was an experience he had already exploited. Ireland was the home of his deepest attachments and the story of the Corners was a composite of Cary family experience.[9] The "unfortunate love affair" in the background of *Castle Corner* was *Cock Jarvis*. Of "measles" or "small pox"—early intentions which have left their marks— *Castle Corner*, too, shows signs. Among these are Chorley the soap maker and Benskin the brewer. Cary intended these sketchy figures to have represented the good and ill in Imperialist commercial influences in a hostile portrayal of a Liberal-backed colonial government in Nigeria which relied on gin for revenue rather than developing the country's abundant resources.[10]

An imbalance in the strength of its three areas of focus largely accounts for the failure of *Castle Corner*. Despite being extensively researched, the English and African sections are thin. Like Felix Corner, Cary approaches the Ireland of his youth with the sensitivity and affection of an exile. Sympathetically observed detail gives the Irish sections of *Castle Corner* the fullness the other sections lack. Here the painter's eye and a sensitive ear complement each other.

In the following passage the serenity of the static natural scene belies the human activity it embraces, and the shifting perspective of watchers and watched describes at once the characters and their world.

> Slatter was already on the watch. It was luckily a fine, clear morning. The sky was transparent after two days of east wind, and the sunlight itself seemed to be brighter and clearer as it fell slanting on the ground. This wintry light, acutely slanted, always made Annish seem unusually solid. The fallow fields like tarnished copper, the black and rusty bog banks, purple in shadow, the black wiry hedges and black trees, the pale gilded branches of the sycamores at the castle, had the weight of metal or heavy ores. The lough, too, undulating all over in smooth, small waves without a break, was more like quicksilver than water.
>
> Cottagers were everywhere sitting at their doors in the sun. They also glanced towards Sandy Point; because the steamer was an event for them. It moved the imagination to the idea, 'That steamer was in Liverpool last night.'
>
> Bridget sat at her door, high up on Knockeen with Finian in

her lap, staring at the narrow strip of the Atlantic on a level with her eyes, which had the peaceful, thoughtless expression of a ruminating animal.

(*CC*, p. 288)

In contrast to such essentially visual scenes Cary sets the lively tone and endless paradoxes of Irish speech. He captures the indirections of speech practised by high and low alike with unexaggerated accuracy. Thus Bridget's approach to the castle, effectively settled already, proceeds through a diplomatic chain from Peggy the housemaid to Mary Corner,

'She [*sic*][11] a dirty slumgalloper, mam, but it would be a Christian act to give her the place, for the Foys are starved.'

Mary Corner then approached Sukey. 'Susanna, I've found you a kitchenmaid and you ought to be thankful.'

'If it's thon Bridgeen, I'd rather a tinker from the road.'

(*CC*, p. 100)

The verbal and active indirections of domestic politics look forward to the narratives of Sara Monday and Nina Nimmo, and to the second trilogy's realisation that "politics is the art of human nature, an aspect of all life".

Again, the fragmented conversation of the Jubilee gathering reveals the complexities of the peasants' private and community life in a time of hardship and change. Con Foy's bitter preoccupation, Bridget's misfortune, the extremes of Sukey's temperament and the people's general ambivalence towards the Corners and the Queen herself link the threads of the novel's theme and action.

He said now, twisting up his face as if he had something bitter in his mouth, 'This is the way we boycott the Jubilee—we're the brave boys in Annish.'

A voice behind said, 'Is it Bridgy? She's as fat as a bonham.'

'Why wouldn't she be fat?' Con said. 'She'd rather ate Jawn's mate at the castle, than mine.'

Alarmed and curious faces turned toward the group. Everybody was anxious to hear what would happen when Con or Sukey discovered Bridget's state.

. . .

'Is it Bridgy's keg?' he exclaimed. 'But that's the leaky wan.'

'What's that,' Con said, confused. Sukey made a plunge after

51

the fellow and screamed, 'Ah, ye dirty devil, and what sort of a drip are ye to be dropped in a medical hall. Let me at him, the pig's dung. But what did he mane at all?' She looked round with open mouth and astonished eyes. Suddenly her expression changed and she cried, 'Look at him, the darling. Has he come to his Sukey.'

Shon, in his red flannel dressing-gown, wriggling between the legs of the crowd, had caught her eye.

. . .

'And haven't we ryalty to ourselves.' old Dan said. He took up Shon's hand and offered it to public view like a treasure from his own collection. 'See that hand, the true share of ryalty. I have it myself. A thrue Corner hand.'

'Aye, a princely beauty,' the ragamuffin said. 'Thanks be to Gawd I saw that one for I never seen him before.'

. . .

'The Corners are the biggest robbers in Annish,' Con said, 'but why wouldn't they rob ye when ye let them.'

'Thrue for you, sor,' the mountain man answered. 'Robbers they are, ryal robbers. Didn't they shteal all Annish?' He turned round. 'All Annish.'

(CC, pp. 206, 209)

Few subleties present themselves in the English and African sections. Cary confessed while writing it that the "English section" was "weak"[12]; it fails of the vitality and the complexity of the Irish scene. Similarly, Felix Corner's deterioration and Cocky Jarvis's adventures left little room for a full presentation of the African natives, although their community is as diverse as the Irish. The ruin of the complacent primitive Laka natives at the hands of Mahomedan invaders enters the novel only as a sideline to the main action, treated as a "set piece" so that it would not slow the novel's progress.

In fact *Castle Corner* is a series of set pieces. Some are dramatic and revealing. John Chass's reckless tandem race, the result of a friendly challenge, gives objective proof of the daring and dignity of the man. Although the scene belongs to John Chass, its flavour emerges from the participation of the watchers. Slatter's lunatic excitement, Darcy's terror, the inevitable offer "from the back" of "two to one on his honour", and old Jebb's violent anger, "Is it the devil or who is it that gave him his luck?" (*CC*, p. 152) provide a tension to match Cary's description of the drive itself and contrast with John Chass's grace and gravity at the reins. And Cary skilfully combines the build-up of furious action and excitement in the race with the drama of Bridget's seduction taking place within the castle. The triumph of John Chass's gratuitous adventure forms a striking and ironic frame for Bridget's perplexed surrender, "And that's all for what ye'd put my soul in hell" (*CC*, p. 154).

Commenting retrospectively on the world of the novel Cary observed that "those who have the keenest intensity of happiness in love and achievement, are those most exposed to suffering in loss and defeat" (*CC*, p. 7). Cary tried to sustain such a pattern in the novel, but exposed as they are, his strongest characters defy suffering: they cope with loss and overlook defeat. Bridget Foy and John Chass Corner are striking examples of this strength. In each Cary realises an individual character who resists absorption into a "universal law". Bridget clings tenaciously to her dreams throughout *Castle Corner.* John Chass devotes all his energies—physical and imaginative—to sustaining *his* dream—Castle Corner itself. And the proof of that doomed creation's substance and vitality is its power to evoke devotion even from the supposedly antipathetic Irish peasants.

An ironic juxtaposition reveals the common strength of these characters despite their superficial differences. When Bridget on Jubilee night refuses to understand the disaster that has befallen her in Cleeve's desertion, Cary says, "Her weakness of the illiterate peasant, credulous in a world of fantasy, was now her strength . . .". And ironically this description of Bridget is followed by this of John Chass Corner, "his voice conveyed perfectly the rich and sanguine character of the man, his instinctive confidence in the rightness of things, as established by natural providence . . ." (*CC*, p. 208). John Chass, like Bridget, refuses to comprehend his misfortunes and it is through this stubborn refusal to be troubled by failure that he survives. These two find a saving faith in themselves while the wiser Felix and the more gifted Philip Feenix are destroyed by doubt and frustration.

Only in these characters does Cary show the "intensity of happiness" successfully. Others are weakened by their subordination to the exigencies of theme or the novel's crammed plot. Cocky Jarvis and Cleeve Corner even in youth stand at the opposing poles of reaction and libertarian idealism. Cleeve and Cocky represent a division of Cary's own character of the sort that he exploited successfully in *A House of Children* and which later enabled him to instill integrity into such diverse characters as conservative Tom Wilcher and creator Gully Jimson. But the characters fail of liveliness and complexity in *Castle Corner*. The character of Harry Jarvis suffers in this novel clearly from having been explored so thoroughly for *Cock Jarvis*. The middle-aged man of that story, moulded by contrary experience and his own idiosyncrasies into a figure at once grotesque and deeply human, was a fascinating creation. In *Castle Corner* Cary took a more detached and simple view of Jarvis. He glimpses in Jarvis's boyhood the attachment to "old things, and . . . old values" (Ms Cary 263, N.54) and the stubbornness that would shape him finally into an uncompromising Tory, blindly loyal to the nation and God of his grandfathers.

> Cleeve, on the funeral day, found Harry still in his blacks with a bowler hat on his head, walking through the yard carrying a fishing rod.
> 'Where are you going, Harry?'
> 'Shooting,' Harry said. His pale thin face, which had by nature a resolute expression, was marked by tears. Harry though fifteen years old had wept violently at the graveside. This had surprised people who had not supposed that he loved his grandfather so much. Harry himself had been surprised and now he disdained to wash his face; he was in a mood of defiance.
>
> (*CC*, p. 41)

Jarvis's sense of humour and his cruelty have the same limit; neither extends beyond his appetite for practical jokes. He cannot laugh at himself, nor does he experience the impulse to triumph over others which Cleeve feels towards General Pynsant and the ragged Porfitt. But his stubborn self-confidence carries him through situations where another's response would be humour or cruelty. He therefore receives Stella's insulting attack on his high collar and offers the vanquished and wounded Emir of Daji his hand and friendship with the same amusing aplomb. Cocky's actions are consistently decisive and immutable.

In *Cock Jarvis* these qualities make life a constant battle and ultimately unbearable for Jarvis. In the latter part of *Castle Corner* Cary avoids the open conflicts between Jarvis and other characters that filled *Cock Jarvis*; his intention was to withdraw Jarvis from complicating situations until, in the third volume, his attitude towards colonial rule could be explored in the African setting.

That Cleeve Corner wants Cary's usual vitalising sympathy reflects the extent to which the character thwarted Cary throughout the series' drafting. Cleeve was to be an advocate of freedom searching for a policy that could provide humanity with the means to be happy, a man involved in politics because of his desire to create the society promised by and for his liberal beliefs. For Cleeve's political career Cary found a pattern in C.F.G. Masterman's pre-war activities. Masterman himself afforded the model of a dedicated behind-the-scenes force, a devoted Liberal whose career faded because of his refusal to sway readily with the winds of change. The sequel to *Castle Corner* was thwarted largely by Cary's inability to invest his fictional character with Masterman's practical genius, to demonstrate the fertility of Cleeve's mind, or to accomplish a convincing portrayal of the morality of his commitment to freedom. It proved difficult to show the fine distinction between a licentious egoist and a humanitarian with a love of liberty, and Cary's drafts rely heavily on such terms as "free spirit" and "demonic reality of freedom".

The difficulties which ultimately defeated Cary in the drafting of the sequels are prefigured in *Castle Corner's* portrait of Cleeve. His erratic nature too frequently requires authorial explanation. His adolescent confusions are insufficiently realised (the sole exception is the incisive and comic confrontation with General Pynsant's decadent settee). As a result Cleeve bears the look—which was unfortunately retained by the brave idealist of the sequels—of a stereotyped spoilt child.

Cary himself saw the weakness of *Castle Corner* as the failure to reconcile his two aims in writing the novel: to achieve verisimilitude in portraying the randomness of day to day life while suggesting a consistency in human character and aims ultimately yielding "universal values". When he looked back on Castle Corner in his preface to the Carfax edition, he acknowledged the impossibility of formulating in a novel—or anywhere—a "final shape of society, to be founded upon the common needs and hopes of humanity". In a free and changing world no shape could be final: at best the artist could articulate men's needs and hopes by discovering a shape within them, not imposing one on them. But to suggest such an intrinsic shape, invisible in life, in a novel which aspired to realism defied Cary's powers. He admitted being thwarted by a "subject" which "was personal character working in a medium which was also personal (but I suppose final) character; that is universal values" (*CC*, p.7).

In writing *Castle Corner* Cary still subscribed to the notion that "general theory of *rambling story* is *the details* by the way", that art must aspire to the randomness of life. Detail in the Irish sections of *Castle Corner* is indeed the stuff of realistic fiction. Con Foy's cottage, the beating of the drums, Sukey's feet, and the landscape itself are unforgettable. But the inadequacy of the *laissez-faire* method in art is plain in the novel. As a vehicle for Cary's coherent "meaning", *Castle Corner* fails. Nevertheless in its representation of that varied and active humanity which lives in its particulars and resists generalisation, the novel offers moments of Cary's most sympathetic art. In such moments of supreme characterisation *Castle Corner* captures—as Cary hoped it would—the reality which any political dreamer or governor neglects to his confusion.

NOTES

1. The transition from *Cock Jarvis* to Castle Corner took place about 1936. In a final attempt to salvage the former, Cary planned a new version in 1935 and the scheme for *Castle Corner* emerged in the following year. *Cock Jarvis*, ed. A.G. Bishop (Michael Joseph, 1974), p. xv. See summary of the projected work sent by Cary to Victor Gollancz in September, 1936, Ms. Cary 268, S.10.D.

2. Cary's plans for the series fill nine large notebooks, one small notebook, and five folders (Ms. Cary 251, 263, 264, 265, 266) some of which also contain notes for *Cock Jarvis* or for *Mister Johnson*. They include research notes, descriptions of characters, comments on themes, and charts mapping the dates and episodes of the work's action. Cary worked on the

series throughout 1936 and 1937. Work from the beginning of April, 1936 to the autumn of 1937 was on *Castle Corner* (Letters to Mrs. Cary 1 April and 6 April 1936 and 18 August 1937, Ms Cary 312) which reached publication in 1938.

Cary wrote over a million words for the series, about one sixth of which were for the sequel to *Castle Corner*. This vast amount of manuscript material more than trebles the total draft material (including the printer's copy) for *Mister Johnson*, and represents between two and three times the average number of words in drafts of his other novels. The quantity of draft material, in which scenes are rewritten numerous times, shows Cary's difficulty in bringing the project under control. The earliest notes and drafts range all over the projected series (Ms. Cary 33, 34, 37, 38, 256, 258, 263, 264, 266, 271). Notebooks describe his intended plots and themes fully. He drafted scenes at random, so that among the early drafts scenes from both *Castle Corner* and its sequel occur. After drafting a number of key scenes, Cary turned his attention to *Castle Corner*, for which he wrote two complete drafts (Ms. Cary 22-9).

3. Notes inserted in Cary Collection of Printed Books, B.402.
4. "Why I am a Liberal", in *Why I am a Liberal*, p. 11.
5. The ill effects of Delia's abstract idealism are seen in her son. Frightened by the liberty she nominally advances, Delia refuses emotional and material independence to her son, Fox. In the third book, Fox is seen as the embryonic Fascist.
6. Joyce Cary, *Power in Men* (Nicholson and Watson, 1939), p. 237.
7. 2 January 1952, Ms Cary Adds. III: 1.
8. 21 January 1952, Ms. Cary Adds. III: 5.
9. See "Cromwell House" for Cary's descriptions of his great-aunt Doll (Dorothea Oakes Cary), the model for Mary Corner; her cook Kate, the model for Sukey; Barney Magonegal, the model for Darcy Foy; Tristram Cary who, along with his brother, Cary's grandfather Arthur Lunel Cary, served as model for John Chass Corner; and Castle Cary, the model for Castle Corner itself. See also Fairfax Harrison, *The Devon Carys*, 2 vols. (New York, The DeVinne Press, 1920); and Lionel Stevenson, "Joyce Cary and the Anglo-Irish Tradition", *Modern Fiction Studies*, IX, no. 3 (Autumn 1963), pp. 210-16; and Foster, pp. 3-12.
10. Cary, in 1917, had violently attacked this connection in a letter to his wife: "Do you know for instance what is the basis of government in Southern Nigeria, what pays the tax, what is the basis of trade, its [*sic*] gin, gin by the millions [*sic*] pounds worth. That very Liberal party that was so mealy mouthed about temperance at home, and the treatment of of [*sic*] subject races stopped discussion on this very matter in Parliament, when it looked like danger to their profits—gin was sacred. And Southern Nigeria is enormously rich—one of the richest palm oil countries in the world—but 75 per cent of the oil nuts rot every year for lack of picking. The government prefers to carry on on gin, rather than develope it" (26 February-1 March 1917, Ms. Cary 306). Probably Chorley's failure, through the closing of Laka palm oil markets, would have been connected with the sufferings of the Laka natives and contrasted with Benskin's prosperity.

11. "She's" in first edition, *Castle Corner* (Victor Gollancz, 1938), p. 132.
12. Letter to Mrs. Cary, 7 August 1937, Ms. Cary 312.

3

Mister Johnson and *Charley is My Darling*

If it were felt that the free development of individuality is one of the leading essentials of well-being; that it is not only a co-ordinate element with all that is designated by the terms civilisation, instruction, education, culture, but is itself a necessary part and condition of all those things; there would be no danger that liberty should be undervalued, and the adjustment of the boundaries between it and social control would present no extraordinary difficulty. But the evil is, that individual spontaneity is hardly recognized by the common modes of thinking as having any intrinsic worth, or deserving any regard on its own account ... spontaneity forms no part of the ideal of the majority of moral and social reformers, but is rather looked on with jealousy, as a troublesome and perhaps rebellious obstruction to the general acceptance of what these reformers, in their own judgment, think would be best for mankind.

J.S. Mill, *On Liberty*

Cary's next two novels dramatise and therefore sharpen the expression of fundamental elements of liberal principle which had been part of the complex "meaning" of *Castle Corner*. *Mister Johnson*, published in 1939, and its successor *Charley is My Darling*, both present a strong central character learning the ways of an unfamiliar world, to assert the importance of the individual and to examine the nature of freedom. Education is again a major issue, for in these novels Cary demonstrates that freedom lies in understanding one's environment and seizing opportunities for personal expression within it. The experiences of his young heroes demonstrate that education is essential to create that understanding and to develop the power for self-realisation.

By and large critics separate these books for discussion, linking *Mister Johnson* to the earlier African novels, and *Charley is My Darling*, as a novel about children, to its successor, *A House of Children*. This separation according to subject matter misleads, for it obscures the significant formal similarity of the two books and the distinct difference between the sociological novel Cary wrote before *Mister Johnson* and the novel of character which was to dominate after *Charley is My Darling*.[1] Such a separation also fails to note the striking similarities in the books' thematic concerns.

The problem of education, diffused throughout *Castle Corner*, is here concentrated in the struggles of individual youths, representative figures of the two classes Mill singled out as needing careful guidance—children and primitives. The theme is clear in the notes for both novels. Of Johnson Cary noted, "Gen idea. that he ought to be taught what is true and right, about the nature of himself and the world" (Ms. Cary 265, N.73). And of Charley: "What Charley is worried abt. is not knowing the ropes". (Ms. Cary 48). Colonial Africa and wartime Britain provide the disturbed and changing worlds in which Johnson and Charley respectively seek understanding through imagination, and survival through ingenuity.

Mister Johnson is an adolescent African clerk from a mission school who serves the British colonial administration. Cary had witnessed the climate of misunderstanding surrounding such a figure in his own sober young clerk, Mr. Graves. When Mr. Graves first came to him from another part of Nigeria Cary wrote, "The world of a clerk is strange. Here he is as much of a foreigner as I am".[2] Johnson's foreignness makes him a curiosity to the other characters. Ironically, many understand aspects of his character. Bamu, his wife, knows his boasts exceed his performance, District Officer Blore knows he is capable of crime, his friend Benjamin knows he is clever, and his ill-wisher Ajali, that he is doomed. Yet no one fully appreciates him. The natives "can't make out whether the boy is mad or only a stranger with unusual customs".[3] The British dismiss him as "Mr. Wog".

The awkwardness of growing up is thus intensified for Johnson; as a stranger to Fada and an African working for the British, the clerk confronts in isolation a world unfamiliar and undergoing profound change. Guides to conduct are few for the scarcely educated native boy. Cary's earliest notes for the novel indicate that these disadvantages would give rise to Johnson's tragedy.

> The book then is the study of a human soul gradually giving way to crime—shewing how it happens, from uncertainty, from ignorance of self. Johnson doesnt know till the end whether hes very wicked or very clever.

> Plot./He is lost in the world, wants help and gets bad help.
> (Ms. Cary 265, N.73)

The corollary of Johnson's disadvantages, however, is that, forced to make his own way, all his activity is creative. In character, Johnson becomes an "artist". Defining artistic activity elsewhere in a note, Cary said, "the artist *receives* feeling, impression, sound, colour", and expresses these "in his characteristic imagination" (Ms. Cary 272, P. 52). Johnson's experience is similar. What others show him he absorbs. For the questions others fail to answer he invents his own solutions. Johnson's actions express a rare personality which, like the creations of the artist, fascinates and influences others.

Cary's choice of subject enforced upon him a new authorial detachment. Even while he was in Africa Cary realised how closed to him were the real characters and lives of the natives. Complaining that he lacked observed subjects for his writing, Cary told his wife, "If I could see the black Borgawa I could write of them. But I can't. I see no more of them in their true lives than you do".[4] The foreignness of his hero called forth greater objectivity in Cary's narrative and a significant use of the relationships between characters.

Cary's enforced objectivity made physical detail the chief means of portraying character in the novel, and dictated the nature of Johnson's character itself. Johnson's mind and body are never long at odds with one another. Thus Johnson's body performs a most effective dramatic monologue, registering his thoughts and emotions for the reader. His legs belie his professed distress at being late for work.

> But his legs, translating the panic into leaps and springs, exaggerate it on their own account. They are full of energy and enjoy cutting capers, until Johnson, feeling their mood of exuberance, begins to enjoy it himself and improve upon it.
>
> (*Mr. J.*, p. 19)

Cary's substitution of physical appearance, gesture and speech for authorial explanation extends to the other characters. A telling simile conveys Ajali's malignancy through his physical posture, "he seems to lurk in the hot, stinking twilight of the shed like a scorpion in a crack, ready to spring on some prey" (*Mr. J.*, pp. 15-16). When Johnson presents Bamu with a costly cloth, Cary captures through dialogue and gesture the self-confidence and perplexity of the eccentric Johnson's young bride, jealously protective of an unexpected and pleasing gift.

> 'Look here, Bamu,' Johnson cries. He laughs and suddenly taking the cloth from behind his back, he stretches it before the two women: 'What do you think of that?'
>
> Falla and Bamu both together drop their pestles and take the cloth. Bamu says indignantly, 'Dragging it in the dust.'
>
> 'Put it in the bokkis,' Falla says. 'Be careful.'
>
> 'I'll be careful.' Bamu goes away, carefully folding up the cloth
> . . .
>
> Johnson, brightening at their reappearance, smiles, strikes an easy attitude and says, 'Well, what did you think of it?'
>
> 'You were spoiling it.'
>
> (*Mr. J.*, pp. 107-8)

Such self-explanatory passages were the fruit of care in tailoring narrative, characterisation and incident to fit Johnson's "own joyful tale". The narrative had to exclude ideas alien to Johnson's world or understanding. Cary was not wholly successful in thwarting the intrusions of the explanatory voice which interprets Fada expressions and old Sozy's actions, and which observes, for example, that Rudbeck "is still, like other young married men, the essential bachelor" (*Mr. J.*, p. 92). He was, however, rigorous in preventing his characters from introducing ideas inaccessible to Johnson's education and experience, or tangential to his predicament. He eliminated a native propagandist for scientific atheism and black nationalism because this figure shed no light on the community's incomprehension of the imaginative clerk. Bamu who scorns Johnson's verbal flights of fancy sums up the local reaction:

> 'But Bamu, don't you 'gree for me?'
> 'No, I don't'
> 'Haven't I done work for you?'
> 'Yes.'
> 'What then do you want?'
> 'You're mad.'
>
> (*Mr. J.*, p. 185)

Similarly, Cary cut away an elaborate plot involving a wide group of characters whose personal inhibitions—born of regimentation, envy, bitterness or frustration—were to have clashed with Johnson's spontaneity. To give perhaps the most telling example: in Cary's original plan for the novel, an affair between Rudbeck and his wife-to-be was to have been crucial. At this stage the novel displayed considerable sexual emphasis. Johnson's lack of inhibition in this area was to affront the whites and provoke his tragedy. The plot of this version is launched and Johnson's downfall foreseen when Rudbeck's fiancée, naturally curious and sexually eager, persuades Rudbeck to take her to the orgiasic *bori* dance, of which Johnson has told her. Excited by the dance, she succumbs to Rudbeck.[5] In each of several versions, the girl turns on Johnson after her indiscretion and he is sacked for insulting her.

These plans clearly made Mrs. Rudbeck's psychological quirks, rather than Johnson's own personality, responsible for his misfortunes, so Cary did away with this aspect of Rudbeck's wife and of the plot. Johnson, once destined to become a shuttle-cock batted about among a wide cast of forceful characters, thus retained the novel's focus. The imagination which is Johnson's gift—inflamed by Gollup, angered by injustice, and desperately inventive—leads him fatally into crime.

Injustice is often Cary's vehicle for discovering the force of necessity which operates in human life. Irony is his vehicle for conveying the quirks of accident and circumstance which challenge men's expectations. The injustice which Johnson feels is his betrayal by the civilization he worships. Although Johnson attributes this betrayal to Rudbeck's ingratitude and hypocrisy, we see it as a failure of education which squanders Johnson's brilliant individuality.

In the interests of making the novel move as freely as Johnson himself, and to convey its ironies through evident contrasts rather than through explanation, Cary reduced a number of passages which had treated the discrepancy between civilization's ideal and its reality at length. Thus, Celia's introduction to Bamu, at first written as a separate section of considerable length, was, for the final version, shortened. As a result, the occasion, a momentous one for Johnson, is seen to be as inconsequential to Celia as observing the pottery-makers. Cary condensed a lengthy, maudlin version of Sargy Gollup's paeon to his family and homeland into a narrative summary, exposing the shortcomings of the "civilization" Johnson idealises.

> He describes how lucky he was to marry his wife Gladys, who was the daughter of a high-class tailor; what a beautiful and good girl she was, and how she forgave him when he got drunk on the honeymoon.
>
> (*Mr. J.*, p. 128)

Elsewhere emphasis on the theme of civilization gave way in the writing to other significant and ironic aspects of Johnson's experience. In the initial version, the opening of Rudbeck's road sorely disappoints its builder, for instead of bringing culture or commerce, the road brings two disreputable young rakes travelling the length of Africa in a flag-bedecked car, who insult Rudbeck and provoke his fatal rift with Johnson. Cary realised that the road was more important as the sign of a creative impulse shared by Johnson and Rudbeck. Not the consequences of the road's completion but the completion itself must produce dissatisfaction in its builder. So in the final version Rudbeck's road opens itself; he does not even see the motor that rattles past, oblivious of the road crew's excitement. Rudbeck's dissatisfaction produces a reaction, however; he sacks Johnson for just such a piece of dishonesty (in taxing road users to procure beer for the workmen) as enabled him to build the road.

The irony of this injustice underwrites the affinity between these two characters and dramatically advances the novel's plot. Elsewhere Cary achieves dramatic irony by carefully juxtaposing events or remarks. Gollup's prophetic warning against boasting ends:

'But look 'ere, w'y, suppose you didn't blow off, suppose you didn't say about being up to anybody and then you knock 'is block off; w'y, it's a bloomin' wonder. It's a surprise, see? That's the game, see?'

(*Mr. J.*, p. 125)

Gollup's confident teaching rebounds with terrible irony when, struck by Johnson's knife, he "says in a surprised voice, ''Ere, 'ere. Wot you playing at?'" (*Mr. J.*, p. 197).

These examples point to a significant characteristic of Cary's technique in this novel. Johnson, whose character directs the action of the novel, is judged not by an omniscient observer but by the action itself, and through his relationship with other characters. The well-defined characters of Ajali and Mr. Benjamin set Johnson's in meaningful relief. Ajali, the unimaginative, envious clerk, torn between admiration and hatred for Johnson, eagerly predicts and awaits Johnson's downfall. His envious hatred of Johnson tells of his own perverse sense of justice and of the forcefulness of Johnson's nature. Johnson the romantic sees the perversity of Ajali's imagination, "you show um a diamond, he tink um broken bottle" (*Mr. J.*, p. 106). Ajali sees the naïveté of Johnson's romanticism, "He perfect fool chile. Dey catch him dis time for sure" (*Mr. J.*, p. 196). Ajali's spite is a foil for Johnson's optimism. Ultimately Ajali's jealousy precipitates Johnson's tragedy.

Mr. Benjamin—a frustrated conservative (precursor of *To Be a Pilgrim*'s Tom Wilcher)—exposes by contrast Johnson's creative nature. Both Johnson and Benjamin are products of mission education. They are victims—in radically different ways—of incomplete education. Education has given both a reverence for British-style civilization and provoked their alienation from the native community. Benjamin's view of civilization is conservative. "The civilization of all people in this country is too unequal. That is why we must depend on government jobs for a long time yet" (*Mr. J.*, p. 49). Civilization for him assumes static forms and will not brook innovation, "I wear clean shirts every day, by very good advice. But I am sorry to hear of a government lady" (*Mr. J.*, p. 57). Benjamin's civilization is encased in protective legalism and morality.

These conservative views contrast with Johnson's dynamic view of civilization, an amalgamation of British liberalism and his own desires, "'I tink some day we English people make freedom for all de worl'—make dem new motor roads, make dem good schools for all people—den all de people learn book, learn to 'gree for each other, make plenty chop'" (*Mr. J.*, p. 130).

Mr. Benjamin is the victim of conflicting desires. The "civilized" values which he has learned fail wholly to suppress the emotional impulse which he has been taught to suspect. Thus he can only offer Johnson indecisive advice.

> If you go for a labourer, they seem to enjoy life. They are so free from worrying about the bad condition of everything. Yes, and not about themselves too. The secret of enjoyment. Perhaps you think you waste your time if you go for a common labourer. I think so too. It would prevent all the enjoyment.
>
> (*Mr. J.*, p. 119)

Benjamin is a parody of nineteenth-century doubt—actually and emotionally caught "between two worlds".

Benjamin's attitude to Johnson, whom he wistfully admires, is revealing of both characters. When Benjamin observes, "You seem so foolish in your English clothes", the remark is eloquent at once of his hero's incongruousness and his own inhibition. Benjamin's habit of following Johnson about parallels his willingness to follow Johnson's imagined paths. Although Benjamin argues that real freedom lies in security, to his emotional self the road offers freedom. Benjamin's sudden "lapse" in the performance of his duties, and his strange, almost wishful suggestion that he may lose his job, imply that his wish to be free is stronger than he knows. But Benjamin's impulse towards freedom is escapist—he dreams of being free to see the world; he unconsciously seeks to withdraw from it to the security of a prison cell. Meanwhile Benjamin remains isolated in his "civilization" from the uneducated and unchristian natives. He even refrains from taking a native wife. The result of Benjamin's education is intellectual and physical impotence.

Amidst the misunderstandings and failures of communication in the novel, Cary unfolds a positive development in the relationship between Johnson and Rudbeck. Creation Cary saw as combined intuition and expression. Rudbeck has, in his passion for road-building, a creative spirit of his own, and subtly in the novel he becomes the agent and inheritor of Johnson's inspiration. The grown public-schoolboy and the mission-school youth have much in common. Like Johnson, Rudbeck responds to the suggestions of those he admires and is hostile to those who belittle him. Johnson rushes headlong through his adventure, carried to its dramatic, tragi-comic end by faith in his own imagined triumphs and his failure to understand a society of lesser imagination and greater convention. Rudbeck is similarly ingenuous. Although more aware of the demands of society, he is scarcely more reflective. We remember Rudbeck's failure even to note Johnson's ability until he startles himself by pointing it out to Bulteel. Rudbeck's failure to see the likeness obvious to Johnson in their practice of illegal financial manipulations, underlines that likeness. So that when Rudbeck grants Johnson's gallows request that Rudbeck shoot him, rather than let a stranger hang him, we see it as the natural consequence of a developing bond between the two.

Ironically, Johnson's request is one more product of his active imagination—his death will be according to the splendid principles of the old Guri judge who considered hanging ungentlemanly. Rudbeck, however, responds to a haunting feeling of real responsibility created by his unthinking identification with the clerk. As with the road, Rudbeck can satisfy himself only by turning the clerk's inspiration into a real creation.

Rudbeck's action comes swiftly and without explanation. Arnold Kettle writes that Rudbeck is "unaware of the implications of what he has done", and goes on to say, ". . . there is about these final pages an incomplete dissociation of the writer from Rudbeck's own sentimental attitudes . . . the horror of this act . . . is somewhat blunted by the underlying paternalism of Joyce Cary's own attitude".[6] Cary's papers show that there is indeed a link between Rudbeck's thought and his own. In 1918 Cary wrote, "I hear they have caught a murderer at Kaiama. Rather a nuisance if I have to hang a man. I shouldn't like that at all . . . It is rather hard to have to try a man and hang him too. I would much rather have him shot".[7] Rudbeck's dilemma epitomised the conflct between personal integrity and official codes of action which Cary's experience had revealed to him as inevitable even in the must humane systems of government. But Cary did not make Rudbeck his spokesman.

One draft of the conclusion had permitted Rudbeck to contemplate the horror and personally disastrous consequences of the act; another made Johnson a stereotype—the black man of whose humanity the white man suddenly becomes aware, and had emphasised Rudbeck's guilt at the cost of diminishing the compelling force of Johnson's inspiration. It is important to emphasise that Cary intentionally thrust into ambiguity the dilemma of the servant of a paternalist system who gives in to a personal impulse of paternalism. He dissociated himself from Rudbeck's train of thought, so that the primary theme of the creative man and his infectious inspiration could dominate. He saw that the view here, as throughout, must remain focussed on Johnson. So in the final version we see Johnson kneeling, peeping through his fingers, his legs inert with fear. We see Rudbeck through Johnson's peeping eyes "with his elbow on his knee and his chin in his hand, looking more gloomy and oppressed than ever" (*Mr. J.*, p. 224). When Rudbeck moves we hear him with Johnson's ears and, with Johnson, see him get up slowly. We are still "peeping" through the boy's fingers when Rudbeck returns with the sentry's gun. And the feeling we are invited to share before the gun fires is Johnson's feeling of exultation and thankfulness.

Only when the act is done does the focus shift, and we are with Rudbeck.

> He is surprised at himself, but he doesn't feel any violent reaction. He is not overwhelmed with horror. On the contrary, he feels a peculiar relief and escape, like a man who, after a severe bilious attack, has just been sick.

> (*Mr. J.*, p. 225)

Objectively, the narrative sweepingly views the startled, horrified natives. When Celia, detached and ignorant of the incident, asks about Johnson's fate Cary treats Rudbeck with the detachment he has maintained towards Johnson throughout. Rudbeck exhibits Johnson's own uncritical spontaneity.

> Rudbeck's forehead wrinkles. He looks, as usual when he reflects on any serious matter, perplexed and troubled.
> Suddenly and unexpectedly to himself, he tells her the story. She looks at him for a moment with the same face as the clerk's
> . . .
> But Rudbeck, growing ever more free in the inspiration which seems already his own idea, answers obstinately, 'I couldn't let anyone else do it, could I?'
>
> (*Mr. J.*, p. 227)

Rudbeck has even, in a Johnsonian manner, given himself up to a firm belief in the afterthought "inspiration". These paragraphs admirably preserve the tone, rhythm and mode of characterisation peculiar to Johnson's story even after the hero has departed it.

The final action represents impulses—Johnson's and Rudbeck's—not "attitudes". Cary's own attitude lodges in the whole action. The novel is not uncritical of the paternalist system which it represents by an ignorant and idealistic boy and a naïf young official whose conventional background has encouraged sentimentality and impulsiveness at the expense of reasoned judgment. Cary's belief in the system of indirect rule is the point from which he criticises its failure to execute guidance and secure fulfilment through education.

That Rudbeck's final action is presented with detachment is significant. We are forced to judge Rudbeck's sentimentality and the murder itself in the context of background events and emotions, as we were made to weigh the extent of Johnson's criminality in the murder of Sargy Gollup. We are made aware of the difficulty of balancing law, morality and justice, and of the relative nature of such judgments. In the ambiguity of the conclusion of *Mister Johnson* Cary anticipates his method in the trilogies. He commits himself to the liberal method of encouraging truth to be discovered in the nature of real events.

In addition, however, Cary has made the imaginative, innovative, ever-hopeful Johnson a triumphant exemplar of the creative power inherent in human nature. Repeatedly along the way, and again—jointly with Rudbeck—at the story's end, the novel calls us to witness a triumph of personal liberation from thwarting or unjust necessity through the fulfilment of an imaginative impulse, in the romantic-liberal pattern which is to characterise the activity of all Cary's succeeding heroes.

Again in *Charley is My Darling* the hero is a boy of lively imagination who, as Cary put it, "likes to be liked". Like Johnson, Charley lacks the experience which might equip him to deal with the present situation. A child displaced from London to the West Country, he is as much a foreigner to the ways of his new environment as was Johnson. Like Johnson, Charley creates an ideal world in words and attempts to realise it through actions. When Charley climbs in a window and becomes the youngest cat burglar in England his intent is not evil. The action itself attracts him, its newness and challenge. "He enjoyed planning and forcing an entry into a house, but he had no taste for rummaging or looting".[8]

Cary began this work with sketches of a "renegade choir boy" called Ro (Ms. Cary 270, S.11.D). Fascinated by religion and strong men alike, this juvenile gangster-crusader is the Nazi spirit in embryo. Efforts to turn his imaginative exploits into achievements lead Ro into crime. The Ro sketches and the three manuscript drafts of *Charley* (Ms. Cary 45-9, 270) show little change of intention or emphasis—indeed, they are inter-changed. But the plot became more clearly defined as the work progressed.

Cary introduced the war and the experience of evacuation, absent in the Ro version, to provide a setting which would exemplify change and injustice in the world and give rise to Charley's peculiar predicament. Ro was isolated, but the reason was obscure. Charley becomes an outcast the moment he has his head shaved and his lousy best suit replaced by an ill-fitting suit of men's clothes and a ludicrous hat. The experience of a delinquent Cockney boy evacuated to Devon was alien to Cary, although he knew the West Country well. In place of experience, therefore, Cary employed research—into juvenile courts, the duties of probation officers, remand homes, even rock gardens.[9]

War supplies a background of social upheaval—the division of families, mixed feelings in the new community about the discipline of youthful offenders, and the upset of the educational system—testing the creative resources of adults and children alike. Nevertheless, Charley and the other children carry on their drama in a world of their own, ignoring the cataclysm of which they are unwitting victims. This device enables Charley's character to remain at the centre of the novel's focus. Cary notes the separation between the "child's world and the war world." The children "take it in to play with—*it* doesn't take *them* in" (Ms. Cary 270, S.11.C). Thus the desperation of Mrs. Galor's "soon as this miserable war's over" passes them by. Ginger sings war songs in the same offhand way he sings hymns or love songs, and Charley follows his enthusiasm for creation, rather than Lina's devotion to the war effort, in building Mrs. Allchin's forbidden rock garden.

From the start the kind of ironic injustice Cary saw everywhere victimises Charley. Those who wish to help him, lacking imaginative sympathy, cause him misery: Lina Allchin and Phyllis Hawes shave his head. But the book's greatest ironies grow out of its theme of the need for education. This need is evident in the clash between Charley's instinctive creativeness and ill-understood social convention. Charley, as intelligent leader in the confusion of evacuation, wins the confidence of his fellow Londoners and his new hosts. While he retains the latter, the de-lousing procedure alienates him from his own group and, finding himself in the "strange misery of not knowing what was the extent of his crime in being lousy" (*CD*, p. 44), he must start again to win the boys' friendship with the daring and imagination which brand him a rascal among the locals.

The artist, Lommax, who refuses to guide the creative impulses he has inspired, and Mr. Brown, who resorts to beating, stand at opposite poles in the dilemma—much discussed by Liberals—of the relative merits, as educational methods, of *laissez-faire* and repressive correction. Cary's belief in responsible, sympathetic guidance is implicit in the disastrous want of such guidance in Charley's experience. When adults fail to define their expectations, Charley's vivid stories, distilled from films and crime magazines, becomes patterns of action for the children in the experience of growing up.

Adult failure to perceive confusion, helplessness, or misery in the children is accentuated by the readiness with which the children respond to such conditions in their midst. The children appreciate each other's needs because the world's injustice is fresh and wondrous to them, their sense of its common impact strong. Thus Cary explains Lizzie's "Poor Gingurr":

> As usual with this expression of pity she seems to be expressing an emotion much wider and much more deeply felt than a passing sympathy with the object mentioned. Children use the same tone, when, on the loss of a doll or a boat, they say: "Poor doll, poor boat." They do not pity the doll or the boat so much as wonder, sometimes with curiosity, sometimes fear, at the circumstances within which dolls and boats can be so helplessly smashed.
>
> (*CD*, p. 110)

Further, the children make the distinction the adults fail to make between their explorative transgressions and evilly motivated actions. Lizzie observes, "A lot of kids is silly . . . I suppose they got to have laws agen the bad uns" (*CD*, p. 341).

In both *Mister Johnson* and *Charley is My Darling* the present tense distinguishes the spontaneity of a childish nature from the adult world of motive, plan and guilt. The hero's thoughts, dreams and plans revolve about the present situation and his actions are one with these mental processes. Both characters are incapable of building judgment on past experience. The childish nature does not connect past and present in continuing action. When Charley seizes a moment's glory by freely admitting to the Longwater police that he alone is responsible for the Twyport escapade, he is shocked to learn that his culpability must lead to arrest. The ignorance of cause and effect implicit in the present tense illuminates character by precluding both an understanding of the nature of crime and a sense of guilt.

Similarly, these characters have no sense of a real future. Both Charley and Johnson dream, but these visions represent a projected present rather than a practical plan. This is evident in Charley's descriptions of how he and Liz will live in America.

> 'Bathroom! I'll ave a swimming-bath—ere, don't think I'm being funny. Swimming-baths is easy. You dig a ole in the garden, see—and put cement round and paint it blue with fishes swimming and then you put a greenus over and flowers in the greenus—palm trees—little uns, of course—you eat the water so you can swim all day and, of course, you'll ave the gramophone playing like Ginje's uke.'
>
> (*CD*, p. 205

Charley's plan, like all dreams, is made of fragments of the present experience that includes childhood, Mrs. Allchin's garden and Ginger's ukelele.

Ignorance of cause and effect does not, however, preclude a sense of injustice, an immediate perception of incongruity. Johnson recognised Rudbeck's hypocrisy in sacking him for the same sort of petty thievery he has committed, "It's all same as Treasury cash book—but don' you tell Mister Rudbeck. I no 'gree for Mister Rudbeck no more" (*Mr. J.*, p. 176). And while Charley denounces the laws that frame their predicament, Liz sadly names the book's great irony, "they didden know about us—how could they if they wurn't us?" (*CD*, p. 341). The children's growing perception of the otherness of others evokes a sense of the isolated self and the subjectivity of all acts of judgment.

If one regards Charley as personally more absorbing than Mr. Johnson it is because his character is more thoroughly explored. Less experienced in his struggle with an anti-creative society than the later mature Gulley Jimson and not as wholly spontaneous as the simpler Johnson, Charley is seen to have moments of fear and loneliness, enthusiasm or boredom which he cannot himself justify or constructively overcome. In this Charley resembles more sophisticated versions of the modern comic hero, finding himself in an atmosphere of irrationality, participating in the laughter of suffering, suddenly and frighteningly face to face with himself.

> Charley was perfectly sane. He knew very well that he was not behaving sensibly, that he was taking absurd risks for very little return . . . It was as though a wall of glass stood between him

and everything rational. He could look at reason, appreciate it, but he was obstinately prevented from making any use of it . . . It was a tunnel of glass set on an incline, down which he was flying. He knew where it ended, in a police-station, but this amused him more than anything else. He made jokes about it in the same tone and manner as his stepmother was accustomed to make jokes about thrashings.

(*CD*, pp. 255-56)

Charley's helpless introspection, significantly conveyed in the past tense, measures his growing maturity. Self-discovery, like discovery of the world, is an empirical process. In the remand home, Charley looks at himself as a stranger. He "noticed that he was included among the dangerous characters and this made him feel strange, as if he did not recognise himself". The old Charley, he knows, would have been proud of the smash-up, but again the double nature asserts itself and "another, more sincere, more experienced Charley, wondered how he did so senseless an act" (*CD*, p. 320).

The double view increases Charley's dilemma by making him (and the reader) more sensitive to his failure to understand. At the same time we see Charley confronted with the physical discomfort, confusion and discovery of growing up. The visible physical transformation parallels the emotional and intellectual struggle of the boy's tumble in adulthood.

The events of the novel show the maturing of a character, and define the nature of that character. Charley's consciousness is at first, as Johnson's is and remains, self-centered. For creative responsibility it substitutes fantasy, concern for his role as gang leader, and devotion to cherished possessions, such as the cave, which constitute a private world. Charley protects the members of his gang in order to sustain his role. This consciousness is like Mister Johnson's, who takes pride in the importance of his job and feels remorse not for failing in his responsibilities, but for public lack of success. Both Charley and Johnson seek the approval of others for their actions. This attitude also has much in common with Wilcher's in the first trilogy. Wilcher's self-centeredness and his dependence on the people and objects of a familiar world are also child-like.

Charley's relationship with Liz replaces self-centeredness with an awareness of mutual dependence, of community. The responsibility attendant on this awareness makes Charley's imaginative plans more practical and domestic. This attitude may be compared to Sara Monday's character which finds fulfilment in serving others. Like Sara, Charley and Liz find themselves at odds with a community whose laws governing "other-regarding" actions censure their private codes of behaviour.

Charley responds to this conflict with the conviction that he must protect Lizzie and their plans from the community's misunderstanding. But the failure of his attempted flight to America teaches him that freedom lies not in escape, but in mastering necessity. At this point Charley and Lizzie recognise for the first time the need to assume responsibility for their individual selves; they must not let the world make them "different". Each reacts to the knowledge positively—Liz with the "courage and instinct" which are the mark of her individuality; Charley, imaginatively: "the two or three years which stretch before him become real to his imagination . . .". Charley's maturity suggests the independence and irrepressible creativeness of the artist Gulley Jimson. Jimson masters necessity through art; in the same way Charley absorbs its possibilities into his imagination and greets even the symbolic smothering darkness with "a tremor of excited anticipation" (*CD*, p. 342).

The notes for *Charley is My Darling* reflect Cary's growing grasp of character as a shaping element in fiction. He no longer began with an idea to which he attached an exemplifying figure. Here Cary drew first a clear, detailed picture of the physical appearance, personality, and background of each of the book's characters and, as he had done with Benjamin and Ajali, he used the other characters to illuminate his hero and his themes. Harry, for example, appears in a list of physical descriptions as "dark . . . brown eyes, snub nose, bandy legs" (Ms. Cary 270, S.11.D). Elsewhere Cary sketches his personality,

> Harry is nervous and affectionate—troubled by cruelty in world—and easily dared. Doesn't want to be left out. Full of terrors. Curious always asking. . . .
>
> (Ms. Cary 270, S.11.C)

The anxious, unoriginal boy Cary envisaged here becomes a foil for the creative Charley. While Harry puzzles over the

injustice and the pain of former beatings, Charley turns a
similar experience into a heroic event.

> E nearly killed me, e did . . . Yers, I deserved it—I was an awful
> cheeky kid . . . Father used a stair rod on me once . . . a brass
> one—the marks lasted six weeks . . . I got permanent marks, like
> a chap oos ad the cat.
>
> (*CD*, pp. 99, 101, 102)

Ginger offers another contrast to Charley by showing himself
wise about the world Charley still tends to treat fictionally. He
tells of his mother's three marriages and her skill with men.
When the others dismiss the "art of love" as something silly,
Ginger remarks, "it isn't silly if you want a lot of husbands.
Everybody has to learn how to do things".

The children's distinctive characters are evident not only in
action but in dialogue and even in their habitual gestures.

> Ginger turns aside in the morning to dig the ditch a little deeper;
> Charley to admire the lamp and polish the cigarette-case; Lizzie
> to leave a bundle of dry twigs in a sheltered corner; Harry simply
> to sit and wonder at the whole construction.
>
> (*CD*, p. 143)

The lesser characters in *Charley is My Darling* are joint
participants with the hero in the tragicomic journey towards
maturity. They participate in the simpler forms of comedy
which support the novel's central ironies. Characters like the
ever-grinning Bert Smith, "toiling and flapping" after the
others in his motley of cast-offs, and Mort, whose twisted
exterior mirrors his personality, partake of the grotesque, as
does Charley himself in his hat and baggy trousers.
Incongruities of talk and behaviour among the children—
Ginger's interjected song lyrics, Bert's fits of giggles, ritual
imitations of adult responses to sex or drink—balance the more
profound incongruities of motive and action in the
sophisticated world. Incongruity of action reaches its climax in
the Burls House evening as the children waver between
assumed adult propriety and childish impulses to masquerade,
boast, and destroy.

The irony surrounding Mister Johnson's dismissal from the
road gang and Gollup's murder was near-tragic in its fatal

consequences. Charley's misfortune is not a fatal one; indeed, its crowning irony lies in the realisation that the extraordinary hero does not incur tragic defeat through a unique fate. In coming up against the prohibitions, misunderstandings and moral postures of the adult world, Charley participates in the universal comedy of the battle with common necessity.

In *Mister Johnson* the only noteworthy symbol is the Fada road. But it is noteworthy because Cary invested the symbol with a local significance for that particular tale. Such local symbols, which also appear in *Charley is My Darling*, operate in two ways in the novels. They carry a conventional import as well as particular associations to guide interpretation of the novel's action. Thus, apart from its conventional associations of communications, commerce, opportunity, revolution, the road in *Mister Johnson* stands for the creative impulse Johnson and Rudbeck share.

In *Charley is My Darling*, repeated comparisons with animals assert the instinctive, amoral nature of the children's actions. In their world, as in the world of animals, if there is cruelty, there is no evil will, shame, or guilt. Darkness, throughout *Charley is My Darling* symbolises worldly necessity.[10] The children's private world appears always as a spot of light or warmth upon which this darkness encroaches. That this world of childhood is illusory is perhaps implicit in the artificial quality of the light, "The white [moon] light glitters on them like the artificial frost of a Christmas card . . ." (*CD*, p. 103). Its impermanence is suggested by the collapse of the children's warm and sheltering cave house, invaded by the wind and rain of a stormy night. Charley's entry into maturity is confirmed symbolically when he is pushed into the police car, "into an opening so small, dark and narrow that he is sure it can never contain him" (*CD*, p. 343). Cary's symbolic description of harvest threshing, which transforms the farmer Hawes into an immortal presider over limitless seas, at once symbol and agent of continuing life, places Charley in the context of endless passing time. It therefore emphasises his own place in the inevitable movement towards maturity.

Because the symbolism he uses belongs to the world that Cary's characters themselves perceive, it provides not only a thematic guide, but additional insight into the scope and nature of each character's consciousness.[11] Burls House becomes for Charley a symbol of artistic achievement, a treasure house worthy of his imagination. For Ginger it is a symbol of never-to-be-attained wealth. The boys' cave takes on added stature once furnished with pieces from Burls. And finally, possession denied, Charley's desperate response to the inspiring and admired structure is to master it through destruction.

Charley's imagination discovers symbols to link new concepts to experience, thus making the concepts intelligible. Charley "has no words to describe a sense of guilt, a conviction of sin, but he feels by nervous imagination what they are". His sensual translation of these concepts, "He feels as if she is trying to push him into a dark place from which he will never escape" (*CD*, p. 324), repeats Cary's use of darkness as a metaphor for necessity, demonstrating the boy's movement into the world of common understanding.

This technique in *Charley* looks forward to its more complex uses in Cary's later work. The harvesting scene, repeated in *To Be A Pilgrim*, takes on added significance there when the threshing occurs in the great Adam drawing room at Tolbrook. The thresher becomes the heartbeat of Tolbrook's new life; its driving band, a vital physical link uniting the old house to the sustaining life of field and sky. The moon recurs as central symbol in *The Moonlight*, but there its conventional associations with light, love or chastity take additional colouring from the associations the characters bring to it. Amanda's experience includes the world of Lawrencian symbolism and the hard feminine self-centeredness of the Aphrodite-moon. Her mother links the moon with the warm passion of Beethoven's romantic sonata. In the first-person narratives of Sara Monday and Gulley Jimson, expression itself is symbolic of character. Sara speaks entirely in the homely, sensual images of the cook's world, and Gulley in the brilliant visual images of the painter's perception.

In many ways *Mister Johnson* and *Charley is My Darling* point to the patterns of Cary's later work. Progressing from formed ideas to novels illustrating those ideas, Cary arrived at the novel in which character shapes theme. A line in one of Cary's notebooks of about the time *Charley* was written reads, "Character centre—*not* problem" (Ms. Cary 269, N.78). Keeping his own advice in mind, Cary turned his natural gifts of sympathy and observation to advantage in the novel of character. From characters acting consistently with a preconceived nature, like Harry or Charley, derived the trilogies' technique of the character who speaks for himself. Mutually revealing relationships between characters in these novels, too, forecast the trilogies.

Further, increasing clarification of his own ideas revealed an intimate link between Cary's interest in character and his view of the world.

> The direction of history is caused by the progress of the imagination, in power and experience towards more rich and satisfactory expression of character, in art for contemplation, in organisation of society, for new experience.
>
> (Ms. Cary 272, p. 52)

The tenacity with which Johnson and Charley seek new experience and opportunities for self-expression, and pursue the reconciliation of their imaginative worlds with the world of actuality, provides the significant action of two moving and meaningful fictions. Here, as in most of his later books, Cary combines interest in the particular with general statement. Johnson and Charley are personally engaging and altogether individual heroes; they are representative of those in society whom Cary, following Mill, regarded as most in need of guidance and most eager for achievement, those in the infancy of personal or cultural development; and both have a typical value, exemplifying the creative spirit fundamental to Cary's optimistic view of human nature.

The tragicomic histories of Johnson and Charley establish Cary's most distinctive exemplar of individualism, the imaginative hero, at odds with society, whose independence and suffering are joint products of his commitment to originality—the type of Cary's most celebrated scapegoat-artist-rogue, Gulley Jimson. Such vital characters at the centre of Cary's novels demonstrate the force and variety of individual creative impulse in the world; they enact its power to secure happiness in fulfilment and to force social progress. They constitute the novelist's appeal for the active promotion of that individual freedom which is the fruit of the cultivation of personal dignity and enlightened power in men.

NOTES

1. This shift has been generally noted. See Foster, p. 352; Charles G. Hoffman, *Joyce Cary: The Comedy of Freedom* (Pittsburgh, The University of Pittsburgh Press), 1964, pp. 54-7; Jack Wolkenfeld, *Joyce Cary: The Developing Style (New York, New York University Press, 1968), p. 103.*

2. Letter to Mrs. Cary, 11-15 August 1919. Ms. Cary 310.

3. Joyce Cary, *Mister Johnson*, Carfax ed. (Michael Joseph, 1952), p. 12. Hereafter abbreviated *Mr. J.* and cited in the text.

4. Letter, 10 November 1919. Ms. Cary 310.

5. This plan might be compared to the fair scene in *The Moonlight* in which Amanda succumbs to Harry Dawbarn. It may be interestingly contrasted with the opposite effect of the similarly explicit *pwe* dance in Orwell's *Burmese Days.*

6. Arnold Kettle, *An Introduction to the English Novel*, II (Hutchinson University Library, 1953) p. 183.

7. Letter to Mrs. Cary, 8 October 1918, Ms. Cary 308.

8. Joyce Cary, *Charley is My Darling*, Carfax ed. (Michael Joseph, 1951), p. 244. Hereafter abbreviated *CD* and cited in the text.

9. Ms. Cary 270, S.11.D. The fruits of these researches often gave rise to authorial digressions which Cary wisely eliminated. All that remains in the novel of a nine page digression on "a pretty sharp division among the magistrates generally and the juvenile court panel in particular on the proper method of dealing with juvenile crime" (Ms. Cary 48) is the down-to-earth admission of helplessness by Mr. Brown who "To Lina's surprise . . . knew all about the controversy between beaters and non-beaters".

10. Cary, who was to use William Blake's poetry schematically in *The Horse's Mouth*, here recalls Blake's use of encroaching night as a token of experience in the *Songs of Experience.*

11. Barbara Hardy discusses Cary's use of "private symbols" in "Form in Joyce Cary's Novels", *Essays in Criticism*, IV (1954), pp. 180-90.

4

A House of Children

> . . . individuality is the same thing with development, and . . . it is only the cultivation of individuality which produces, or can produce, well-developed human beings. . . .
>
> J.S. Mill, *On Liberty*

A House of Children, which followed *Charley is My Darling*, stands at a transitional point in Cary's career. It is the last of his childhood novels, and the last to have education as its overriding theme; it is the last to make direct use of autobiographical material. It is Cary's first use of the reminiscence and of the first person narrative. The late-Victorian or Edwardian character is depicted and subtly analysed in the figures of Mr. Corner and Pinto more precisely and economically than it was in Felix and Cleeve Corner, and *A House of Children* looks forward to Cary's most memorable canvas of the Edwardian scene in the lives of the Wilchers of *To Be a Pilgrim*. Its women characters, too have a vitality and individuality which foretells Sara, Nina, Tabitha, and the Venn sisters. And here, as elsewhere, the growth of an individual discovers and reflects a world of continuing evolution.

Between 1940 and 1942 Cary published four novels. The proximity in notebooks of material relating to the various novels, as well as the similarity of their themes, leads one to speculate that Cary was, as usual, working on several books at a time during this prolific period. The appearance of *A House of Children* only nine months after *Charley is My Darling* suggests that Cary, having called forth abundant childhood memories for the previous novels, turned readily to the reminiscence. Initially, he set out to write another family chronicle about the lives of Frances and Delia, modelled upon two of his young Irish aunts.[1] Probably the recollection of the activities and the uncertainties of the years he had shared with these girls steered Cary from the chronicle to a "narration of development" (Ms. Cary 269, N.81), about "children trying to form ideas of life" (Ms. Cary 270, S.11.I).

> General plan is the battle between Frances and Delia . . . Events throughout—picnics, games, rides, drives, boating, bicycling parties, plays, operas, dances, in which the children or young ones are eager for some *teaching experience* i.e. atmosphere of enquiry from children and anxiety, hope, about their lives. and on the other hand wilful or unconscious suppression and misinformation.
>
> (Ms. Cary 269)

Cary's young aunts were among several members of his family who appear as characters in *A House of Children*, but the novel is not wholly autobiographical. Cary borrowed or created figures from outside the Cary family to make the Corner family circle a more complete microcosm of the age. Evelyn Corner's father is Cary's own, the "sportsman and man of the world", purposeful, honourable and responsible, who is a hero to his children.

> In idea, he belonged to his own time. But from his father and through him from his great-grandfather, as I knew from a great-aunt, born in 1810, he had certain courtesies which belonged to the great age of polite forms and social ease.[2]

Victoria's reign spawned many such figures, the most notable being her own son Edward VII.

Evelyn's father contrasts with the children's other hero, the erratic bohemian Pinto, the reverse of the late-Victorian coin. The confrontation of these two in chapter 51 of the novel, which astounds the children by its amicableness, epitomises an Edwardian tolerance which cushioned and concealed sharp contrasts and momentous changes in society.

Cary's maternal uncle Jim Joyce, the opposite to his father in temperament, is the almost unrecognisable source behind the

Uncle Herbert of the novel. Cary's drafts richly characterise "Uncle Joyce", a "fierce" bachelor whose position and self-confidence were shattered by the Irish Land Acts and the coming popular power in Ireland, and whose fits of literary ambition dissolve in despair and drink. The political implications and personal tragedy of Jim Joyce's life were inaccessible to the childish consciousness which shapes *A House of Children*, and so Cary created instead the embittered and conservative Uncle Herbert. Uncle Herbert remains a mystery to the Corner children because they are oblivious of the hurt he suffers in finding his station meaningless, his life useless. Herbert's fastidious indolence which the children only vaguely sense as despair and his sterile self-centeredness which they do not know for a self-erected defence, assume tragic meaning in the novel through the evident contrast between his shrinking world and the ever-expanding landscape of imaginative growth in which they dwell.

Inspiration for *A House of Children* came from literature as well as life. Fellow Irishman George Moore's *Hail and Farewell* trilogy supplies Cary with the model, in an uncle of Moore's called Dan in *Ave* and Joe Blake in *Vale*, for Evelyn's uncle, Major James Foley, the lively recluse who shares a large, partly furnished house on a hill with his maid Pegeen. Moore's uncle raised horses and lived with his cook and mistress Bridget in a house where a piano and a collection of pictures furnished an air of comfortable culture. The Major's concerns are sport and "a boundless interest in the affairs of the world, as mirrored in three or four neighbouring families" (*HC*, p. 201) (the latter a trait borrowed from the stock of Uncle Jim Joyce's eccentricities). The young Moore felt a respect for Bridget akin to Evelyn's shy sense of "something formidable in the look of [Pegeen's] bright eyes and set, firm lips" (*HC*, p. 199). Both narrators express concern about the future of the girl in the light of her anomalous position. Cary follows Moore's lead in demonstrating the artistic vision by drawing a compelling portrait of the girl whose existence is both an integral part of the uncle's character and an engaging story in itself.

Cary's "narration of development" reflects the influence of Bergson's views on perception and memory. Complementing this influence is that of Proust who made involuntary memory

essential to form in his fiction. Although Cary rarely acknowledged his debt to Proust, whom he read during the years
in which *A House of Children* was written, the debt is evident in
this novel and Cary's succeeding works.[3]

Up to this point Cary's novels were conventional in their
treatment of time; a series of events led progressively to a
consistent conclusion. Motive was explored through the
observations of an objective narrator and manifested in action.
But Cary certainly shared Proust's conviction that the
achievement of art is

> To lay hold of our life; and also the life of others; for a writer's
> style and also a painter's are matters not of technique but of
> vision. It is the revelation, impossible by direct and conscious
> means, of the qualitative difference there is in the way in which
> we look at the world, a difference which, without art, would
> remain forever each man's personal secret.[4]

Here Proust was guiding Cary towards recognition in art of a
problem which had exercised many of the late nineteenth-
century writers and thinkers who had coloured his outlook, the
relative nature of truth as discovered in personal experience. He
had touched on the dilemma is *Charley is My Darling* (in Lizzy's
"They didden know about us—how could they if they wurn't
us?"), and in *Castle Corner*'s recognition of the myriad individual
impulses towards happiness. The artist was privileged and
challenged to express *his* truth, even to record that truth as
changing in changing circumstances. For a liberal artist
committed to the value of individual truths, the challenge was a
crucial one. Thus Victorians who had feared the implications of
relativism had been driven to reassert a divine verity overriding
personal impulse, as Tennyson did, or to despair as did the
Arnold of "Empedocles". But others had found in relativism
license for empirical observation and a new kind of dramatic
integrity in art. The self-revealing portraits of Browning's
monologues are the obvious and striking example. Browning
found that by adapting the Liberal posture of tolerance for
individual opinions and for the historically changing nature of
value, he could, as an artist, allow his judgment to remain
implicit and, as Robert Langbaum puts it, "tentative". Such a
posture "allows the case to establish itself in all its particularity,

and to be judged according to criteria generated by its particularity".[5] Cary was to follow a similar course. Recognising that relativism stood between the committed artist and objective truth, he made relativism a mode of art, allowing truth to discover itself through the juxtaposition of opposed cases in his novels; the relative attitudes of childhood's phases in *A House of Children* constitute a prelude to the contrasting first-person narratives of the first trilogy and the revealingly juxtaposed memoirs of the second.

In preparing *A House of Children* Cary began to take note of Proust's lesson. "Narrative straight on, and taking all *scenes (but scenes important)* in its stride . . . and keeping in minds—always the operative mind. In narration of development, break up the same conversation or flow between two scenes and places . . ." (Ms. Cary 269, N.81). To better embody his own world view and to better expose the meaning of a character's relationship to his world, Cary readily introduced into his fiction involuntarily remembered sensation, and experience represented as continuous.

Proust described the effect of an involuntary recollection in a passage which Cary noted,

> And yet should this day from the past . . . rise to the surface and spread itself over us whom it entirely covers, then for a moment the names resume their former meaning, people their former aspect, we ourself our state of mind at the time, and we feel, with a vague suffering which however is endurable and will not last for long, the problems which have long ago become insoluble and which caused us such anguish at the time. Our ego is composed of the superimposition of our successive states . . . Incessant upheavals raise to the surface ancient deposits.[6]

Such an enveloping recollection provided the inspiration for *A House of Children*; its forcefulness enabled Cary, like Proust, to recreate in fiction an actual past enlivened by the sustained mark of authenticity. The formula for these, the novel's opening lines, is to be found in chapter one of *Swann's Way*:

> The other day, in an inland town, I saw through an open window, a branch of fuschia waving stiffly up and down in the breeze; and at once I smelt the breeze salty, and had a picture of a bright curtain flapping inwards and, beyond the curtain, dazzling sunlight on miles of crinkling water. I felt, too,

85

expectancy so keen that it was like a physical tightening of the
nerves. . . .

$(HC, \text{p. } 9)$

Cary was later to evoke similar impulses in the minds of wholly
fictional characters, investing the dissimilar motives and
actions of the conservative Wilcher, the artist Jimson, and the
emotional Ella Venn with the vitality of personal truth.

Cary consciously avoided intrusions which would break the
spell of the reminiscence by going outside the novel's setting or
the child's consciousness. Allusions to the narrator's adult
experiences and the future of the children were removed, in the
novel's drafting, as were scenes involving coarse or corrupting
behaviour by the adults. It was not necessary to portray the
children's reaction to abnormal adult behaviour; the
momentous for the child lies in the ordinary. So the children
wonder at Frances' marriage without love or Uncle Herbert's
fear of novelty, stories told by adults against themselves, or
Evelyn's crushing failure to "make a sensation" at the Maylins'
party. These events reveal the complexity, the injustice, or the
moral ambiguities of the adult world—and are, hence,
disturbing and even corrupting. In contrast, the apparent
normality of such established facts as the Major's mistress,
Pinto's dependence on drink, or Delia's elopement renders
these innocent to the eyes of the children.

In this novel Cary skilfully achieves the Proustian sensation of
passing time by showing the successive changes in personality
which individual characters present to the constant observer.
The "varying aspects" of each character which, in Proust's
description, make him "seem like successive and different
characters"[7] parallel in the adults the lines of development
evident in the children. This is particularly true of the women
characters. The usually placid, generous and flirtatious Frances
bewilders the children by turning into an unpredictable creature
who marries a dull, reliable lawyer only to mock him and make a
slave of him. Her subsequent fierce ambition for him, "He's
determined to be a nobody all his life—he won't even go on the
council" (HC, p. 181), creates a new character for Frances,
quickly succeeded by another, equally astonishing to the
children, upon her entrance into motherhood.

Frances was once more caught up in events, to which she yielded with obvious joy. She seemed to welcome them as a guiding fate, for which she had waited. But she was making small decisions all day along, and since she was now a mother, they were important to everybody and gave her dignity even in Delia's eyes.

(*HC*, p. 188)

Frances' successive stages are merely facets of a consistent personality. The charming but passive woman bestows love and ambition on others so that she may claim her own fulfilment in enjoying their successes. Similarly, Aunt Hersey who labours to effect compromise in a household of conflicting personalities, and wastes her life "in trifling anxieties" (*HC*, p.35), surprises the children by acts of physical agility or indulgence in childish jokes, "for we thought of her as a fussy old lady, whereas she was really a charming and active woman of forty-two . . ." (*HC*, p. 31). When Pinto's influence brings a change in her routine and manner, the children see her for the young woman she still is, and also glimpse the gay and charming girl who had been "a toast in her Dublin season" (*HC*, p. 83).

The changes in Aunt Hersey's character give point to those observed in her impulsive daughter Delia. Delia's unconscious but driving sense of purpose makes her leader of the childish band, an aspiring professional artist, and later a diligent student. When Dunamara falls under the spell of Pinto's enthusiasm for his Shakespearean production, Delia suddenly emerges in the role of responsible manager. She takes the neglected household as well as the most trivial needs of the play company into her charge. Indeed Delia's responsibility, in contrast to Hersey's liberation from it at this juncture, is a sign that her search for a purpose, thwarted in respect of art and study, has found an object in Pinto. The love, the energy, and the ambition evident in her previous characters, manifestly equip her to succeed in the marital venture she undertakes with characteristic impulsiveness.

In Cary's "narration of development" the childish growing consciousness affords the Proustian heuristic narrative centre. The limitations of this consciousness compelled Cary to allow events and sensations to override explanation in the narrative. Cary relates the process of personal discovery to the theme of education, and the novel becomes a portrait of the way children employ imaginative experience to comprehend their world.

Cary comments, in the Preface to the novel, that Evelyn's elder brother Harry "is also myself, and I suspect that I divided myself in this way because I realised by some instinct (it was certainly not by reason) that the two together as a single character would be too complex for the kind of book I needed to write . . ." (*HC*, p. 7).[8] A more precise reason is that Evelyn must be only vaguely aware of his own development. Harry's actions and those of the other children supply a continuing comment on Evelyn's. Cary measures development by exploiting the childish tendency to adopt, through imitation, a *persona*, always regarded as original and individual. Thus Evelyn copies Harry and feels a slight shock every time his brother outdistances him and turns to new interests, often themselves patterned after his cousin Robert.

Robert's failure and success at school, Harry's interest in words, then in the drama, and finally in facts themselves, and Anketel's unconscious creative imagination draw lines of development along which, by likeness or contrast, Evelyn can be seen to move. Cary noted, "Each main scene and period, carries one character forward or introduces a character, reflecting on *our development*, and the period of it" (Ms. Cary 270, S.11.I).

Imitation and sensation are the children's primitive modes of discovery. As they grow more sophisticated, the abilities to reason and express themselves follow.

Imitation is an important aspect of expression and a path to understanding. Through it the children progress from self-centeredness to new worlds of interest. Evelyn watches Anketel make himself ridiculous by copying his own spontaneous witticisms, and then receives a shock himself when informed that his poems on The Mouse, The Fly, The Tit, and The Microbe are all repetitions of his first success, The Ant. Anketel finds renewed happiness and expanded interest in adopting the mannerisms and concerns of the local boy Oweny. Evelyn "recognises" his earlier error and finds a new originality in writing epics in imitation of Shakespeare.

Throughout the novel the children seek to understand their feelings and, through them, their world. Evelyn lives in a world

of feelings he is at a loss to explain, but Anketel gains understanding through sensation. He describes this process when,
dabbling with his foot in the water, he says, "I was only feeling
at it" (*HC*, p. 54).[9] Imaginative comprehension, too, is for
Anketel a matter of sensation. To grasp the concept of a sheep
grazing on a cliff above a cave, "he went back into the cave to
know what it felt like with a sheep overhead" (*HC*, p. 38).
Harry, on the other hand, with his more mature grasp of a world
grounded in explicable fact, directs his imagination towards
technical achievement. On unburying two old fish boxes on the
beach, he draws an imaginative link between this discovery and
the known facts surrounding buried treasure and sets about
building "a Spanish galleon out of them" (*HC*, p. 55).

The problem of understanding is linked to that of expression.
An unconscious sense that meaning is concealed in the shape of
words provokes Anketel's funny remarks, while Harry indulges
in a constant quest for the word which by definition is most
appropriate to convey a meaning already conceived. Evelyn
finds that words open up worlds of hitherto unnoticed meaning.
The description of a whale "ocean bathing too" reveals "the
magnificence of sharing bathing-places with a whale. We both
used an ocean" (*HC*, p. 11). When Freeman says "I suppose the
fish takes us for a bird", Evelyn sees himself

> with a fish's sideways glance, darting through the pale iridescent
> firmament, like a transparent pearl, which is a fish's sky, just as a
> swallow, with short wings, appeared to us in a sunset twilight, as
> it dived after a maybug. The boat was a bird and a boat at the
> same time; we sailed and flew. . . .
>
> (*HC*, p. 10)

He has discovered the substance of a metaphor.

Imagery in this novel enmeshes itself in the visible
development of a character. Real things have the quality of
images for the children. A sword symbolises courage; a lofty
masthead embodies a challenge to independent action which
Evelyn can neither resist nor explain. Conversely, the effort to
comprehend relationships is an imaginative exercise which
forces the children to dwell in a world of images. The sea
provides a continual source of these exercises, as the above
examples show.

As *A House of Children* progresses, the shifts from activity to boredom to new activity become more frequent, each change bringing new interests and new understanding. As the paths of development become more divergent each character becomes more of an individual. The quality of imaginative experience defines itself in relation first to the adult world, then to art itself.

The children make contact with the social community through their father and Pinto. Pinto and Mr. Corner aid the children in their quest for understanding by taking their questionings seriously and by stimulating their imagination. Both translate experience into metaphor which stirs the childish fancy. Further, they reassure the children by the consistency of their own divergent modes of behaviour. An active imagination motivates Pinto and shapes his life. In a draft version Cary describes Pinto as

> possessed by a mysterious spirit which perpetually drove him into actions which ran counter to his own private advantage, which set him standards of perfection far beyond his powers of achievement . . .
>
> (Ms. Cary 55)

The infectious state of enthusiasm thus described is strangely like that of the childish nature, also compulsively seeking knowledge and achievement with the insistence of air filling a vacuum. In this essential likeness of motivation the children and their tutor strike a sympathetic chord.

Pinto's character allies itself to that of the children in another important sense. Cary's drafts emphasise that Pinto typifies the bohemianism of the period.

> [Pinto] was a compound of William Morris, the early fabians, pure Victorian sentiment and the special bohemianism of the nineties . . . He had always been a provincial. But in those days there were plenty of young men equally cut off from the direct influence of the London set, who shewed the same characteristics, who belonged, even at first sight, to the same period . . . The tramps and the dandies both seemed to say, and often did say, in various forms "I am born out of time—I came at the end of things."
>
> (Ms. Cary 53)

Pinto follows the fashions of the time and in this sense is like the children who follow their leaders, never suspecting their actions are anything but original.

In Pinto's faithfulness to his bohemian *persona* and in their father's consistency of character, the children find a valuable reassurance of the validity of their intuitions. There is profound truth in the father's joking reply to Pinto, "I can act myself only too well, but I don't think I could act anybody else" (*HC*, p. 186). Evelyn finds in his father's every action reassuring confirmation of the heroic and responsible character he has conceived him to be.

The confidence the children's father inspires in them mirrors the sentiments of the nation which banished its fears before the reassuring figure of a monarch at once typical and heroic. On Edward's death the *New Age* wrote

> His love of sport, his aversion to the aesthetic, his love of travelling and mixing with men of the world, his indifference to the scholar and student, his love of pleasure and his rigid practice of duty, were shared by him in common with the vast majority of his subjects. These qualities were understood and appreciated exactly because they were common; and in their magnified form they made of King Edward the most popular and representative king that has perhaps ever sat upon a modern throne.[10]

In Pinto and Mr. Corner, as in the king, may be found that typification of common impulses, which later astonishes Evelyn in Shakespeare's characters.

These two figures link the children's world to the world at large. Their father belongs to the world of "patriotism and imperial sentiments; but all with stress upon duty and responsbility" which Evelyn glimpses in the teaching and traditions of his private school. That the clash between these traditions and the new ideas of social organisation represented by Pinto mirrors a conflict in the world at large becomes evident to Evelyn only in retrospect. The children reflect the transition of which they are only dimly aware; their sympathies embrace the old order and the new.

Nevertheless, change in the world outside makes itself felt as part of the novel's atmosphere of evolution and growth. The casualties of history's march such as Uncle Herbert, and the casualties of childhood's loss—Robert, Anketel, Evelyn himself—merge in a comprehensive picture of the nature of all life as evolution, all change as progress. The two aspects explain each other and, in the Proustian manner, it is the immediacy of the childhood recollection that gives to the narrative not only the sense of time passed, but of change unchartable and inevitable.

Art reveals to the children the community of experience and feeling. *The Tempest*, performed by Pinto's dramatic society, is the climax of the novel's action and focusses the delineation of the children's characters. For Evelyn it is an epiphany, revealing the correspondences among words, feeling and action.

> It was the poetry, I thought: "I didn't know poetry was like that," and then at once it seemed to me that it was not the poetry, but the people, the brave boatswain, the wise Prospero. "But it was not the people—it was the way they felt," and it seemed to me that I felt like them; that this was the way real people felt. Words like beauty, death, love, took living form and sang in my head like angels.
>
> (*HC*, pp. 227-28)

The play teaches Harry that the drama is not a crude imitation of experience but a meaningful re-shaping of it, and shows Evelyn that feelings can be expressed because they are, after all, shared.

The episode finally marks the divergence of Evelyn's intuitive nature from Harry's reasoning one. Harry, through his study of words and facts has trained his critical faculties; his involvement is thus with the statement of the play and the faults of its execution. Evelyn succumbs uncritically to the magic of the "whole experience", finding "happiness so intense that it left a permanent memory" (*HC*, p. 226). But the lesson that imaginative expression has it roots in reality is not lost to him. He abandons his epic, but the sketches in blue chalk of diving men which creep onto its pages signal a new immediate relationship between life and art.

This novel's scope is limited to the period of childhood and in substance to the elements of the childish consciousness, but its implications are clear and wide. As the childish personality grows into understanding of the world, the character of the world reveals itself as one of continuing evolution. The child becomes the man, but the man is seen as part, in his turn, of an everlasting process of change, of the creation of new forms out of the common fund of imagination. Cary's return to the theme of the evolutionary nature of the world in *To Be a Pilgrim* takes on a wider scope. Assured in his mastery of the reminiscence, Cary there combines individual development and historical portrayal in Thomas Wilcher's narrative. He uses the technique in conjunction with a disturbing actual transformation in which the man becomes the child again in his innermost desires. Wilcher's memoir poses the challenging question of the finite limits of an individual's capacity to be a creative part of the inevitable evolution in which his lifetime occupies only a brief moment.

NOTES

1. Ms. Cary 269, N.81; Ms. Cary 53. The contrast drawn between Delia, unsophisticated, capable, and immune to injustice, and Frances, ambitious, frustrated, and embittered, is the prototype for Cary's explorations of womanly natures in *Herself Surprised*, "The Captive and Free", and *The Moonlight*.
2. Joyce Cary, *A House of Children*, Carfax ed. (Michael Joseph, 1951), p. 186. Hereafter abbreviated *HC* and cited in the text.
3. The direct link between *A House of Children* and Proust is confirmed by a typescript in Ms. Cary 301. Cary writes: "Proust entered childhood by taste—the taste of his madeleine cake. I knew a man who was moved only by sounds, and certain sights, like that of fuschia, especially when it is being blown about in a wind, can always take me to Donegal . . .".
4. *Time Regained*, pp. 246-47.
5. *The Poetry of Experience* (Chatto and Windus, 1957), p. 107.
6. *The Sweet Cheat Gone*, p. 176.
7. *Letters of Marcel Proust*, trans. Mina Curtiss (Chatto and Windus, 1950), p. 188. Cary Collection of Printed Books, B.237.
8. Proust, too, used the method of fragmenting one character into several.
9. Compare Bergson's description of "pure perception", *Matter and Memory*, trans. Nancy Margaret Paul and W. Scott Palmer (Swan Sonnenschein and Co., 1911), Chapter One.
10. *The New Age*, VII, no. 2 (12 May 1910), pp. 25-7.

93

5

The First Trilogy

Cary's romantic notion of "creation" as the activity which likens man's nature to God's and gives its "character" to an ever-changing world dominates the first trilogy, *Herself Surprised, To Be a Pilgrim* and *The Horse's Mouth*. "The trilogy", Cary wrote in a descriptive note,

> was planned before *Herself Surprised* was written, but it was not published as planned. Sara, Wilsher [*sic*] and Gulley were all partly realised characters in different sketches and the trilogy was a separate enterprise intended to shew the same world over the same period of time from three different points of view[1].

The "world" of the trilogy was England of the period 1880-1939. Cary's aim was, by portraying individual creative activity in morals, government and art, to epitomise "the character of the English civilization" (Ms. Cary 279, S.16.B) (a character reflecting the "dominating mind" of liberalism, in evolutionary or measured change, individualism, the Christian faith, and democratic institutions). As in *Castle Corner*, Cary's intention was to give history a three dimensional depth "as a related order of change". This time, however, the nature of this order was to be implicit in the structure of the trilogy itself. As in *A House of Children*, the first person narrative and a controlled multiple perspective would order the trilogy's world view. "Each character was not only to reveal himself, but to be seen through the eyes of the other two. In this way, I hoped to give my characters also a force of reality which would increase their value as witnesses"[1].

Cary used *To be a Pilgrim*, the central panel of the "triptych", to portray English civilization broadly, through the necessarily historical view of a character wedded to the past and sensitive to the changes which identify society's progress. Wilcher's narrative extends from his remembered childhood in the 1870s to the present of the late 1930s. The Edwardian years are crucial to Wilcher; in this era he both touched the pulse of history and resigned himself to a life of conservatism.

Sara and Gulley dwell in the same nation at the same time, but because Sara is oblivious of the extent to which her life is shaped by that "world", and because Gulley strives for detachment within it to create a balance between his power to shape a world in art and the world's shaping powers, the wider world is glimpsed rather than contemplated by these characters. Sara recounts the events of her womanhood, dwelling on the years shared with Jimson, a span of about twenty years around the time of the First World War. Gulley's narrative covers only the final year of his career, on the eve of World War II, dominated by his three uncompleted last works, The Fall, The Raising of Lazarus, and The Creation.

In writing the trilogy Cary recognised the difficulty of making self-revealing characters the vehicle for historical generalisation. The theme of creation, realised in the occupations as well as the dispositions of the characters in the trilogy, provided a bridge between the personal and the historical. Each of Cary's creative individuals is also a type—of humanity at large, of an aspect of Cary's traditional "English civilization", and of its Edwardian-Georgian moment.

Cary defines the creative experience, embeds it in the social setting of the trilogy, and further evokes the English liberal character through the crude adaptation of two philosophical views. The Lockean view of sensation as apprehension, which was later sophisticated in the Utilitarian assignment of pleasure as the basis of moral action, is epitomised in Sara Monday's sensuous relationship to the life around her. Cary sees this relationship as socially anarchic because its form is dictated not by systems of law or idealism, but by individual intuition.

Gulley's admiration for William Blake introduces another view traditionally opposed to the Lockean, but here comp-

95

lementary to it. Blake envisaged a humanity fallen, through progressive stages of individuation, away from a whole, ceaselessly creative divine existence, and striving to rise again to that wholeness. Through this constant activity man realised the divinity in himself. Here again social anarchism signals the rejection of the laws of code or custom for the intuitive compulsion towards unrestricted creative activity. This anarchic individualistic bent Cary saw as a perennial vitalising element in "the English civilization" and a reflection in that particular "character" of the creative nature of humanity at large.

Cary's treatment of creative activity is often obscured by his own statements that each character in his fiction "creates" his own "life" or "world". Cary does not susbscribe to the "decadent" view of a man's life as a self-conscious work of art. The form of a life is not calculated; it emerges as the visible pattern of characteristic activity, that activity through which the individual, subject to necessity (social, economic, emotional, or accidental) and creating in response to desire, exists. The paradigm might be Blake's Los.

The importance of activity in Cary's view of creation clearly derives from Bergson as well as Blake. Cary had shared with his friend Murry a youthful enthusiasm for Bergson's aesthetic of intution, interpreted as "no mystical surrender of personality",[2] but as an assertion of personality in the creative response by which the individual character assimilates experience and imposes its own ordering vision on the beauties and novelties of a fluid, active world.

This creative response, Cary saw, was necessarily expressed in the form of a life—most completely in the God-like activity of the artist who reassembles forms, giving them a new quality of activity, discovering for them a character unique in a world of multiple character. Gulley Jimson's activity epitomises this idea.

> Even the worst artist that ever was, even a one-eyed mental deficient with the shakes in both hands who sets out to paint the chicken-house, can enjoy the first stroke. Can think, By God, look what I've done. A miracle. I have transformed a chunk of wood, canvas, etc., into a spiritual fact, an eternal beauty. I am God.[3]

Just as the laws of nature and causation shaped the world's

form, the artist's materials and his own physical character, though limitations on his creative power, were inseparable from the product of his creative impulses. As Gulley Jimson puts it,

> Sun coming up along a cloud bank like clinkers. All sparks. Couldn't do it in paint. Limits of the art. Limits of everything. Limits of my fingers which are all swole up at the joints. No fingers—no swell, no swell, no art.

(HM, p. 17)

In his view of necessity Cary modifies the romantic *and* the utilitarian views of human creative power which primarily shape the trilogy. That man can create like God is qualified by the observations first that God is subject to necessity, and then that the human form divine is not merely enchained by a material world but derives his existence from it, finding the stuff of creation not in his own or a divine mind but in that solid world. Further, man cannot, in Cary's view, control necessity, finally shape (in a utilitarian-idealist way) his society. He can only act in pursuit of enlightened desire as part of the forces which, shaping him, are ultimately also shaped by him.

This emphasis on material necessity leads to a further element in Cary's portrayal of the English civilization and its individual members—an element not primarily at issue in the novels, but clearly present to Cary's consciousness. The period in question is that in which Marxism—as theory and as a source of the evolving forms of English socialism—became part of the English consciousness, an element in the transferral of liberal allegiance away from the principles of economic and governmental laissez-faire to those of constructive control. Although the novels contain only oblique or passing references to this element in society (in Sara's daughter Belle who "took up a little communism to have something of her own", or Gulley's description of the 'twenties ethos, "Modern democracy. Organised comforts. The Socialist state. Bureaucratic liberalism. Scientific management. A new security"), the trilogy at every point reflects a preoccupation with the economic bases of the individual's social existence and of social change. In addition to the manifestations of necessity I have already alluded to, Cary recognises an economic necessity which moves historical events, defines a climate for the world of the arts ("Through cash to culture", Gulley remarks), and acts upon all individual lives.

Although Sara does not reflect on history as Wilcher does, or analyse society's attitudes as Gulley does, all these three share the same point of contact with social necessity: money. Bills bring Sara's downfall, as financial security ties Wilcher to Tolbrook and money limits the practice of Gulley's art. Cary has rooted material necessity in this trilogy in the specific dehumanising force attacked by Christians and Marxists alike and cited by Mill as a false standard of happiness (*Utilitarianism*, p. 34). The work is thus invested with a wide historical relevance which both grows from and extends beyond the dilemmas of Cary's individual characters. Sara and Gulley defy this element of necessity and both, as a consequence, enjoy a rich and highly developed sensibility—Sara's primarily physical, Gulley's both physically and conceptually creative. Wilcher succumbs to it, incurring the impoverishment which expresses itself in Christian terms as lack of faith, which an economic interpreter might call lack of productivity, which Cary, as a liberal, sees as a failure of personal fulfilment in the creative activity which distinguishes men from beasts or machines.

Cary's concept of character as mutually defining form and activity gives the first trilogy its shape. *Herself Surprised*, *To Be a Pilgrim* and *The Horse's Mouth* anatomise the world's flux by deriving a representative fate from an individual characteristic pattern of activity. Sara's physical preoccupations determine her activity; she serves her "flesh" not least by serving others. The desire to give and to receive satisfaction shapes her life as a servant, and the form of her perception is rendered through her language. Gulley's characteristic activity is creation, and the practice of art defines his character. By moving steadily towards pure unity of activity and intuition, Gulley reveals the essence of creative activity.

If, however, the creative instinct is fundamental to human nature it is by no means a solitary instinct. Sara, following the uncomprehended promptings of an animal female nature, and Gulley, receiving his inspiration from a spiritual "horse's mouth", form an incomplete picture of human motivation. Cary was acutely alive to those other sentiments, bred from man's awareness of the transience of his life and world, which vie with the creative instinct, urging the human to conserve that which he has made.[4] The central volume of the trilogy, therefore, belongs to the conservative Wilcher; his deathbed narrative introduces the conflicts, psychological and historical, which give the world of the trilogy its appropriate complexity.

Herself Surprised

> A person whose desires and impulses are his own—are the expression of his own nature, as it has been developed and modified by his own culture— is said to have a character.
>
> J.S. Mill, On Liberty

As Cary stated, Sara, Wilcher and Gulley were initially "all partly realised characters in different sketches." Initially Sara's story displayed a triple pattern, with Matthew Monday completing a triad of social types: liberal, conservative and artist.

> Matley is a study of Liberal trying to do the impossible as anarchist. Gulley is study of possessed artist. The mysterious drive of art . . . Willsher is study of conservative virtue decay no creative outlook or outlet except in evil forms.
>
> (Ms. Cary 81)

This pattern proved unsatisfactory, for, apart from the physical, there were no grounds for shared interests between Sara and Matt, such as those which link Sara to Gulley and Wilcher. Sara loves her flesh and the art which praises it; Gulley loves his art and the flesh which physically and aesthetically inspires it. Wilcher responds to Sara's instinctive faith in providence and, in turn, Sara delights in his care for the literature and habits of the Victorian past no less than in his gratitude for physical comfort. But Monday's political interests, like the rigorous ethics and manners of his class, are alien to Sara's background and beyond her intellectual ken. Monday was to be an idealist surprised by the shortcomings of reality, a conformist baffled by changes in tastes, morals and social habits, a pacifist confronting the reality of war. His idealism and that of the Liberal party were to be signalled by his faith in mutual trust among nations. But his expression of the liberal crisis of confidence in 1914 could only issue as a detached monologue in the narrative of a wife for whom a political party was an afternoon social affair. Cary recognised the inappropriateness of the political theme to Sara's world. Instead, he permitted the conflict between idealism and reality to show itself in Matt's reaction, shared by Sara, to Jimson's art: "He said that Jimson was not even a true artist, for the true artist was never spiteful or cruel. It was impossible, because if he was inspired it must be by God".[5] Matt's reversal of sympathy towards Jimson parallels his subsequent horror and disillusionment when confronted by irrational cruelty on a grand scale in the outbreak of war.

Sara's surprised response to her own physical appearance— in the novel's opening scene—possibly another glancing allusion to Bergson's idea of pure perception—is a model for the delayed self-recognition which signals her impulsiveness and fundamental innocence throughout.

> I remember the first time I saw myself in my true body. It was on my honeymoon, in Paris in a grand shop . . . I seemed to be looking into the next saloon, and I thought 'Look at that fat common trollop of a girl with a snub nose and the shiny cheeks, jumping out of her skin to be in a Paris hat . . .'
> But in the same flash I saw that it was me.
>
> (*HS*, p. 10)

Her reaction, too, is characteristic: "If I'm a body then it can't be helped, for I can't help myself".

Sara's body which mediates her perceptions and performs her various pleasure-giving activities is her point of contact with the world. Indeed, her "flesh" has an entity of its own and she is ever mindful of its needs. She guards its health, on which her livelihood depends, and its beauty which secures her pleasure. She accords it respect and comfort, "I could never bear cheap stuff anywhere near my skin" (*HS*, p. 183). And her sense of justice is nowhere stronger than in her sense of the appreciation due her flesh.

> I will admit that when I stood in my bath and looked down upon myself, I have cried to think that I was done for, and thrown away upon a living tomb, pitying my flesh as well as my skill.
>
> (*HS*, p. 139)

Sara's resignation to her nature—physical and emotional—precludes moral reflection. Her spontaneity expresses itself intellectually in forgiveness. She forgives herself, "That's the way I'm made" (*HS*, p. 14), and others, not according to ethical formulae, "not, I mean by words, for words would have brought it all up for talk and talk is dangerous in such a case."(*HS*, p. 32), but actively. Sara's impulsive forgiveness is the creative basis for further action, new relationships, progress through experience.

Sara's amorality defines itself through clashes between her impulsive behaviour and the "world's eye"—that social arbiter of opinion which, Mill says, prevails in every age—which judges her actions before she herself grasps their implications. Miss Maul's disapproval, statements of the judge and the prison chaplain, and Gulley Jimson's comments on her motives compose a view of Sara through the world's eye. Where the world's eye sees lawlessness or guile, Sara sees none. Only when she hears herself characterised as a criminal does she regret her indiscretion. Nor does Sara grow significantly in awareness. As she ages, Sara's unselfconsciousness restores her youth, "I would be gay all evening, as if I had been a young girl coming from a party or from the communion. Not knowing yet my own self or the traps of the world" (*HS*, p. 163). Sara's amorality is intrinsic to the narrative—a moral negative capability, a resignation to the providence she calls her "luck", different in foundation from Jimson's acceptance of vicissitudes, but complementary to it.

Sara's language, like her morality, is the constant expression of her character. It derives from her experience and affections. Her delight in nature emerges through metaphorical references to the domestic things she loves, the objects of the cook's pride, the housekeeper's happiness. What Wilcher calls "wisdom" is merely the unthinking utterance of platitudes. Such formulae, derived from a tradition of shared experience, bring the comfort of shared irresponsibility for the inevitable.

The immediacy of Sara's consciousness is evident in her literal reception of language. Despite the duplicity in her own conduct, Sara is completely insensitive to verbal innuendo. Gulley's sarcasm eludes her. So does the import of Wilcher's first suggestion that she become his mistress, "Now when he said that, all at once I had the feeling that he was going to propose marriage" (*HS*, p.172).

The limitations of Sara's experience and consciousness define her relationship to art. The familiar settings of Charlotte Yonge's novels enable Sara to find in them a mirror of her own life, or guides to conduct. "'Many thoughts floated through Theodora's mind; but whether the better or worse would gain the advantage seemed rather to depend on chance than on herself' and it might have been written for me" (*HS*, p.351) But she is incapable of responding to Jimson's unrepresentative art.

The quality and impulse of all Sara's expression derives from sensation. Sara apprehends her own emotions and those of others sensually. Happiness can be tasted. Lack of purpose lies "like a big hiccup . . . on my chest" (*HS*, pp. 88-9). Regret has a physical basis in the waste of her bodily powers. Even her mother's Christian teaching is "in my blood, the best part of me" (*HS*, p.147).

Through physical evidence Sara penetrates the feelings of others. When Matt's face grows red, Sara recognises "nature working in him" (*HS*, p.15). Her relationship to Jimson has two parts, the intellectual and the sensual, the latter interpreting the former. "So that my mind was laughing at little Jimson when he held my hand and told me he could make me so rich and give me furs and jewels; yet my flesh delighted in his kindly thoughts" (*HS*, p.92). A fine day and a physical reference reveal Nina Jimson's religion to Sara. "She said to me that it was a day when God seemed so close that you could hear him breathe" (*HS*, p.56). Similarly, Gulley's practice, not his explanations, make his code of conduct clear to her, "Then I remembered that I had never heard Gulley swearing and from all I knew I think that was Gulley's religion. Not to trouble about his ups and downs" (*HS*, p.72).

Sara's social consciousness, too, has a physical basis. She is well aware of the importance of physical attributes in determining a person's career in the world. Rozzie's gaudy clothes, Matt's long nose, ladies whose coats and skirts fit "like a coat of paint", Wilcher's "long blue upper lip", Clary's face powder, measure for Sara the nature and social status of these figures and the success or difficulty in store for them, dwelling — as they must — in the world's eye. Though she admits she could never understand " the minds of that class" she serves, Sara learns the manners of the upper bourgeoisie in terms of dress, and it is these terms that she views the character of society in Edwardian Britain, "Life was nothing but joys and new dresses" (*HS*, p.76).

Out of her characteristic preoccupations Sara evolves a personal morality of pleasure and utility. Just as waste is the sign of a badly run kitchen or household, waste of one's powers, abilities or lifetime is the chief evil in Sara's world. It is the enemy of life itself. Life is a gift of providence, perceived in moments of happiness. Such moments — seized and remembered — are therefore waste's counterpart, sources of grace and the measure of one's blessedness in the world. These forces operate in nature itself. The waves of the sea only seem to waste their work when there is no onlooker, "but then it was a comfort too, to think that they would always be there, whether anyone was looking or not; such is the bounty of providence, to pour out pleasure" (*HS*, p.99).

These guides determine Sara's conduct, "I even made it seem welcome to please the man, for I thought, if I must give him his pleasure, it was a waste not to give him all that I could" (*HS*, p. 93).

Jimson's disappearance provokes rage and regret in Sara because her own creative activity has been thwarted. The ambition which Sara displays on behalf of Matt, her daughters and Jimson is not materialistic, but a campaign against waste. She merely wishes to ward off emptiness in their days, to ensure their chance for fulfilment: marriage is essential for Nancy "to make up to her for all her disadvantages" (*HS*, p.55), Matt's political activity makes him "more fearless . . . more happy and more easy in his mind" (*HS*, p.42). The sense of waste measures Sara's incomprehension of Gulley's art. She grasps its innovative quality and only objects to its inutility. "It's like the fashions. A hat may be as new-fashioned as you like, but it must stick on a woman's head" (*HS*, p.89).

Sara evaluates her days in terms of waste and happiness. Her joys with Gulley are active, "I did not want to sleep, either, because it seemed waste to sleep away such an afternoon" (*HS*, p.128). Her careless happiness at Woodview lacks the wisdom of experience which makes her appreciate her good fortune at

Tolbrook, "So it was really waste of my days and their proper delights" (*HS*, p.149). Sara's efforts to fill her days with the greatest possible amount and quality of pleasurable activity illustrate a fundamental sense of freedom. Her active pre-occupation with the needs of her flesh presents in the simplest physical terms the concept of freedom as the scope for self-fulfilment within the limits of the individual character.

The "luck" which providence bestows is merely Sara's way of understanding Cary's freedom. It is the opportunity provided by a home, an occupation, the companionship of friends, for Sara to exercise her abilities. Change is no threat to this luck, but the sign of its continuing operation. It was, Sara says "providence Himself that had taken me by the hand and led me back to the kitchen" (*HS*, p.149). Wilcher's kitchen is the epitome of Sara's luck, the climate of her freedom. In this place Sara recognises that her character as "a born servant in my soul and heart" makes her also "mistress of my own world in my own kitchen" (*HS*, p.149). Here necessity and possibility are one, for the confines of kitchen and kitchen garden are limitations which correspond to the bounds of Sara's interests.

Here Sara's powers find expression in an activity as vital as nature's own processes. "You would say I was putting out in buds like a shallot with my big kitchen heart in the middle and my little hearts all round in the empire of those good faithful offices" (*HS*, p.150). Every object in this realm serves necessity, "For the great beauty of my jewels was that every one of them was needed", and thereby reveals, in the absence of waste, a triumph of creative possibility. Further, Sara's activity fulfils not only in rewarding herself but in bringing physical and spiritual pleasure to those she serves, "conquering hungry stomachs and bad tempers" (*HS*, p.150).

Though incapable of self-analysis, Sara recognises in herself an inexorable and sustaining sense of purpose. "I never had Rozzie's art", she says, "not to care for anything and to keep myself going on like a horse without any kind of happiness or hope or proper object in life" (*HS*, p.118). This object often overshadows, in Sara's consciousness, the nature of the means employed to realise it. Hence she procrastinates, lies or steals in order to preserve herself for the greater creative activity of promoting pleasure. Her sense of purpose pushes Jimson into his exhibition, sends Tommy through school, and accounts for her pride in the fittings of her kitchen. Yet its workings remain as unpremeditated, instinctive, and ramifying as the budding of the shallot. This purposefulness drives Sara into the exercise of her freedom, makes her sensible of the blessings of providence, and allies her with the forces of change. It ultimately rings from every sentence of her final statement.

> Neither had my luck left me, for just when I was fretting for our quarter day at Gulley's and Tommy's bills on top of that, this kind gentleman came from the news agency and offered me a hundred pounds in advance for my story in the newspapers, when I come out. Paid as I like. So that will pay the school bills, at least, and I've no fear then. A good cook will always find work even without a character, and can get a new character in twelve months, and better herself, which, God helping me, I shall do, and keep a more watchful eye, next time, on my flesh, now I know it better.
>
> (*HS*, p.220)

Sara's history tells a remarkable tale of social mobility. Marriage to Matt Monday transforms the servant into the mistress of Woodview. Her debts and her arrest for fraud deprive her of this comfortable existence, but she finds occupation living with Jimson and keeping house for Miss Slaughter. When left by Jimson, her capital exhausted, she returns to service in Wilcher's household. There she rises from cook to house-keeper and is on the verge of again marrying her master when she is arrested for theft. The pattern of her activity is one of rise and fall.

In keeping with Cary's view of existence as character, Sara's social progress grows as much from her nature as from social accident. The same bold sensuality which attracts and wins Matt Monday causes Sara to succumb to the admiration and advances of Hickson and Jimson. She rejects the conventional comforts of social propriety for the enjoyments of active service and pleasure-giving. Sara's flesh is thus the agent of her fall as it was of her rise.

Cary retained a persistent interest in the capacity of people, particularly women, to progress downward socially,[6] for he saw its roots in the same consistency of purpose which accounted for the social rise of a Chester Nimmo, a Lloyd George — or a

Hitler. The social regression of Sara Monday or Gulley Jimson reflects a personal purpose which outweighs social concerns. Sara can move freely up and down the social scale because her character as a "born servant" is not dependent on her occupation, but on an attitude. She practices pleasure-giving with equal artistry as wife or cook. Her social flexibility is therefore the exterior condition of a consistent character.

The narrative which primarily reveals Sara's character also offers a secondary comment on the nature of social change in the period of the trilogy's historical interest. Sara's experience reveals a movement in national life away from the Victorian and Edwardian world of servants and masters into the post-Great War world. Here, as in Forster's *Howards End*, industrial progress signals the decline of country houses and an agricultural economy. Sara, with a common view but an idiom unavailable to Margaret Schlegel, sees suburbs encroaching on the countryside "like mould in a bread bin". The middle classes retreat into "rows of little houses, red and green with pink roofs" (*HS*, p.200), and small kitchens physically preclude the separate households of family and staff. Sara observes these changes in the same unanalytic way that she records changing fashions, which raise and lower skirts and render face-painting first acceptable, then familiar, as they impinge on her experience. There is no need for her to speculate on their causes; the prosperity she enjoys as wife of a foundry owner in Bradnall explains the ravages Sara sees the town suffer. The trends discovered in Sara's narrative continue through the trilogy. Tolbrook's decline, evident in Sara's tenure as cook, finds its explanation in Wilcher's story, and Gulley's discovery of Sara amidst an atmosphere of steam and soapsuds in Byles's tenement "in a little desert of asphalt" in *The Horse's Mouth* completes the trilogy's portrait of social change which finds an unconscious mirror in Sara's life.

Sara Monday's limited experience intimates to her the nature and inevitability of social progress. Sara understands better than Wilcher the impossibility of preserving the past, "I often thought that you couldn't go back on a fashion. For say what you will, fashions never do go backwards . . ." (*HS*, p.195). Like Jimson, she understands change as the search for personal development. In this understanding she exposes the failure of

Matt's conservative liberalism.

> He quarrelled with Belle for her politics, because like all young
> people with natural spirits, she did not agree with him and took
> up a little communism to have something of her own; and he
> complained of Edith because she was so set on leaving home. But
> why not? Thank God for the ones that know what they want and
> want something sensible.
>
> (*HS*, p. 71)

Self-reliance, the ability to forgive herself and others their
weaknesses, liberates Sara. Her life takes its form not from
possessions or concepts, but from activity. The form of her
expression is work—the essentially and uniquely human
productive activity—but its object is happiness. Sara, in the
reality of her strengths and her idosyncrasies, both approaches
and qualifies the liberal-utilitarian ideal.

To Be a Pilgrim

> The despotism of custom is everywhere the standing
> hindrance to human advancement, being in unceasing
> antagonism to that disposition to aim at something better than
> customary, which is called, according to circumstances, the
> spirit of liberty, or that of progress or improvement.
> . . . the only unfailing and permanent source of improvement
> is liberty, since by it there are as many possible independent
> centres of improvement as there are individuals. The progressive
> principle, however, in either shape, whether as love of liberty or
> of improvement, is antagonistic to the sway of Custom, involving
> at least emancipation from that yoke; and the contest between
> the two constitutes the chief interest of the history of mankind.
>
> J.S. Mill, *On Liberty*

Cary's sympathy for the conservative impulse in human
nature gained forceful utterance in an article of 1953.

> Adjustment to the revolution of the arts is easy for one who is
> not himself a practicing artist . . . Can anyone fail to suffer in face
> of the continued ruin of good men, good things, of all that is fine,
> true, delicate, in civilisation built up over centuries by the
> devoted labour of generations? Can everyone console himself
> with the enjoyment of all that is fine, true, delicate, in the new

arts, new aspirations which arise every day? It may not be possible to do so. We may be too old, too tired. We may be too lonely. Change may break our hearts.[7]

This tragic possibility lies at the heart of Thomas Wilcher's memoir; the narrator of *To Be a Pilgrim* is an old lonely man unequal to the challenge of change. Wilcher, born in 1868, is a man of his age, the late Victorian and Edwardian. A Liberal in politics, his is the liberal character bred from a Whig tradition and shocked by the radicalism of his contemporaries. It is significant that Cary did not, though he contemplated it at an early draft stage,[8] make Wilcher a Tory or an Empire man. Wilcher's conservatism is neither the product of traditional policy nor power-thirst, but instinctive. Thus Wilcher practices the law, an intrinsically conservative profession. A religious man, he is an English protestant of the Low Church variety. His roots are among the landed gentry. Wilcher belongs firmly to the order which, manifested in "the Landed System, the Established Church, the Popular Religion", C.F.G. Masterman described in 1905 as "in peril of change".

Wilcher, thus, is typically disposed to a conservative frame of mind. But in his old age an awareness torments him that the happiest people he has known seem not to have conserved. His failing days see him engaged in an effort to assess his relationship to these personalities and to overcome the fault of his compelling attachment to material things. Ironically, the effort is a large conservative gesture, the recording of those memories whose substance will be lost with his death. The symbol of Wilcher's world is Tolbrook, the family home which has been the lifelong object of his conservative efforts. That Tolbrook is also a monument to change dawns on Wilcher as a revelation. Tolbrook mocks Wilcher's fear of change, but its survival enables him to take the measure of his own life.

The conservative impulse, Cary acknowledged in a note for the novel, could be positive or negative.

> The conservative in fact has to *recreate*, to *maintain*, his activity is protective and maintaining. He must contrive a flexible defence of standards and must *believe* in those standards. To lose faith in the standards is to lose motive for creation (which may be unconscious) i.e. you can be passive conservative, a mere

parasite or a creative maintainer. A man *can* be quiescent and merely receptive of reflexes.

(Ms. Cary 71)

Wilcher's conservatism, is manifested in a love of possessions, an inability to cast off things. "I never liked lodgings. I was too fond of my dear ones at home. And what if they were trees and chairs and furniture and books and stones?" (*TBP*, p. 342). It became clear to Cary that this conservatism must be antagonistic to faith. Faith must be continually self-renewing; it must grow. Cary was quick to realise that Wilcher's fear of political disintegration and moral dissolution "because he has lost touch with the reality of growth" (Ms. Cary 274, N.87) must be the outward sign of an inner failure of growth, affecting faith and love as well as ideas and opinions. Wilcher's inability to exercise complete faith in God leads him to seek a surrogate object of duty in the world so that Tolbrook becomes "a sacred trust". This conservative materialism in turn can be seen "gradually removing him from faith" (Ms. Cary 71).

Lacking faith and the essential belief even in his professed standards, as evidenced by his political and religious vacillations and his deviation from the moral rigidity he defends, Wilcher's conservatism has all the bluster of insecurity and none of the action of integrity. In his notes Cary singled out that passage in *Pilgrim's Progress* where Christian learns the powerlessness of law in the absence of faith. Wilcher, the man of law, finds beyond him the act of faith necessary to be a pilgrim, to ally himself with progress, spiritual or temporal.

The temporal progress evoked by Wilcher's history unfolds in the events of the Edwardian transition. In the brothers Thomas and Edward Wilcher Cary splits the Edwardian liberal character as he had formerly split *A House of Children*'s central childish character into the separate personalities of Evelyn and Harry. Tom is the doubting Thomas of his age and his actions are not creative, but imitative. He epitomises that Edwardian "Civilisation" which, said Masterman,

> speaks with a voice less certain than in former days; being itself perplexed why, after the long journey has been attempted and all the miracle achieved, it cannot at last see clearly on the horizon the walls and towers of the Golden City of men's dreams.[9]

Rapid change, always foreseen by Edward, always wounding to Wilcher perplexes the narrator. For a time he joins the revolutionary forces. "I shouted the pilgrim's cry, democracy, liberty, and so forth, but I was a pilgrim only by race" (*TBP*, pp. 341-42).

Wilcher's torment lies in his inability to assess the nature of change in an age of change. Revolution fires his imagination to enthusiasm while at the same time striking fear and confused disapproval. He wavers, now the agent of change, now its antagonist.

> Indeed, I was enjoying at that time, in my renewed friendship with John, a resurrection of hope and enterprise. I had instituted in the office, the new reform of wearing short coats; and also of typing, instead of engraving our wills, bringing us up to date in both respects.

> And suddenly the idea came home to me and I was frightened . . . As if there were an infection of change in the very walls, books and Edward's bent figure, white hair and hollow cheeks.
>
> (*TBP*, pp. 275-76)

The source of his confusion is his conservatism, his hatred of the destruction of a familiar world.

The failure of faith which distorts Wilcher's personality is akin to that which beset the old liberalism. Cary's notes make this plain.

> The movement of politics in W's time. The Tory belief in all its *logical force*. Giving way to a vague laissez-faire in that class. *A dying class*. Trusting without faith. The election, he is shocked and horrified 1905, again shocked by Edward's violence. But Edward trusts *life* on a cynical basis. The war forgets fears in faith in humanity. Afterwards disintegration.
>
> (Ms. Cary 274, N.87)

Wilcher's two-mindedness mirrors that of the liberals of his time, poised on the traditional brink, uncertain whether to retreat from reform or to advance into areas of incalculable risk. No liberal is more honestly revealing of this uncertainty than C.F.G. Masterman:

In no panic fear, certainly with no acquiescence and despair, the reformer to-day will contemplate the possible future of a society beyond measure complex, baffling and uncertain in its energies and aims. But the warning, always useful, but now more than ever necessary, cannot be too strongly emphasised: that with the vertical division between nation and nation armed to the teeth, and the horizontal division between rich and poor which has become a cosmopolitan fissure, the future of progress is still doubtful and precarious. Humanity—at best—appears but as a shipwrecked crew which has taken refuge on a narrow ledge of rock, beaten by wind and wave; which cannot tell how many, if any at all, will survive when the long night gives place to morning. The wise man will still go softly all his days; working always for greater economic equality on the one hand, for understanding between estranged peoples on the other; apprehending always how slight an effort of stupidity or violence could strike a death-blow to twentieth-century civilisation, and elevate the forces of destruction triumphant over the ruins of a world.[10]

Wilcher's character emerges as a trope for the spirit of his class and age. His frequent recourse to the imagery of seafaring and the journey, so popular in late Victorian poetry, echoes Masterman's prose and reflects the mood of escapism and the sense of drifting progress which characterised the Edwardian mind. With his substitution of materialism for faith, of nostalgia for constructive thought, his desire for quietude and fear of decisive action in a world of change and risk, he is the embodiment of Masterman's assessment of the condition of England's traditional responsible classes in the hours of decline.

Edward, as his name affirms, is the quintessential Edwardian. His political principles and activities reflect the most significant public Edwardian developments. "Civilization" is dear to Edward whose cultural tastes are as fine and unerring as his political insight. Yet Edward's awareness that his own order has been superseded produces not bitterness or reaction, but a constructive purpose to assist the new order in its efforts to achieve an equally meaningful civilisation. Edward never doubts the inevitability or the desirability of change. Politics, war, reform all have their base in human restlessness, in hope.

A government has to show energy and do something, and that

111

means making changes—sometimes, I daresay, unnecessary changes. But do you know, one of the things I'm beginning to realize in the last few weeks is that a lot of change starts by itself simply because there happens to be a new government. There's a change of feeling and expectation which is like a change in the weather . . . And, of course, the expectation is always beyond what any government can do. People want a new heaven and a new earth before the end of next week.

(TBP, p. 196)

In *Prisoner of Grace* Chester Nimmo wonders at the ingratitude shown by the working classes for the fruits of Liberal reform. Edward suffers the ingratitude of his party for their inspiration. A draft passage compares Edward to other notable intellectuals who failed to make a distinctive mark on the politics of the day and were eclipsed. "Look at all the men who went out of politics", Wilcher exclaims. "Morley and Masterman, it's a common thing". Edward replies, "Yes, but politics is the art of making your own circumstances" (Ms. Cary 63-4).

Wilcher, along with Edward's young wife, accuses his brother of lacking ambition, but Edward's ambition is of a fragile nature. He lacks the class ambition of a Lloyd George or a Bevan; personal ambition shows itself less in the thwarted desire for high office than in a wish to see his perceptions rewarded by respect and action. The detachment which enables Edward to take a wide view of events makes him a victim when the groundswell of popular passion begins to overturn the benevolent intellectualism of Liberal reformers. As in the Nimmo trilogy, Cary here reads the Liberal triumph of 1906 as the paradoxical moment of Liberal eclipse.

> "The cloth caps came to Parliament in 1906, and their cry was not for eternal life and the judgment of God, but for the world's life and justice on earth. A revolution deeper than the French. Rousseau said 'Trust human nature to do the right thing.' But now they say, 'By our will we shall remake the world and humanity also.'"

(TBP, p. 199)

Able to see, but not to share, the hope of the "cloth caps", Edward retreats into detachment, then to despair. Lacking the conservative impulse as well as the drive to action, Edward loses what is precious to him—his fame, honour, wife, even Tolbrook.

"You must have an object in life . . ." Wilcher tells Ann, "something big enough to make you forget yourself" (*TBP*, p. 52). Politically such an object now motivated the socialists. The Liberal party—like Edward, concerned for "self-respect" in his time of defeat—floundered in a confused effort of self-preservation which diminished its usefulness and integrity alike. "To accept all and to reject all are in this case equally desperate courses", warned Masterman, commenting on the rapidity and shock of Edwardian progress. "To turn aside in despair, to hold aloof in disdain, to proclaim from the heart of comfort an easy approval, are policies traitorous to the public good".[11] Torn between acceptance and rejection of radical developments at the close of that era, Edwardian Liberals found themselves out of touch, if not with the public good, certainly with the popular needs of the nation. Like Edward Wilcher, his party found after the Great War that "Even the foundations have shifted". And like Edward, the party was "too old to begin a new education" (*TBP*, p. 275).

Politics was but one aspect of the drama of the Edwardian transition. Cary presents, through his characters, a full picture of its other aspects. The king was the epitome of aristocratic extravagance at the time and his delighted followers were many. Edward Wilcher displays the blend of culture and dandyism which characterised men of substance who were also men of fashion. His dress is as impeccable as his wit is unfailing. In financial difficulties he does not stint in the maintenance of habitual luxuries. Edward is always in the fashionable and cultural vanguard. In 1906 he buys "an enormous motor car"; in 1910 he buys Cezannes.

The flavour of internationalism which wafted through English society in the van of King Edward's predilection for foreign sojourns and foreign friendships, enlivening English art and reshaping foreign policy can be felt in Edward's cosmopolitanism. In Julie Eeles, the Ibsen actress and friend of the artists of the '90s, Cary captures the vitality, the daring, and the transience of the Edwardian aesthetic splendour. Julie is regarded as decadent in the hour of her creative blossoming;

she is worshipped by another generation in the pathetic days of her personal decline. Wilcher's first visit to her flat is an entry into romance.

> I had never seen a room with plain walls, plain curtains, with no gilt frames or silver ornaments; with no decorations but the austere prints. For even Beardlsey in his black and white was priest-like. I thought, "It is like a cell, of one whose faith is in beauty and love, but a noble beauty, a proud and reserved passion."
>
> *(TBP*, p. 148)

The cell becomes, in time, a prison where, twenty years later, Julie in her loneliness still reads George Moore.

The portaits of Bill and Lucy round out Cary's picture of the Edwardian milieu. Bill serves Britain's dying imperialism. Contented to serve providence and his superiors without question and eager for information unshaded by opinion, he combines an active temperament and wide range of interest with the character of an "idiot" in the Greek sense—a "private citizen".

> he had begun to show that thirst for exact knowledge which, as with many soldiers of his corps, grew all his life. Bill was always anxious to get to the bottom of things. Yet he would never read the books we recommended to him. He was suspicious of learned works.
>
> *(TBP*, pp. 93-4)

Bill epitomises the island man who conquered an empire. His values and interests are traditional British ones—service, the best public school education for his sons, his garden. Masterman's portrait of the average Englishmen at the opening of *The Condition of England* might have been a description of Bill Wilcher:

> . . . he drives ahead along the day's work: in pursuing his own business, conquering great empires: gaining them by his power of energy and honesty, jeopardising them by his stiffness and lack of sympathy and inability to learn. So he will continue to the end; occupying . . . that locality whose jolly, stupid, brave denizens may be utilised for every kind of hazardous and unimaginable enterprise; fulfilling the work of another, content to know nothing of the reason of it all; journeying always, like Columbus,

"to new Americas, or wither God wills."[12].

Bill's conservatism is that of Cary's "creative maintainer", and akin to that of his nephew Robert who "saves" Tolbrook by changing it. His little garden is at once a monument to his privateness and his creativeness. "I just had an idea about the place" (*TBP*, p. 261).

Lucy's world reveals another side of Edwardian life, the flourishing nonconformity which spread from rural pockets to the great urban centres of the late Victorian industrial revolution, assisted by the liberalisation of laws regarding education and Dissent. Sects like the Benjamites were the breeding ground of radicals, people whose religious energies found a kindred spirit in the energetic zeal of reforming politicians. Edward Wilcher benefits from their support.

> The Benjamites and a dozen other strange sects did vote for Edward, in force. They seemed to like his violent speeches, his denunciations of their political sins; as much as they enjoyed the hellfire threats of their preachers.
>
> (*TBP*, p. 69)

Such religious radicals shared the Liberal love of individualism and of freedom. Their political loyalties were not class loyalties nor the tenets of an ideology. The sense of class which, Edward claims, drove Lucy away from a dying aristocracy into the arms of Puggy Brown "to give herself the sense of nobility" remains with her. Thus Lucy scorns Edward's optimistic view of change. "Progress downwards, through the stink of oil and tar. Hell is fired with petroleum . . . these are the days of trial—when the devil has a free hand" (*TBP*, p. 290). Industrial progress, democracy, bourgeois expectations of material or spiritual advancement are the enemies of her reactionary individualism. Her penetrating awareness of the joys of life scorns the hope of the masses and rejects the progress of which Edward sees that hope as the fountainhead.

Lucy's scorn of the lower middle class, scathing in the Jones episode, and her insistence that Robert be raised a gentleman, reflects the egoism of these nonconformists which enables them to humble themselves with pride. Such individualism within the grass roots support of the Liberal party, together with the detachment of its upper strata, brought the party to disarray before the organised ideological challenge of the post-war socialists.

Cary brings the events of his novel up to the narrative present of the 1930s through Wilcher's involvement in his nephew John's career. John leaves university for war and returns to join the family law firm. Wilcher shares a brief period of sympathy with his nephew at a time when both look forward to a new world of peace and freedom. But the new society belies this ideal, and as Wilcher retreats into his conservatism, John embraces the post-war spirit of life for life's sake. He allies himself to the mechanical revolution, leaving the law firm to sell automobiles; failure brings about his dissolution and wasteful death.

Explicitly acknowledging the source of his narrative method for the book which was to reveal personal development and the atmosphere of an era, Cary wrote in a notebook that *To Be a Pilgrim* was to be "a *Proustian* book" (Ms. Cary 71). The elderly Wilcher's return to Tolbrook in the care of his niece Ann sets off the chain of involuntary memories which return him to the world of his past and the company of his family.

> It was a breezy morning, and every knock of the blind, on the window ledge, brought something fresh and gay and austere into my spirit. A sensation from the past, which I could not place.

> "Of course," I said, "I am simply a child again. This expectation is the feeling of getting up in the morning. I am getting well after some illness and waiting to join the others in the nursery. ["]

(TBP, p .14)

A few moments later, when Wilcher pronounces the name of his sister Lucy, a startling echo voices the phrase, "To be a pilgrim." Immediately, the scene is set for the novel's chronicle of Wilcher's history, and the conflict evoked which will occupy his mind throughout the narrative. The first passage, filled with details of the Tolbrook surroundings and bespeaking the indulgent enjoyment of old familiar sensations, contrasts with Lucy's urgent message. Lucy changes in the moment of memory from the child to the young woman and challenges Wilcher from afar to abandon worldly indulgence, urging him not to dwell in expectation, but to act.

Involuntary memories, sparked by a chance encounter in the present—with a chair, a tree, a sound carried on the air or a fragrance wafted through a window—are selective and immediate. Thus Wilcher's narrative is punctuated by episodes linked to the unconscious stream of present thought and remembered with the clarity and vitality of newly experienced sensation. Their chronology is fitful; Lucy's voice whispering "To be a pilgrim" expands into the memory of Bunyan's hymn roared from the "thick swollen lips" of Puggy Brown, striking fear and attraction in the heart of Wilcher. The vision of the rebel Lucy spawns another earlier memory of a childish Lucy scolding her errant brother who is late for the walk to church. Each memory is characterised by complete detail of sensation and surroundings.

> I am walking along the drive, through red mud, with my hand firmly locked in Lucy's. I wear a long yellow coat with large buttons and a round hat. Edward in a bowler and a smart overcoat, Bill in a cape, swaggering his broad shoulders, walk in front. Edward I think is even carrying a walking-stick. My father, in a flat-topped felt hat, and my mother in a tight-waisted sealskin and little round ermine hat, are already fifty yards down the drive.
>
> (*TBP*, p. 25)

Details of clothing and of physical gesture throughout the compendium of remembered episodes form their own chronicle of social change and register the effect of altering age and attitude in individual characters. The little boy in his yellow coat will become the Oxford dandy apeing his fashionable brother, newly elected to Parliament in 1885. "Both of us are dressed in the extreme of fashion. Our overcoats are long and tight waisted; our top hats have fall-to sides and curled brims; and we wear little curled moustaches" (*TBP*, p. 71). The one young man talking philosophy and practicing dandyism at university, the other praising Corot and Whistler embody the spirit of the coming Edwardian society. By 1910 Wilcher is dressed in the tall hat and frock coat of his profession and

Edward, prematurely retired from politics "to enjoy that civilization which he had given so much energy, so many years, to defend" (*TBP*, p. 205), is still in the vanguard of culture, pronouncing Cezanne among "the greatest in the history of art" (*TBP*, p. 206), in the very year that the British public mocked London's first post-impressionist exhibition.

The divergence between Wilcher's attire and the fashions around him marks the emergence of a new generation to which John Wilcher and his promiscuous wife Gladys belong. Evident contrasts in fashion become moral *exempla* for the ageing Wilcher in his protest against civilization's decline. Gladys, Wilcher remembers, mocked his tight trousers with the epithet, "Lucifer legs". Wilcher's justification of his attire condemns the degeneracy of Gladys and John's generation: "My good city tailor quite agreed with my dislike of seeing men drape their legs in two skirts, and my trousers were cut on the old manly basis, to show the limb" (*TBP*, p. 273). Similarly, a decade later, when Ann arrives to take charge of her dangerously ill and mentally suspect uncle, Wilcher defends his sanity, and again condemns the present generation, in terms of haberdashery.

> My hatter tells me there is only one man in England beside myself, who still wears a curly-brimmed bowler. But he agrees with me that there has never been a better hat, that hats, in fact, since the last war, have gone to the devil. And are getting more degenerate, more slack, more shapeless, every day.
>
> (*TBP*, p. 10)

Details of appearance record the natural as well as the fashionable changes time brings. Wilcher's father's progress towards the grave is measured by the transformation of his bearing and gait from those of an upright soldier to those of a rambling farmer, and finally to an animal-like waddle. Such physical details also convey the peculiar individual consistency of each character. Lucy, once she has gone her independent way, never loses the gypsy-like appearance which hard living and innate restlessness have given and preserve. Amy Sprott Wilcher, Bill's wife, though transformed from a rosy blushing girl to a silver-haired matron, is always the same red-faced Amy whose constancy and independence are proclaimed by her unfailing costume of ill-becoming blue. The reappearance of such detail in varying contexts unites each portrait, making the episodic flashes of observation into a coherent whole.

Successive glimpses of Wilcher himself unite the portrayal of his character. His faithlessness is a continual embarrassment and a torment. The timid child who lives in fear of being made the butt of a joke becomes the old man who believes his niece is poisoning him. The young rationalist enthusiastically arguing God's existence who suddenly realises that "To believe in God is an act of faith" (*TBP*, p. 141), and is unable to make that act, becomes he old man who says of Lucy's adventurous faith, "That faith has come to me now. At least, I hope so" (*TBP*, p. 55).

Wilcher's lack of personal conviction is evident in his reluctance to form independent political opinions. Edward's canny foresight repeatedly earns Wilcher's immediate criticism and later enthusiasm. In company with the majority of his countrymen he utterly fails to read the coming and import of the First World War. His initial pacifism is no less fervent than his later belligerence. His quarrel with the curate arises from that man's accurate reading of the future effect of the treaty of Versailles. The book's conclusion finds him, on the eve of the Second World War, committing the same error with regard to Hitler's Germany that he had made in the case of the Kaiser's. This political impercipience is mirrored more tragically by Wilcher's failure of depth or progress in personal relationships. The little boy who got on his mother's nerves and followed Lucy around like "a lost dog" grows into the man who joylessly haunts his mistress's bed and can only respond to the crises of family deaths by substituting officious meddling for personal sympathy.

Wilcher shies away from love with terrible regularity, for love inevitably threatens self-sufficiency and alters the *status quo*. He fails to give both his parents the sympathy they seek in their last hours of life. Similarly, Wilcher abandons Bill and Amy's fireside during the war when the death of their son threatens to make demands on his emotional self-sufficiency, "I can bear my own grief, but I can't bear that of other people . . ." (*TBP*, p. 257). He quarrels with Lucy up to "within half an hour of her death" in a pact to ignore death's imminence and the awkwardness of its emotional demands.

Recognition of his past failures does not alter the pattern of Wilcher's self-centredness. While lamenting Edward's loneliness or his mother's, he cannot comfort Ann. Indeed, the stirrings of sympathy cause him to turn away from the girl's manifest misery, as he fled from Bill and Amy's grief, "I could not bear her unhappiness so close to me" (*TBP*, p. 163).

Wilcher's readiness to relate to things, rather than open himself to the demands of people, enables him to sacrifice the happiness of even his loved ones to the exigencies of finance and the fancied "needs" of Tolbrook. When Bill dies Wilcher is too preoccupied with his brother's material improvidence to offer spiritual comfort; and when Amy is left penniless he finds excuses to deny her a home at Tolbrook, lest concession in this respect bring disruption of his ordered routine. To protect this routine he deprives Edward of Julie and, in turn, flees the prospect of marriage to Julie. Again, Tolbrook provides his excuse. "I felt perhaps that to bring a Julie to Tolbrook would be an impiety to my father's house, now in my care" (*TBP*, p. 209).

In the present Wilcher uses Tolbrook in place of sympathy in his attempts to gain the attention and cooperation—the love—of Ann and Robert. He rails against their refusal to be bribed by his hints of a will in their favour. Yet he refuses to respond even to Ann's love of the home, leaving his will unsettled lest he disturb himself through the giving of Tolbrook. "I thought that I was entitled to some peace on my death bed" (*TBP*, p. 335). Cary annotated a passage in Jeremy Taylor's *Holy Dying* which throws ironic light on this episode. Taylor admonishes the dying, "let thy charity out-live thee, that thou mayest rejoice in the mansion of rest, because by thy means many living persons are eased or advantaged".[13]

Peace is Wilcher's obsession, but he obstinately denies himself the peace which a child finds in sharing its delights, which Lucy found in the service of God, which Amy found in a life of self-sacrifice—the peace of giving. This final gesture reveals the negativeness of Wilcher's conservatism. The motive which might have been noble, to save Tolbrook and preserve the traditions it represents, has turned to motiveless grasping; he clings to the family seat to the very last and thus ensures that like his memories, it will come to an end with his death.

Wilcher fears responsibility and seeks reassurance from others throughout his life. The least flattering approval from those around him comforts him. Bill's assurance that "Anything we can do for Edward is worth doing" (*TBP*, p. 176), Amy's tacit confidence that Tom will not abandon Tolbrook, Julie's admission, "Perhaps I need Edward to use me and you need Tolbrook to use you" (*TBP*, p. 177), and even Edward's "You've got what you wanted. You always meant to live at home" (*TBP*, p. 175), absolve Wilcher of the responsibility for sacrificing his grand ambitions to his conservative inclinations. Edward's approval and Julie's own acceptance permit him to perform what he knows to be a debasing gesture in stealing his brother's mistress. Political exigency seems to him a satisfactory reassurance that he has done right in thus depriving Edward of one of the true sources of aid and comfort in his life. This desire for reassurance underlies Wilcher's anger against Ann and Robert who refuse to pander to their uncle's childish wishes for compliance, despite their generosity in caring for his physical needs.

Wilcher secures an infallible escape from responsibility for his failures by cultivating his belief in an evil will. If Wilcher has sinned he must be forgiven, but his lack of faith makes it necessary that he should not require forgiveness. Therefore Wilcher's recourse is to the devil. The devil in others—Lucy and Ann—points out his hypocrisy and therefore need not be believed. The devil in himself provokes those "bold and scandalous" adventures in which Wilcher indulges after Lucy's death, and the loathing and triumph they inspire. "Part of that triumph, which proved it to be the devil's was in its distortion of the whole moral world" (*TBP*, p. 307). Wilcher is not slow to acknowledge his corruption, but the demonstrable presence of the devil's guidance absolves him of responsibility for it. He responds with a campaign comical in its irony, on behalf of the devil; that is, to prove the devil real in order that his contribution to the state of the world may be properly respected.

Wilcher's attack on the socialist curate is the high spot of this campaign. When his "proofs of the devil's real existence" fail to convince, he challenges the cleric,

"This matter is too serious for logic-chopping—the point is simple, do you believe in your own professed creed or not? Do you believe in the devil and the need for fighting him and for supporting any measures, military or otherwise, to defeat his purposes?"

(*TBP*, p. 248)

Wilcher's diabolism results ironically in severance from the Church, "For I could not take communion from the hand of a blackguard who had betrayed the creeds, and denied the devil, at such a time of crisis" (*TBP*, p. 248). After this Wilcher carries on his Manichaean campaign in private literary efforts, preparing a book "on the need for a new statement of the Christian belief, with special regard to the positive power of evil; and the real existence of the devil" (*TBP*, p. 262).

Characterisation in *To Be a Pilgrim* is enhanced by the diverse viewpoints which emerge within Wilcher's reminiscence. Wilcher's view, always predisposed to find greater worthiness in the friends of a bygone era, is tempered by the memory of judgments those friends pronounced upon each other. Such judgments qualify Wilcher's retrospective view of himself as one continually seeking liberty and continually burdened by responsibilities. Lucy pronounces him a "wretched little pettifogger" (*TBP*, p. 161). Yet when he threatens to resign as Edward's agent, Bill protests against the abdication, "I never thought you would let us down" (*TBP*, p. 176). Edward, at the height of his success, regards his brother as "one of those poor creatures, lawyers, bankers, the little clerks, who haven't the spunk to take a risk" (*TBP*, p. 176). Later, in acknowledging his own failure, Edward views Wilcher's conservative materialism from a contrasting though uncontradictory point of view, "You knew what you wanted, Tommy, and you made for it, from the beginning. It's the only way . . . You gripped something. I hit the air" (*TBP*, p. 282). Each judgment contains a measure of truth. The attitudes of these characters towards Wilcher's conservative spirit uncover both its shortcomings and its positive use.

Where Wilcher's perception of another's character or motive is lacking, Edward, Bill, or Lucy often supplies the understanding necessary. Lucy's flight to the Benjamites, read by Wilcher in the past as a disgraceful and wasteful sacrifice and in the present as a noble gesture of independence and faith, strikes Edward as an act of class pride.

> "My impression is that Lucy hasn't any religion at all. But she has a great sense of class. She has turned herself into a char because she feels that her own class is finished. She doesn't feel grand enough as a mere lady."
>
> (*TBP*, p. 76)

Bill on the other hand, regards Lucy's motives as religious and conjugal duty. "Scrub for the glory of the Lord. Why not?" (*TBP*, p. 76) he asks matter-of-factly, and when Lucy returns at a moment's notice to her unfaithful husband his approval is unhesitating, "and a good thing too. She's quite right . . . Dammit, you don't want her to separate from her husband, do you?. . . marriage is marriage" (*TBP*, p. 98).

Lucy's behaviour, inexplicable to herself, combines all these motives. Duty is not an ideal for her, but a fact of life. "I have always fought against God, and it's my plain duty to do His will and go back to the master" (*TBP*, p. 96). But pride is as forceful a motive as religion, "I don't need God's command. It's common sense" (*TBP*, p. 97). Her impulse to leave comfort finds its rewards in sheer enjoyment of life.

> "And with the master, too, praise the lamb—I've been happier still with the poor master. Yes, it's been glorious sometimes—to hear him speak, and feel how he moved those savages, it threw a glory on the whole world. . . . How I love being alive. . . . I can't imagine myself dead and the world going on without me."
>
> (*TBP*, p. 295)

In the final analysis Lucy's motives combine Edward's notion of rebellion against a class which has lost its function, and Bill's of duty to a faith and a husband. They find a curious affinity with the womanly impulses which make Amy the family slave which Lucy's pride of place forbade her to be. "Rubbish, Tommy," she exclaims when Wilcher challenges her motives, "I must go back because I'm needed" (*TBP*, p. 296).

Wilcher's understanding is baffled by generations succeeding his own; he regards them with stereotyped views, and this is the way Cary portrays them in the novel. Thus, John is a typical post-war peacetime casualty, Gladys a caricature of the hard modern women of the 'twenties, and Ann the stereotyped career girl of the 'thirties steeped in psychology and intellectual independence. This device, unhappily, introduces into a novel rich with character a group of characters who lack the full personality and motivation of Lucy, Amy, or Bill.

Nevertheless, these young figures illuminate the preceding generation's behaviour. Edward's comment that John is "standing aside" is less convincing as an assessment of that sketchy character than of Edward's own failure and the inadequacies of the detached liberal minds of his age.

> "People like John feel that they aren't wanted—that there's no place for them among the turmoil, the chatter, the spite and the nonsense of all sorts—he was born to serve some independent truth—he could have made a first-class researcher or scientist". . . .
>
> (*TBP*, p. 277)

Gladys's flagrant immorality and boastful materialism are set against Julie's decline and Wilcher's own regard for property and success. The ironic juxtaposition both labels the later generation as tawdry in its values and reveals Wilcher's propensity to romanticise his own age. "A bit too civilised" is Robert's comment on his uncle's society, and Wilcher is forced to acquiesce in the diagnosis of a complacent attenuation of liberal ideals. "A universal tolerance, based on a universal enjoyment. They were faithful to friendship, to kindness, to beauty; never to faith. They could not make the final sacrifice." (*TBP*, p. 205).

Wilcher is enraged when Ann belittles the revolutions which he himself supported with trepidation twenty years earlier. But if Ann's assessments show the foreshortening effect of time, her observations often explain those conflicting reactions which have puzzled Wilcher in retrospect.

> "My dear girl, I've never faltered in my belief in democracy."
> "Yes, you believed in it, so did Daddy. But you didn't like it. . . ."
>
> (*TBP*, p. 236)

Ann and Wilcher stand at opposing temporal poles. Despite her nostalgia for her father's world, Ann can enter it only objectively, by recreating its physical features and analysing its motivations. Wilcher views Ann's world with a harsher, calculatedly distancing objectivity; he turns away from the frustrating sense that this world harbours common emotional needs with his own. Ironically uncle and niece find common ground chiefly in their retrogressive love of Tolbrook at the very moment when that symbol of a tradition based on change is once again stepping into a new character in welcoming the throbbing life-beat of Robert's thresher into the classical beauty of the Adam drawing room.

In addition to the characters' comments on each other, another form of comment emerges to deepen characterisation in the novel. The imagery of his narrative offers implicit qualifications to Wilcher's explicit statements. Wilcher claims that in the course of his reminiscence he accomplishes an intellectual progress which he failed to make in his active lifetime. The title of *To be a Pilgrim*, its journey motif, through which Wilcher interprets and assesses the personalities of his family and nation, and its extended chronological scope all indicate that progress is central to the novel's theme. Throughout its action the novel questions the nature of the personal and historical progress observed and the nature of progress itself.

Historical and personal progress evoke the theme of the pilgrimage shared by England and her individual members. But the image of the pilgrimage exposes again the duality of Wilcher's thought. On the one hand Wilcher sees his "pilgrims" as wanderers free of materialistic preoccupations and the fetters of responsibility. In this mood he praises the irrational gestures of Lucy and Brown, the unquestioning adaptability of Bill and Amy. England herself, he says "was born upon the road, and lives in such a dust of travel that she never knows where she is" (*TBP*, p. 342).

At other times Wilcher finds this aimlessness uncongenial and considers the pilgrimage in Bunyan's or Chaucer's terms, as a purposeful journey. "A pilgrim is not a lost soul, I thought, nor a wanderer" (*TBP*, p. 313). Such a view reveals the faults of Edward who loses his purpose, or Lucy who surrenders herself to the simple joy of life itself.

125

The imagery of the voyage in *To Be a Pilgrim* also echoes French poetry of the late nineteenth century and carries with it, as a further gloss upon the sense of decadence in the Edwardian atmosphere, the Baudelairean idea of the voyage of jaded spirits seeking heaven or hell in response to a need for novelty.[14] Wilcher's own personality entertains such impulses in his period of perversion.[15] In a travesty of Edward's vision he sees the impulse operating throughout society.

> You would say whole nations grow suddenly bored at the same moment; and tear off their clothes to dive into vice; or fascinated by some dark unknown sea, draw nearer and nearer to it, walking on the very edge of war and destruction.
> All breaks, all passes save God's cry to men.
> Break all, die all, that ye be born again.
>
> (*TBP*, p. 311)[16]

Each aspect of the pilgrimage simultaneously attracts and repels Wilcher. To journey faithfully requires a purpose which Wilcher lacks or an innocence which he condemns. Bill's happiness is that innocent joy of the monk in his cell, which regards the world outside "from a security and faith as strong as a child's surrounded by the unseen care of its mother" (*TBP*, p. 108). The imagery of monks, seafarers, and children describes the weakness of the faith in providence which Wilcher rejects— its lack of initiative and responsibility. "I think it's our duty," says Wilcher, "under providence to use some foresight . . ." (*TBP*, p. 243). Ironically, Wilcher's dread of change makes Edward's foresight equally unattractive. Wilcher recognises that Lucy abandons herself to Brown and his sect in an escape from responsibility more active but no less complete than Bill's, pursuing with the Benjamites an evangelical escape into enthusiasm.

Yet at the same time that he condemns, in his father or Bill, the soldier's unquestioning faith, or, in Lucy, the enthusiast's forgetfulness of self, Wilcher delights in such irresponsible ways to happiness as a stretcher-bearer in the Great War. Further, he envies the child's peace in forgetfulness and "the unseen care of its mother". The clouds of Wilcher's seafaring England, with which he longs to identify, are those snow clouds called "Mother Carey's chickens", the same image Cary used to evoke

126

the sense of childish insignificance and dependence in *A House of Children*.

Longing for escape underlies Wilcher's own desire to be a missionary. He sees himself as a contemplative Eastern mystic, "renouncing self" to find "a final peace and joy" (*TBP*, p. 199). Significantly, he adds, "So I have felt of women; of Julie and Sara, but especially of Julie". Woman thus becomes an additional and revealing symbol in Wilcher's narrative. The female guided by instinct is the faithful servant and the agent of a natural providence.

> That was Sara's religion which served her like her pans, her rolling pins, her private recipes for clearing soup and saving a burnt stew. . . .
>
> (*TBP*, p. 328)

> Amy and Sara, countrywomen both. They didn't submit themselves to any belief. They used it. They made it.
>
> (*TBP*, p. 339)

Like providence itself this womanly nature is at once creative and protective.

Ironically, it is the fear of enforced independence which drives Wilcher to his single positive act in the novel. He sets off for London to claim Sara as his bride because he fears that Ann, his guardian, has left him for good. "I don't expect she's ever coming back" (*TBP*, p. 292), he tells the housekeeper, and he is suddenly terrified at the demand for responsibility this fact implies. Despite his quarrels with Ann's modernity, Wilcher has grown comfortable in the care of this young mother, as he did in his relationships with Julie and Sara. Years before, when shut in a laundry basket in childish play, Wilcher willingly believed that his brothers and sisters and even his mother had made him the victim of a murderous plot. In the same way the unfounded conviction of Ann's abandonment grows on him, "this very kindness convinces me that she will not come back" (*TBP*, p. 298).

His resort, therefore, is to Sara, the maternal figure who has once before shielded him from his own irrational impulses. Wilcher compares his sense of freedom in London to a child's. "I was young again, without a care. For that is what it is to be young; to be careless. The young are born pilgrims" (*TBP*, p. 301). Like a child's, Wilcher's new confidence rests in the expectation of Sara's love and protection, that security of the "unseen mother."

In the perversions which overtake him in later life Wilcher seeks not novelty, as the psychiatrist flatteringly proposes, but final surrender to irresponsibility. Wilcher performs his exhibitionism and sets fire to his London house in confident expectation that his sins will be discovered and that someone— the police or the lunatic asylum—will take care of him. The girl in Hyde Park echoes this unspoken motive when she replies to Wilcher's advances, "I should think you'd better have someone to look after you" (*TBP*, p. 306).

In terms of England's wandering journey Wilcher is a failure because of his inability to abandon worldly concerns, to accept "all possibility" and to say "I am ready. Anywhere at any time" (*TBP*, p. 342). In terms of the purposeful journey forward, too, he fails, for his purpose in conserving the past from irresistible change, is retrograde. The imagery which defines Wilcher's state is not the freedom of the journey, but enclosure. Change evokes this imagery:

> I seem to be thrust into a long tunnel from which I shall never again escape until I reach the speck of light at the far end. That light is my death. But the tunnel is not dark. On the contrary, it is lighted throughout by a kind of pale sad gleam in which everything is exceedingly clear and long familiar. I see the chairs, tables, pictures; and even my London office ... They have already that dejected look of things at a sale, where everything seems to say, "We are betrayed—there is no faith or trust in the world."
>
> (*TBP*, p. 176)

The tunnel, the boy locked in a clothes basket, the old man left alone at Tolbrook so that "the house became a coffin and it seemed that I had been shut up in it alive" (*TBP*, p. 299)—all are images for the terror of a man imprisoned in an uncreative individuality which fears its own company and clings to a familiar world because it lacks the faith and resource necessary to make a new one.

Wilcher survives beyond the age to which his character belongs, but he does not move forward with the times. The personal character falls behind the nation's progress, "England took me with her on a few stages of her journey. Because she could not help it." Cary effects the split between Wilcher and England with skill and consistency by creating a paradoxical progress in the man's personality. As he grows increasingly to acknowledge and follow his conservative impulses, Wilcher longs for rebirth, that he may escape the burdens of his own conservatism. But rebirth proves impossible. As inexorable as historical change is the natural fact of human progress from birth to death. Lazarus, the dead man raised by a miracle of faith, whose countenance will be seen to elude even Gulley Jimson's imagination, haunts Wilcher and perplexes him. Rembrandt's resurrected Lazarus, Wilcher observes, greets the world with a face "of haggard amazement" (*TBP*, p. 291)—the new world, he finds, is the same one in which he has always lived. "I don't suppose Lazarus enjoyed his resurrection" (*TBP*, p. 215), Wilcher comments, for intuition tells him that rebirth removes none of the conflct of this familiar world.

Wilcher's response, therefore, is to seek a rebirth not of faith but of escape into illusion. The illusion—clarifying the parasitic nature of Wilcher's conservatism—is one of the peace of childhood, the comfort and security in the protection of a mother's love. Wilcher's reminiscence carries him back to the hours of joy in his mother's bed, and on her breast, in fulfilment at last of his own prophecy, "Those who cling to this world, must be dragged backwards into the womb which is also a grave" (*TBP*, p. 37). Notes for Cary's drafts emphasise this backward progress. "He is creeping into his mother's bed, into the womb, into the grave . . . at end returns to an earlier age, and to the mother again—the idea of the womb and England's earth" (Ms. Cary 71). Thus the old man returns with relief to the nursery, wanders for comfort to his mother's sitting room (*TBP*, p. 30), and later to her bedroom (*TBP*, p. 292), and as death approaches, finds bliss again in the memory of waking "in paradise" in her bed (*TBP*, p. 334). Wilcher's retrogressive mental progress to the threshold of the womb in search of rebirth is the reverse of creativity. There is a bold irony in applying the scheme of Gulley Jimson's paintings to the scheme of the trilogy itself, for Wilcher can only be seen as a faithless Lazarus for whom no miracle is possible, and therefore a deluded Lazarus, the "amazed" man of his own world-bound vision. In fact Wilcher is no Lazarus, but an ordinary man who finds this world a changing, baffling place, and who accepts at last the security of release from bafflement in the certainty of death.

To Be a Pilgrim asks and answers the question, what is progress. By capturing the sense of time passed, the Proustian reminiscence proclaims the inevitability of change over any period of time. As Proust measured personal development against the historical foci of war and the Dreyfus case, Cary measures the attitudes of his characters against the cataclysm of the First World War. From the war emerged a modern Britain with a new social orientation, new tastes, and demanding new forms of political action. Wilcher's inability to see as individuals those younger characters to whom he applies the generalising label "modern" measures the progress which has made them strangers to his understanding, just as his own reaction to the values of his parents measures the distance between Victorian and Edwardian frames of mind.

Cary uses the medium of character to define the source and nature of progress and in doing so cements the link between the novel's theme of progress and the trilogy's overall theme of creation. Individualism marks the strength of those characters who win Wilcher's admiration as pilgrims, people who "cut out their own destinies" (*TBP*, p. 55) through faith and action. Progress is implicitly defined as the compendium of individual acts of self-assertion, acts of will.

Faith is the novel's term for the individualism that believes in its own power and serves its will. Cary rejects the temptation to which Wilcher's disappointed conservatism succumbs, to place a negative construction on individualism, to care for no one and nothing rather than to endure hurt at the hands of loved ones and cherished possessions. Caring for nothing is self-negation. Wilcher is therefore forced to recognise the flaw in Edward's lack of self-assertion, and the strength of Lucy, Bill, and Sara in acting upon commitment, however eccentric or trivial.

Cary does not attempt to answer the question which haunts Wilcher, whether the progress he has witnessed is good or bad. He adopts the view that it is simply inevitable, revealing in this the Edwardian liberal cast of his own mind. The narrative which captures through Wilcher's perplexities the equivocation and evasiveness inherent in the Edwardian liberal outlook, synthesises the progress of that age of transition whose creativeness baffled even its most percipient members. Through the failures and triumphs of the novel's forceful characters, Cary affirms his liberal belief in freedom of action as the key to personal fulfilment and in diversity of activity as the root of social progress.

The Horse's Mouth

> Persons of genius, it is true, are, and are always likely to be, a small minority; but in order to have them, it is necessary to preserve the soil in which they grow. Genius can only breathe freely in an *atmosphere* of freedom. Persons of genius are, *ex vi termini*, more individual than any other people—less capable, consequently, of fitting themselves, without hurtful compression, into any of the small number of moulds which society provides in order to save its members the trouble of forming their own character. If from timidity they consent to be forced into one of these moulds, and to let all that part of themselves which cannot expand under the pressure remain unexpanded, society will be little the better for their genius.
>
> J.S. Mill, *On Liberty*

The "godlike" artist was, for Cary, a type of the human character in its highest state of fulfilment. A return in 1942 to Edinburgh where he had studied art stimulated Cary to celebrate this divine humanity and to exploit his own ideas about art in the third novel of his trilogy.[17] Cary himself recalled, in a note about his religious history, that his experiences as a student in Edinburgh first suggested to him a common spring of aesthetic and religious intuition.

> I suspect that it was here at The Art School and in this odd encounter with Reffalovitch [sic] and his friend[18] that I began to uncover a train of thinking and experience which became afterwards important to me. For it was almost entirely through the aesthetic experience that I came to a true faith, that is, a faith which I believe so entirely that nothing has shaken it, or could shake it.
>
> (Ms. Cary 293, S.22.K)

In his philosophy notes of around 1942, Cary characterised this source of intuition, which experience transmutes into art and faith, "The forms, the colours, the fundamental aesthetic qualities are *given*. They come from *The Horse's Mouth*" (Ms. Cary 272, p. 52). It was to this undefined source of the world's character that he was to pay tribute in Gulley Jimson's story.

The artist had been a presence in Cary's fiction before this time. Artists appeared as minor characters in both *Charley is My Darling* and *A House of Children*. Among the notes for the latter novel appear sketches of an artist called Tom Jimson (Ms. Cary, 55-7), and further notes of this time reveal the themes and even the plot of *The Horse's Mouth* beginning to take shape[19].

Shew artist (?Moore). struggling against spite & enmity. . . .

His sense of religion and god—'god is an artist.' His humility, his [[clowning]], his secret pride and happiness. His vices which do not affect him. His anger at philistine world which does not care, his pity and contempt.

Conflict here bet. Moore & the ph[i]listine world the f[a]ther and m[o]ther in law who take away wife and wreck him—the bogus art[i]st & critic with his foolish followers. . . .

(Ms. Cary 269, N.78)

Real experiences were behind the novel. In 1905, while in France, Cary visited the artists' colony at Etaples. There he met an elderly painter who wept while telling his young visitor of his eclipse by new fashions in art. The episode haunted Cary, working itself into the background of *The Horse's Mouth* through the sketch of Jimson's father, and reappearing as an example of changing aesthetic taste in *Art and Reality* and elsewhere.[20] Its influence appears among the earliest notes for *The Horse's Mouth*. "The exploded artist (J) and his family, struggling, the academy picture rejected. His bitterness . . ." (Ms. Cary 269, N.78).

Many artists of Cary's acquaintance probably helped to shape his conception of Gulley Jimson's character and style. Gulley's sensitivity to the creative spirit all around him recalls the painter J.D. Fergusson whom Cary and Murry met in Paris, and who applied the term "artist" to anyone who had "the courage of his being . . .".[21] In a pseudo-critical note on Jimson's style Cary confirms the debt, often suggested by critics, to Stanley Spencer, ". . . allegorical works in a styel style of [*sic*] compounded of W. Blake and the extreme modern school represented by Stanley S. the Spencers . . ." (Ms. Cary 82). Stanley Spencer's small stature and his liveliness, his complex relationships with women and his predilection for large works, all no doubt contributed to Jimson's portrait. Like Jimson, Spencer associated aesthetic and religious inspiration, valued work as a fundamental expression of human creativeness, and acknowledged sex as a source of inspiration.[22] The nature of his compositions, full of activity and rooted in experience, but symbolic of his own religious intuitions, provided a pattern for Jimson's style.

Literary influences too, probably contributed to Jimson's characterisation. John Bidlake, the artist in Huxley's *Point Counter Point*, which Cary acquired and probably read in 1931,[23] sees "whole chunks of anatomy in leaves and vapour and swelling earth".[24] He transforms views of clouds, trees, and hills into cherubs, a Nereid's belly, paunchy Silenus or Diana's breasts in much the way that Jimson sees pepper pots and grey monks in cloud configurations, and Rubens angels in the Thames tide. Gulley's ability to project onto a pristine wall the picture with which he would transform it recalls the artist Jim Browne in George Moore's *Vale*.

> An intense moment of appreciation was when he said that no gallery in the world afforded so many beautiful pictures to his sight as did a dirty ceiling. He had only to half close his eyes to see Last Judgments finer than Michael Angelo's, and if he closed his eyes a little he could rediscover his Battle of Arbela.[25]

Finally, William Blake's life and thought inform Cary's characterisation of Jimson. "The *stoic* English view but he *enters into freedom and individuality* through experience *As individual* fights government and so does Gulley" (Ms. Cary 82). Cary thus synthesised elements of character from the entire range of his experience to make his typical artist figure at once true to fact and universal.

Gulley's personal and family history chronicles the revolutions in art and politics from 1800 to the present.[26] Jimson's introduction to the upheavals caused by changing tastes in art recreates Cary's Etaples experience. "I couldn't forget seeing my father, a little grey-bearded old man, crying one day in the garden" (*HM*, p. 51). Gulley's reaction to the experience is to escape from art into the bourgeois security of an office. Ironically, however, the turn of the century was bringing changes to this middle class security. Gulley's fated rediscovery of art is contemporaneous with the challenging of the Victorian social order by Darwinism and social democracy. Gulley participates in society's moment of change when his early classicism is quickly swamped by the Impressionist wave.

Gulley's Impressionist period is the era of the Sara Monday nudes. Gulley's style is like Sara herself, "pure sensation without a thought in my head" (*HM*, p. 53), and Gulley outgrows it as surely as society outgrew laissez-faire Liberalism and looked for new classical structures in the forms of mathematics and Marxism. "Cezanne and the cubists . . . All services. Modern democracy. Organised comforts. The Socialist state. Bureaucratic liberalism. Scientific management. A new security" (*HM*, p. 55). Each new form generated by society's activity remains secure only until that activity yields a new form. The heat of the activity, as Edward Wilcher observed, melts the old and forges the new, and when Gulley's activity carries him beyond cubism after 1930, it is in the context of a world feeling the stirrings of Fascism, uncertain of the form to come, doomed to suffer in the clash of warring inspirations. At this point Gulley's art itself discovers activity, the importance of patterns "coming and going", rejecting static subjects for the subject which links the process and product of activity. The Creation. It is at this point that the action of *The Horse's Mouth* takes place, in a world where activity seeking its appropriate form, in Gulley's life, his art, and the world at large, reveals a world whose formal existence is perceived in a flux of activity.

Initially *The Horse's Mouth* was set in wartime London.[27] The war was to affect Gulley personally by thwarting his art. His enforced abandonment of painting during the bombing of London was conceived of as a plausible reason for his resort to verbal expression, "He could tell story to someone in blackout . . ." (Ms. Cary 82). As the novel developed, however, Cary realised that a full and sympathetic characterisation of wartime London would overshadow the peculiar predicament of the artist. He therefore preferred to lodge the thwarting necessity in everyday, rather than cataclysmic, events. "Have it before the war 1939. Gulley can't pay his rent" (Ms. Cary 82). By locating the novel's action on the eve of the war Cary was able to focus the personal and political character of the constituent members of London society around the coming upheaval, while retaining as his central action the artist's own struggles against the injustice inherent in the world's day to day existence.

Delight in self and excessive introspection had permitted Sara's and Wilcher's narratives, respectively, to flow readily. Jimson's mode of self-expression, however, was his art. Cary justified the self-forgetful outpouring of Jimson's deathbed memoir by making it an extension of an inner dialogue which Gulley has carried on all his life. Gulley recognises in himself a tendency to indulge a grievance against injustice. Such indulgence signals a dangerous turning inwards, implying a loss of sympathy with the whole of creation. To indulge a grievance was to accept, albeit grudgingly, the laws of necessity, instead of joining the creative battle against them. The continued effort, even at death, to resist such an anticreative state provides coherence and purpose in the narrative.

By recording the events and impulses which brought inspiration or enjoyment, or stirred his grievance, Jimson documents his struggle. At the same time his vivid language and characteristically visual apprehension reveal the springs and nature of his creative activity. In observing the world and people about him, Jimson names the elements which become the forms of his painting, Coker's forearm, Harry's stumpy leg, a blot of ink like "a map of Australia" (*HM*, p. 97), trees "solid as whales" (*HM*, p. 213). In dialogue with others Gulley discovers the meaning of his own intuitions, "I didn't know what I meant till Plant asked me" (*HM*, p. 120). Be recapturing successive moments of illumination Gulley himself traces their coherence into his final work, The Creation, and into the hitherto unformulated philosophy which enables him ultimately to announce to the nun that laughing and praying, both spontaneous expressive activities, are the "Same thing, Mother" (*HM*, p. 289).

Gulley's representative place in the "character of the English civilization" is interpreted through Blake's poetry. The artist's character achieved universality as a Blakean everyman, victim of injustice, champion of freedom, and above all, proponent of activity.

Gulley's interest in Blake reveals the book's argument without requiring Gulley to indulge in abstract philosophy. "If one could find 300 linked quotations from Blake to run through book", Cary noted, "with argument, and the pictures . . . Wanted the links between injustice, luck and freedom (Jerusalem. Los). *Gulley's own world*, illustrated by Blake" (Ms. Cary 82).

Gulley's predicament derives from the paradoxes inherent in a world of freedom, the identity of possibility and necessity, form and activity. The unpredictable elements of such freedom could be seen as luck—a moment's inspiration—and as injustice. Further, the two were often inseparable. Blake provided an interpretation of these phenomena. Proclaiming the sacredness of creative activity, he recognised the unity of good and evil, "Tyger, tyger burning bright . . . did he who made the lamb make thee?"

> Whole books deals with injustice and so emphasis, from Blake, that evil is real. And inevitable because of the creative freedom of the *individual*, and because of *luck*.
>
> (Ms. Cary 82)

The interpretation was by no means rigid. What Blake might not supply as a gloss for Jimson's story, Cary was prepared to provide himself. "Look in Blake for the creative. And luck. If nothing of luck, Gulley must shew it."

Gulley's paintings in no way illustrate Blake's theories, but Blake's words contribute to an understanding of Jimson's intent and inspiration. The real world in Blake is that of Eternity. To recognise the universal in individual forms is to participate in the eternal act of creation. Gulley calls art the thing that "Keeps on . . . keeping on", and creation the thing that "GOES ON GOING ON", allying the individual act to the unending process. Imagination is the power which perceives the "eternity" of the forms of the material world, thus making them real.

> For, as Billy says, "There exist in the [*sic*] eternal world the permanent realities of everything we see reflected in this vegetable glass of Nature." And I thought, in the works of Gulley

Jimson. Such as red Eves and green Adams, blue whales and spotted giraffes . . . and all the dreams of prophets whose imagination sustains the creation, and recalls it from the grave of memory.

(HM, pp. 227-28)

Gulley's intimate perception of Sara's individuality reveals her to him as the eternal woman. Aspects of her character are illuminated by a variety of Blakean concepts. She is now Oothoon the eternal innocence, , now Enitharmon the materialistic feminity. "Women on the grab" (Ms. Cary 82).

Blake's poem "The Mental Traveller" elucidates for Gulley various aspects of his experience.[28] The poem reveals a cyclical conflict between vision and necessity or law. The former is characterised by a new born babe, the latter by an old woman. Necessity fetters the babe and ages him. Triumph over the established order renews his infancy. Gulley's aesthetic experience derives a rough gloss from the contrast. A new vision restores him to infancy, "The famous Gulley Jimson, whom nobody knows, is perceived laughing like an old goat and skipping like a young ram . . . second childhood" (*HM*, p. 111). The idea itself comes like a birth, "And I felt a kick inside as if I was having a foal" (*HM*, p. 34). Jimson follows Blake in characterising necessity as an Old Woman.

Sara's possessiveness forces Gulley repeatedly to break away from her, ultimately to destroy her. Coker's mother puts art to the service of necessity, patching her roof with Jimson's painting. But this act in turn enables Gulley to master necessity, for the destruction of The Fall opens the way for The Creation and the cycle of necessity transformed to possibility works itself out in Gulley's experience.

Gulley's use of Blake is completely idiosyncratic. He casually applies Blake's terms to real people, "They're phantoms, spectres" (*HM*, p. 177), and freely injects his own words into Blake's lines, "Amidst the lustful fires he walks, and polishes his door knob" (*HM*, p. 31).[29] Cary's use of Blake in the Beeder episode enhances the themes of liberalism and creation. The Beeders are wealthy liberals, removed by their wealth from mundane care, liberated by it from intolerance. Gulley calls the Beeder's world Beulah, Blake's place of comfort where inhabitants of a fallen world can receive rest and inspiration.

> There is a place where Contrarieties are equally True:
> This place is called Beulah. It is a pleasant lovely Shadow
> Where no dispute can come, Because of those who Sleep.
>   . . .
>
> Beulah is evermore Created around Eternity, appearing
> To the Inhabitants of Eden around them on all sides.
> But Beulah to its Inhabitants appears within each distict
> As the beloved infant in his mother's bosom round incircled
> With arms of love & pity & sweet compassion. But to
> The Sons of Eden the moony habitations of Beulah
> Are from Great Eternity a mild & pleasant Rest.[30]

Cary's notes refer to Beulah as "visionary element, dreamland, means of spiritual influence," to its daughters as "temporary perceptions of ideal beauty" (Ms. Cary 273, S.12.G).

In Blake's scheme the fallen man must strive towards regeneration through ceaseless activity in the generated world. This activity, translated by Gulley Jimson, means using the materials of the present world to forge the new. The individual creates a new world by transforming (in fact or vision) the old; it is this drive to transform and control which rejects Spinoza's fatalism and finds a congenial climate in progressive liberal government. In a note on Blake's individualism Cary makes the transition to Jimson's interpretation:

> As *you*, you must use the world and the *government*. You must serve
> God and mammon, and make em serve you. Descent into
> generation . . . the artist—the man-God makes the new world.
>
> (Ms. Cary 82)

Thus when Alabaster asks Gulley if it is possible to "serve Mammon and Art at the same time" Gulley's answer is flippant in its tone only, "It is . . . or there wouldn't be any art. Through cash to culture" (*HM*, p. 139). Money provides education; the rich or the public custodians of wealth do not produce art, but they create the climate for its appreciation.

> But what a government can do is to encourage art schools and
> artists, and when you get a lot of art schools and bad artists, you
> get a lot of people trying to steal an idea from somebody else and
> the people they steal from are the original artists. So you get an
> encouraging atmosphere for original art.
>
> (*HM*, p. 140)

Gulley's analysis recalls Mill's comments on originality and his observation that "a government cannot have too much of the kind of activity which does not impede, but aids and stimulates individual exertion and development" (*On Liberty*, p.169); and, though cynical in tone, Jimson's remark builds upon Sir William Beeder's liberal sense of good emerging through evil in a climate where the two freely mingle.

> 'The slump' said Sir William, 'certainly did much to push forward social legislation . . .'
> 'That's another advance we owe to the Great War,' said Sir William, 'Medicine. Especially in mental cases and plastic surgery.'

$$(HM, \text{pp.}147\text{-}48)[31]$$

Beeder's world, where money gives Lady Beeder the freedom to practise her amateur art, gives Jimson the fundamental necessities of food and shelter, essential to *his* art.

This Beulah, therefore, is no less a place of inspiration for being built on material prosperity. Its limitations reside in its passivity. While Gulley battles against evil or injustice, the Beeders wait for the emergence of good. They partake of the somnolence of the beneficient limbo. This contrast is emphasised in the final scene where the Beeders, unwittingly thwarting Jimson's greatest creative act by their reluctance to take an innovative step, are overwhelmed and forced to retreat by the active executors of Jimson's vision, the boys and girls made "invulnerable" by their part in the creation.

Evil in Gulley's world resides not in misguided activity, such as the Beeders' unadventurous taste or a government's indiscriminate spending, but in abstraction. Practically, Gulley prefers an active government to none, "But unless you spend millions you don't even get mistakes — you have nothing at all" (*HM*, p.141). "Spectre" is Blake's word for the inactive, rationalising and self-centred aspect of a character, opposed to the active hence creative, "emanation". Spectre is the word Gulley applies to government in the abstract, as it exists in the minds of a people, rather than as it manifests itself in activity, through individuals. Gulley calls Tom Wilcher a spectre, for Wilcher is a man who permits concepts to dominate his activity. Such a character is dangerous, for lacking a sense of its own active being, it is insensitive to the individuality, the life, of others. Gulley also rejects theoretical anarchism, like Plant's, which is as much an abstraction as its antagonist the law. Gulley opposes to the law his individuality. He does not attempt to make a new world, as Chester Nimmo does, by changing his surroundings; he makes art, transforming his world in the products of his characteristic vision.

Jimson's vigilance against getting "in a state", too, has important Blakean connotations. In Blake a "state" is a temporary condition. Cary annotated Blake's admonition, "Distinguish therefore States from Individuals in those States".[32] Pity, hatred, righteousness, are states, and to give way to them is to belie one's true character, to distort one's perception of the world and to act in character with the state itself. Gulley, therefore, tries to free himself from emotions which distort the world or draw attention from the forms of reality — the materials of creation — to the self.

The main subsidiary characters in *The Horse's Mouth*, although roundly characterised, function as further illustrations of Jimson's Blakean world view. Gulley's view witnesses Sara's transformation from the ever-innocent sensualist to the determined preserver of her own past. It is in this guise that Sara is a threat to Gulley, withholding from him the means to achieve his own rejuvenation in creative activity. Materially, Sara thwarts Gulley's activity by refusing to let him sell her favourite drawing. But she also tempts him to love of the past. Gulley must fight Sara's comfortableness no less than her obstinacy.

Sara is more intimately related to Gulley's art than any other character. As the sensual Eve-Oothoon, she is his inspiration; as Enitharmon who weaves the forms of law and necessity she is his chief antagonist. Cary noted Sara's place in the novel's thematic scheme. "Sara as engulfing law and order. The maternal state which thinks it knows whats good for you" (Ms. Cary 82). Gulley's battle with Sara is a fight to the death, for it is a clash of two vital activities, Sara's sensuality and Gulley's creativity. For either to dominate is for the other to be destroyed, and so after a lifetime of tension caused by the

simultaneous exchange of gifts and hurt, love and enmity,
Sara's life is sacrificed to Gulley's art only to be reborn in that
art.

Plant, as his name suggests, epitomises the character of the
vegetable world, Blake's term for the level of existence which
eschews creative strife and hence enjoys only the most
rudimentary growth. Plant follows Spinoza in accepting
injustice, not as an element of freedom, but as the sign of an
inscrutable fate. His stance is contemplative and conservative,
"on grounds the world can't be any better" (Ms. Cary 82).
Plant discovers an illusive security in his unproductive
resignation. As such he is the foil for Jimson's belief in the
creative power of the individual.

For Plant abstractions are the only realities. His God is
distant and unapproachable. He therefore clings to his
Spinozan philosophy and makes a hero of Jimson, while
regarding with suspicion the government, Jimson's art, even
the reality of the weather or the pavement under his feet.
Indeed, Gulley feels threatened by Plant's need to "get him in a
pigeon hole", under the label "genius". In contrast, Gulley's
relationship to his God is undefined and immediate. He
receives inspiration, from the horse's mouth, and shares in the
divine creative activity. The form of his relationship with other
creatures is not hero-worship, but love, and these relationships
are not static but many-sided. In short, Jimson's individualism
conforms to the liberal ideal; it is not abstract, but active and
social. By discovering the error in Plant's suspicion of
governments which rely on human wisdom to direct change,
Gulley clarifies his own anarchism which welcomes human
progress, but opposes static legalism. His rejection of Plant's
conservative anarchism reveals the implicit liberalism of
Jimson's outlook. Similarly, discovering the uncreativeness of
Spinoza's fatalism, the inactivity of the ever-watchful "old
diamond eye", enables Gulley to formulate his own Blakean
view of creation as ceaseless active battle against necessity.
"Freedom, to be plain, is nothing by THE INSIDE OF THE
OUTSIDE. And even a philosopher like Old Ben can't judge
the XXX by eating pint pots. . . But what you get on the inside
is SOMETHING THAT GOES ON GOING ON. . . It's the
creation" (*HM*, pp.94-5).

141

Plant rises from his defeat because unconsciously he, too, creates. By insisting on the moral value of the art he does not understand, the rectitude of his own conscience, and the meaningfulness of uncomfortable situations, Plant "invents a fiction" which he believes. His creations, typically, are abstractions — "dignities and responsibilities" — but they enable him to survive and make the most of his luck.

Pride, in Blake's scheme, is a form of vitality, and Coker, with her pride and her enforced self-reliance not only lives through trouble, but nurtures new and healthy life. Coker, who practices Blake's dictum, "Go love without the help of any thing on earth", is an important foil for the other characters; her forceful individuality is neither selfish nor demanding.

The lesser characters of *The Horse's Mouth* provide a rich social background to the novel as well as contributing to its Blakean themes. The world at large is seen through two groups in society among which Gulley moves, the proletarian environment of Greenbank and the world of the bourgeois liberals, Hickson and the Beeders. Ironically, though neither group comprehends his art, both respect it; and though neither alleviates Gulley's material need, it is his poverty that cements Gulley's relationship with both communities, evoking generous solicitude from Greenbank, a response of "richesse oblige" among the wealthy.

"Walrus" is Gulley's generalised term for the Thames-side working class figures in the narrative, but the variety of occupations discovered among the Greenbank group is matched by a spectrum of personal peculiarities and outlooks. The physical attributes of these figures can be seen to reflect their characters. Cary pointed to this intention in a note, "If Nosy has a stammer it must affect him i.e. make him isolated and therefore more obstinate and determined" (Ms. Cary 82). The effect of such serious observation in Gulley's narrative is to deepen Jimson's own character as a sensitive observer of his fellows in a fallen world. Nineteen year old Franklin, uncomfortably learning the meaning of necessity, is ever on the lookout for injustice and hopeless to alter it. His boils epitomise his personal suffering; Hitler signifies to him the injustice in the world. He scorns idealism and talk. Bert the boatman, who "wears a jersey to show he's on the boats and moleskins to show he's on the hard," is secure in his place in the world, proud in his self-sufficiency. The clothes of Mr. Moseley the bookie, "suits and shoes so beautiful that they make you look again" (*HM*, p.61), announce his success as a worldly "prophet". These individuals, as self-contained as Albert's deaf cat, are nevertheless a community linked by local solidarity and common interests — gossip, the war, fundamentalist religion. Active friendship towards Jimson focusses their communal identity in the novel. Their common predicament emerges in their preoccupation with the impending war. Successive gatherings in the Greenbank pubs reveal, as Hitler's voice issues over the radio, first the stirrings of a destructive idea which develops parallel to Jimson's deepening artistic intuition in the novel, and then its fruition, "Another raid on Warsaw, poor old Warsaw". A liberal society is Cary's antidote — and Jimson's — to such events. If the genius suffers, as Gulley knows he must, the madman cannot triumph where all enjoy the freedom of individual expression.

The community of the walruses — embracing Bert's scepticism and conservatism, Plant's fatalism and Coker's pride — is a microcosm of the world at large. Nosy Barbon, sacrificing his tidy lower middle class home and his "true bent . . . for commerce" (*HM*, p.221) to the love of art as Jimson did, is a link between Jimson's eccentricity and the creative impulse common throughout society. A similar link is found in the history of the inventor Rankin, Gulley's brother-in-law, whose struggles as a technical artist parallel Gulley's own history. Both exemplify the irrepressible creative spirit which is source and victim of progress, and — because of its unrestrainedness — agent and victim of injustice. Jenny Rankin demonstrates undemanding and ill-rewarded love.

Gulley unfolds the tale at significant moments in his narrative. To Plant's preoccupation with the meaning behind injustice Gulley opposes Jenny's active unquestioning devotion to Rankin, which again exemplifies for him the wisdom of Blake's "Go love without the help of any thing on earth". The battle between Rankin's inventiveness and the conservatism of the technological planners illustrates, as Gulley tells Nosy, that imagination is both the enemy of government and the force of necessity to which government is a response. Rankin's ultimate sacrifice of Jenny to the advancement of his inventive career forecasts Gulley's sacrifice of Sara to the pursuit of his art.

Within the class of "boorjays" too, Cary draws distinctions. Professor Alabaster's fraudulence shows through the tatters in his clothes. The Beeders and Hickson live in mansions surrounded by eclectic gatherings of traditional art. Although both patronise Jimson, the nature of their patronage differs. The Beeders display a *laissez-faire* generosity. If Gulley's efforts in their studio come to no material fruition, the place of inspiration leads him towards his greatest conception. Meanwhile their unwitting assistance enables Abel's sculpture to be completed, illustrating the chance achievements of uncalculated provision.

Gulley calls Hickson his "oldest friend", but Hickson's patronage is fundamentally exploitive, not creative. His relationship with Hickson twice lands Jimson in jail, but Gulley recognises these setbacks as the inevitable injustices of a system whose benevolence is subject to the limitations of its materialist basis. Opposite to the Beeders and Hickson is Wilcher, whose conservatism is sterile and who can be dismissed in a few Jimsonian phrases, "Genus, Boorjwar; species, Blackcoatius Begoggledus Ferocissimouse. All eaten up with lawfulness and rage; ready to bite himself for being so respectable" (*HM*, p.175). The opposition, however, emphasises in a crude schematic way Cary's sense, shared by Gulley, that for all its limitations the liberal pattern of activity is more positive, more creative than the detached self-centredness of those who withdraw behind the established forms of propriety and preconception, "political systems and religious creeds".

Throughout the development of *The Horse's Mouth* Cary sought a scheme which would lend order to his plot. The history of the Jimson family was such a scheme, but it proved too generalised. Blake's "Mental Traveller" usefully outlined the theme of necessity. In early notes Cary constructed a crude symbolism out of Jimson's characteristic vision, with such equations as

fury of life and   3. Surry side all in a blaze.
injustice and   Clouds sending up golden
corruption   with[[flecks]] Lettuce green
                         to cabbage green. River
                         [[disappeared]] . . . old willow
                         trembling and wheezing together.
                         as if in an old man's fright.

(Ms. Cary 82)

Gulley's creative activity gradually defined itself through a schematic use of his paintings. This scheme emerged late in the writing. In early drafts Gulley's first painting was to be Genesis, but Cary altered this, permitting the artist to work his way upward from the fallen material world to the divine act of creation itself. A note reveals the dawning of this scheme, as a two part structure.

> 1st part. Picture the fall. . . Through love of real into love of God and the spiritual life of vision. Free to enjoy life and like people. Get away from injustice.
>
>   . . .
>
> 2nd part. Creation. The fall by passion passes into the toils of Adam's creation, *with* God. All meditation and quotation on free creative side. . .

(Ms. Cary 82)

The final structure of the novel clarified the pattern of fall and rise. Gulley's three paintings, The Fall, The Raising of Lazarus and The Creation, epitomise in their subjects the artist's necessary immersion in the real world of his experience and humanity, his reception of inspiration, and his participation in the god-like act of creation.

Gulley's story begins with a return to his painting of The Fall. Although he continues to work on The Fall for a time, the content of the painting is less important than Gulley's relation to it. He is at first proud of the work, then dissatisfied with it. Out of the dissatisfaction grows a sense that what the composition lacks is motion. But a more significant discovery is that this lack extends to the picture's conception. "The Fall is a frost, I said. It's iced all over. It's contemplated from the outside" (*HM*, p.95). Because he has regarded the fall of man as a static event, Gulley has failed to capture its enduring

145

significance as a universal action. Understanding the fall not
simply as a symbol of man's disobedience, but, humanistically
and romantically, as an action typifying his quest for mental
and physical development, leads Jimson to reinterpret the
legend. Cary noted "Fall, entry of imagination into
experience". Eve's impulse towards knowledge is at once a
departure from innocence and the first step towards
regeneration. The scene in Eden is a type of the human quest for
fulfilment.

> It's not pleasure, or peace, or contemplation, or comfort or
> happiness — it is a Fall. Into the pit. The ground gives way and
> down you go, head over heels. Unless of course, you know how to
> fly, to rise again on your wings.
>
> (HM, p.95)

Later Gulley tells Nosy The Fall wasn't solid enough because it
failed to embrace the duality of the state of freedom it heralded.

> . . . what was the Fall after all. The discovery of the solid hard
> world, good and evil. Hard as rocks and sharp as poisoned
> thorns. And also the way to make gardens.
>
> . . .
>
> . . . love doesn't grow on trees like apples in Eden — it's
> something you have to make. And you must use your
> imagination to make it too, just like anything else.
>
> (HM, pp.164-65)

The Fall thus teaches Gulley the nature of his own creative
activity, but it is only when necessity — in the form of old Mrs.
Coker — forcibly deprives him of the painting that Gulley is
freed from his attachment to that work to exploit the
possibilities its evolution has opened to him.

The Fall revealed to Jimson the nature of human striving
towards creation, but the source of Gulley's inspiration, of the
"solid forms of the imagination" now seizing him, remained for
him to discover. And this discovery emerges from the second
picture, The Raising of Lazarus, sketched out on the Beeders'
studio wall. The theme of the painting advances the schematic
progress from fall to regeneration. But Gulley only succeeds in
covering the wall with feet before necessity again steps in to
drive him from the work. Nevertheless, the composition is

significant, for, as Stockholder points out, Gulley's vision is of "the feet of man, and the feet of God walking in the same earth".[33] Here God is sharing the world of his creation. In Blake's scheme Christ's incarnation and self-sacrifice demonstrate for humanity its unity with the divine character; Christ's activity is the type of man's regeneration.

> . . . Lo, the Eternal Great Humanity,
> To whom be Glory & Dominion Evermore, Amen,
> Walks among all his awful Family seen in every face:
> As the breath of the Almighty, such are the words of man to man
> In the great Wars of Eternity, in fury of Poetic Inspiration,
> To build the Universe stupendous, Mental forms Creating.[34]

The Christian theme of resurrection thus again unites with Blake's vision to promote Gulley's understanding of the creative process. Fallen man is no longer striving alone. The inspiring deity is present in his creation just as creative man participates in divine activity. But Lazarus' raising is a miracle; the free man cannot passively await the miracle; he must forge his own rebirth through activity. The Beeders' return, which drives Gulley from his painting and back into the world of necessity, clears the slate once again in preparation for the book's climactic creative effort.

The painting of The Creation brings together all the thematic strands of *The Horse's Mouth,* as the composition itself brings together into formal coherence the objects and symbols which have been massing in Jimson's consciousness throughout the narrative. Here in a final frenzy of activity necessity and possibility join. Luck brings Jimson the wall he requires; "Twenty five by forty. Windows bricked up and all smooth plaster round. Sent from God". The wall itself partakes of the material world and the spiritual, once a chapel, then a garage.

Heedless of the limitations of the structure and his own health, Gulley now seizes upon the hitherto limiting forms of his experience, ready to give them a new formal existence.

> And all the time, the forms were growing out of my egg-like [*sic*] cracker snakes. Coker and Sara and Lolie and Churchill's hat, white and red and blue, legs and arms and bottoms and a great black shape like a relief map of Iceland, with a white oval just by

147

the north-east corner. God knows what it would have to stand for — He would give me the tip.

(HM, p.234)

By incorporating the people, objects and institutions of his environment into his painting Jimson "throws the loop of creation" (HM, p.213) around necessity at last.

Gulley knows the wall is doomed to crumble, as he knows that he is dying. As Cary's notes make clear, The Creation is Jimson's final desperate bid to sustain his characteristic activity by giving it objective form.

> If Jimson sees the danger to the chapel but carries on — i.e. really playing a game. Art for art's sake. . .
> General feeling not friv. but desperate. Gulley feels he hasn't long. He wants to put it over. Creation — point is world of imagination and. The way to live . . .

(Ms. Cary 82)

Gulley's ultimate endeavour is thus, both in form and purpose, art for creation's sake. The painting names the form, as it consumes the activity — mental and physical — of Jimson's character.

The collapse of the wall provides a grand dramatic finale to the novel's action. Throughout, tragedy and comedy have been closely allied; tears and laughter, one activity. Cary makes us laugh as Gulley sobs to the whale and to Sara in a comic prelude to the final fall. Not only tears and joy are one, but life and death as Sara lives again, identified with the whale, the central figure in the new creation. "'Oh dear, Oh dear, I ought to know what life is.' 'Yes,' I said. . . Practically a MATTER OF LIFE AND DEATH you might say, or thereabouts'" (HM, p.284). as the whale smiles and bends lovingly towards Gulley, form itself becomes active, and with the collapse of the wall, laughter triumphs.

> When the dust began to clear I saw through the cloud about ten thousand angels in caps, helmets, bowlers and even one top hat, sitting on walls, dustbins, gutters, roofs, window sills and other people's cabbages, laughing. That's funny, I thought, they've all seen the same joke. God bless them. It must be a work of eternity, a chestnut, a horse laugh.

(H.M, p.287)

148

Gulley is the author and object of this universal joke. He stands in immediate relation to the assembly as both God and man. In Gulley, victim of injustice and master of creation, the dualities of existence are resolved. Gulley's experience illustrates the inextricability of creation and destruction in the inevitable activity of the world's existence, which Cary sees as progress. Gulley's story solves no moral dilemma for society. His personal triumph, in understanding and practising creation both evokes and defies injustice. At best, by characterising the creative activity through which man realises his freedom and his personal potential, Jimson's story points to the need for such activity to be recognised and promoted.

Cary's fiction offers no absolutes, for to uphold absolutes, moral, legal or aesthetic would deny the vision of a world, active in character, changing in form, growing. The only absolute, insofar as it is seen as inevitable, in this view is creation itself. From his triumphant expression of the nature of creative activity in *The Horse's Mouth*, however, Cary was empowered by his own formulated understanding to go on, in succeeding novels, to further analysis of its varying social, political and religious forms.

NOTES

1. MS. labelled "Note on Trilogy for U.S.A.", Ms. Cary 292, N.148.
2. John Middleton Murry, "Art and Philosophy", *Rhythm*, I (Summer 1911), p. 9. Cary Collection of Printed Books, C.549/1.
3. Joyce Cary, *The Horse's Mouth*, ed. Andrew Wright (authorised ed. George Rainbird in assoc. with Michael Joseph, 1957), p. 161. Hereafter abbreviated *HM* and cited in the text.
4. See, for example, *Art and Reality* (Cambridge University Press, 1958), pp. 72-4.
5. Joyce Cary, *Herself Surprised*, Carfax ed. (Michael Joseph, 1951), p. 51. Hereafter abbreviated *HS* and cited in the text.
6. The unfinished "Marta" told of such downward progress. (Ms. Cary 175, 263, 264, as did a draft version of *Prisoner of Grace*. Rose Venn in *The Moonlight* rescues her sister from a slum, and an early version of *The Horse's Mouth* emphasises the pride with which Jimson's mother, loyal to her husband, progresses from a "woman house proud . . . to a simple village char", MS. Cary 82.
7. "On His Own Method", TS. in Ms. Cary 237, p. 10. Labelled in Cary's hand "Preuves 1953". Published as "Notes sur l'Art et la Liberté", *Preuves* XLII (August 1954, pp. 28-32).

8. Ms. Cary 275. Cary also altered the sentence, "The young people call me an old Tory", which appears in the printer's copy to "The young people think me an old fossil", *To Be a Pilgrim*, Carfax ed. (Michael Joseph, 1951), p. 78. Hereafter abbreviated *TBP* and cited in the text.

9. C.F.G. Masterman, *The Condition of England* (Methuen, 1909), p. 260.

10. *The Condition of England*, pp. 302-3.

11. *The Condition of England*, p. 305.

12. *The Condition of England*, p. 18.

13. Jeremy Taylor, *Holy Dying* (Halifax, Milner and Sowerby, 1852), p. 194. Cary Collection of Printed Books, B.177. Cary's copy of *Holy Dying* is dated 1942, the year *To Be a Pilgrim* was written.

14. Among other poems, Cary annotated "Le Voyage" in his copy of Baudelaire's poems. Charles Baudelaire, *Les Fleurs du Mal*, ed. Enid Starkie (Oxford, Blackwell, 1942), pp. 134-40. Cary Collection of Printed Books, B.204.

15. Wilcher's search for peace and the frustration it engenders recalls a passage Cary annotated in a letter of Flaubert to Louise Colet: "But one must never think of happiness, that allures the devil . . . The conception of Paradise is at bottom more infernal than that of Hell. The hypothesis of a perfect felicity creates more despair than that of a torment without cease. . . ." C.H. Charles, *Love Letters of Great Men and Women* (Stanley Paul, 1924), p. 186. Cary Collection of Printed Books, B.106.

16. A kindred example in Victorian poetry of the journey contemplated with a sense of purpose but harbouring escapist undertones is Tennyson's "Ulysses".

17. Letter to John Dover Wilson, December 1942, Foster, p. 366. Cary studied at The Board of Manufacturers School of Art, later the Edinburgh College of Art.

18. Marc-André Raffalovich, literary man and a member of a cultured cosmopolitan family, and his friend Father John Gray, whose new chapel at Torphichen Cary visited.

19. For a discussion of this material see Charles G. Hoffman, "The Genesis and Development of Joyce Cary's First Trilogy", *PMLA*, LXXVIII (September 1963), p.. 431-39. Hoffmann's transcriptions are not always accurate.

20. See *Art and Reality* (Cambridge, Cambridge University Press, 1958), pp. 74-6; "The Art of Fiction", *The Paris Review*, VII (Fall-Winter 1954-55), p. 68; "Notes sur l'Art et la Liberté", p. 31; "The Novelist at Work", *Adam International Review*, XVIII, nos. 212-13 (November-December 1950), p. 22; and "The Way a Novel Gets Written", p. 91.

At Etaples Cary visited the artist Leandro Ramon Garrido, whose pupil his Aunt Hessie had been. B. Obumselu, in "The Theme of Creativity in Joyce Cary's Novels", D. Phil. thesis, Oxford University, 1966, p. 25, claims that Garrido is the artist of whom Cary speaks. This is unlikely. In "Notes sur l'Art et la Liberté" Cary states that while visiting Garrido he met the artist of the tale, an impoverished man in his sixties, with several children, who lived in a farm nearby. He repeats this description in all the works cited above. Obumselu bases his claim on a note in Cary's copy of "The Novelist at Work". The change occurs in a reference to the artist with whom his aunt studied. In the sentence "She's been taught by him and I met this man who'd been a well-known painter in England and had sold his pictures", Cary circled the word "him" and wrote "Garrido". I believe Cary's intention was to make the distinction between the two artists, made elsewhere. It is unlikely that the reference was to Garrido who was at the time only 37 years old, in good health, with a baby daughter, at the height of his popular success (he was elected Sociétaire of the Société Nationale des Beaux Arts in 1906), and sympathetic to Impressionism. J. Quigley, *Leandro Ramon Garrido* (Duckworth, 1913), pp. 2, 99.

21. John Middleton Murry, *Between Two Worlds* (Jonathan Cape, 1935), pp. 153-54. See also F.A. Lea, *John Middleton Murry* (Methuen, 1959), p. 20, and Cary's Paris Diary, Ms. Cary. 253.

22. Maurice Collis, *Stanley Spencer* (Harvill Press, 1962), and Gilbert Spencer, *Stanley Spencer*, (Victor Gollancz, 1961).

23. Aldous Huxley, *Point Counter Point* (Chatto and Windus, 1930), Cary Collection of Printed Books, C.367. Signed "Joyce Cary 1931".

24. *Point Counter Point*, p. 579.

25. George Moore, *Vale* (William Heinemann, 1920), p. 65, Cary Collection of Printed Books, C.488.

26. Cary considered giving the novel a broad historical orientation, conveyed through the story of Gulley's family: "Family life of Jimsons *and history of taste throughout period 1840-1940*" (Ms. Cary 82).

27. The novel was to be set "among war scenes shewing ordinary life continuing" (Ms. Cary 274, p. 36). Notes suggest that Jimson's son might be killed in the war, that the tale might be told in a bomb shelter, and that Gulley might, at the end, be found in the river, "probably on account of the blitz" (Ms. Cary 82).

28. Cary drew up elaborate schemes for the correspondence. See Ms. Cary 82.

29. Quotations from Blake are from the Everyman edition which Cary annotated in preparing *The Horse's Mouth*. References to *The Complete Writings of William Blake*, ed. Keynes, are given in parentheses. Blake's line reads "Amidst the lustful fires he walks: his feet become like brass", *America: A Prophecy*, 1. 74, annotated by Cary in William Blake, *Poems and Prophecies*, ed. Max Plowman (Everyman's Library, J. M. Dent, 1927), p. 66. Cary Collection of Printed Books, B.98. (Keynes, plate 8, 1. 16, p. 199.)

30. William Blake, *Milton*, Book II, plate 33, 11. 1-3, 8-14, *Poems and Prophecies*, p. 146 (Keynes, plate 30, 11. 1-3, 8-14, p. 518.)

31. Similarly, in *A Fearful Joy*, when John is seriously injured in a car accident, his recovery is promoted "by the very rapid development of surgery due to the concentrated practice of the war," Carfax ed. (Michael Joseph, 1952), p. 197. Hereafter abbreviated *AFJ* and cited in the text.

32. *Milton*, Book II, plate, 35, 1. 22, *Poems and Prophecies*, p. 149 (Keynes, plate 32, 1. 22, p. 521).

33. Fred Stockholder, "The Triple Vision in Joyce Cary's First Trilogy",

Modern Fiction Studies, IX, no. 3 (Autumn 1963), p. 242.
34. Blake, *Milton*, Book II, plate 33, 11. 15-20 *Poems and Prophecies*, p. 146 (Keynes, plate 30, 11. 15-20, p.519).

6

The Moonlight and *A Fearful Joy*

> The business of a woman's ordinary life is things in general, and
> can as little cease to go on as the world to go round.

> There is nothing, after disease, indigence, and guilt, so fatal to
> the pleasurable enjoyment of life as the want of a worthy outlet for
> the active faculties.

J.S. Mill, *The Subjection of Women*

"No one who doesn't know womankind knows anything about
the nature of Nature," says Gulley Jimson in *The Horse's Mouth*.
A portrait of womankind focusses Cary's view of human nature
and its collective creation, historical progress, in *The Moonlight*
and *A Fearful Joy*. Cary posed woman's nature as one of the
constant elements in his view of human progress as a pattern of
consistency in change. Revolutions could be seen to affect
woman's social role, not her essential instinctive character.

Woman's nature is one of the most consistent formulations in
Cary's schematized view of humanity. "He imagined an entity
called 'woman' . . . ," Enid starkie recalled. "He saw her
motivated only by the characteristics which made her a woman.
. . ."[1] Cary attributed to woman a limitless depth of emotional
vitality. But he permitted her a degree of initiative
circumscribed by the natural functions of wife and motherhood,
and assigned a monopoly of conceptual inventiveness to the

male. He elicited support for this view from his reading. George Moore observed,

> that the great gift Nature has bestowed upon woman is the power of enjoying things as they go by—a great gift truly it is, and sufficient compensation for lack of interest in religion and morals. It may be this is why women have not written a great book, or painted a great picuture.[2]

The usefulness of this generalised view enabled Cary to overlook its obvious exceptions. "I do not think that he possessed any scales capable of weighing such a woman as Madame Curie, whose most individual self would not have registered in his balance" commented Enid Starkie.[3] Cary does not analyse, as Mill did, the social and educational conditions which, resticiting individuality and promoting only amateurism, traditionally made the outstanding woman philosopher, scientist, or artist a rarity; nor does he follow Mill in viewing a female intuitive perception and pragmatism as the foundations for intellectual and practical achievements equal to those of men, and equally worthy of primary professional pursuit. Indeed, Cary's view of women, though warmly sympathetic, is entirely in keeping with that "established custom" to which Mill, a century before, had attributed the unreasonable subjection of women.

Cary generalised both on the basis of woman's evident physiological makeup and of an established social role. He resented that some women were denied self-fulfilment by their inability to marry; he felt, too, that women should enjoy the freedom to choose a career *and* a family. But the conventional aspects of his liberal stance are evident in his commitment to natural law viewed through a pattern of relationships entrenched in the mores of Western society, a pattern of family organisation towards which his attitude is wholly conservative. It is one of the ironies of Cary's liberal viewpoint that the freedom to choose, on which he insists in "The Revolution of the Women" and *The Moonlight*, admits only the choice of action in accordance with maternal instinct or as a subsidiary part of a male-oriented society.

Cary elaborates in his fiction the "power of enjoyment" he and Moore recognised in women. Gulley Jimson defines the "eternal female" as fusion of Eve, the wife and sinner, and Blake's Oothoon the ever-innocent virgin: she who "falls every night to rise in the morning. And wonder at herself. Knowing everything and still surprised. Living in innocence" (*HM*, p. 32). Moore's "lack of interest in religion and morals" emerges along with a general passivity in Cary's females as a corollary of woman's fundamental inability to conceive her own purpose. Nature or a man supplies this purpose. Thus women's religion is at its best a pure expression of love or service: Tabitha's heartfelt cry for life to the master of creation, or Sara's "religion which served her like her pans. . . ." Elsewhere religion masks the superstitious faith to nature's purposes prompting Amanda to let herself be made a mother, or the egoistic impulse of Lucy Wilcher's pursuit of independence in a service of her own designing.

Cary's women do not formulate their religion, because as creatures of instinct they are essentially unreflective. Tabitha, Lucy, Sara all respond to the demands of the moment. Cary triumphantly portrays in Ella Venn and Nina Nimmo women who rationalise continually without performing the mental links between past and future action which give rise, in Cary's men, to a coherent plan or aim. All Cary's women share Sara Monday's conclusion, "If I'm a body then it can't be helped, for I can't help myself" (*HS*, p. 10). Such figures, passive even before the onslaughts of their own emotions, rely on a life of service to provide them with an opportunity for fulfilment. Sara, a servant by profession as well as inclination, epitomises this conception. Aunt Hersey and Delia, rescued from purposelessness by Pinto in *A House of Children*, Coker, given purpose by her baby in *The Horse's Mouth*, Nina compelled to service by Chester's grace, swell the ranks of Cary's illustrations.

Cary does not distinguish women—as he does men—as creators or conservatives; in them the two impulses join to to construct and sustain family relationships. The object of female conservatism is life itself. Gulley Jimson sums up the paradoxical nature of a women's selfless and compulsive role of service: "And I thought, she's got something to live for, Cokey, and it will kill her by the painful method specially patented for lucky mothers. She'll be a hag in five years, and she'll never die till she's dead" (*HM*, p. 276).

155

Although Cary implies that lack of conceptual vision limits women's achievements in the arts, it is significant that those who turn to art in an instinctive search for emotional fulfilment (Tabitha, Delia, and Ella all demonstrate musical skill at an amateur level) are those who find that fulfilment in personal attachments and the service of love. Similarly, Amanda's studies serve her not as an end, but as a preparation for understanding and carrying out her timeless role in a modern world.

Cary distinguishes from his typical women those who deny themselves fulfilment by suppressing feminine impulse or misreading their purpose. Women, in his view, frustrate themselves by trying to assume the male role. A note (for *A House of Children*) naming "K.M." as the model of a frustrated woman who "wants greatness" and "*does mischief*" (Ms. Cary 53), probably referring to Katherine Mansfield's erratic personal life, and another explaining that Tabitha "wants music to escape and achieve (like a man)" (Ms. Cary 283, N. 134), make this clear. Both *The Moonlight* and *A Fearful Joy* contain such characters whom Cary actively disliked. Significantly Kit in *A Fearful Joy* and Kathy in *The Moonlight* share the same name. These "emancipated" women who assume a masculine authority and intellectualism degrade their sensual role and despise the emotional bases of family life. Cary's contempt is embodied in their characterisation. Kathy, dull, sterile and calculating, speaks like a psychology textbook. Kit's intellectualism is cold, shallow and imitative. Her actions are not only unthinking but destructively irresponsible.

Cary's view of women emerges as conservative and typifying. Nevertheless, he has deserved praise as a masterful creator of women characters. A lifetime's affectionate observation of aunts, cousins, his friends and his wife enabled Cary to draw women characters whose vitality seems self-generated. Physical detail rendered with sympathy, thoughts conveyed with idiosyncratic selectivity, unselfconsciousness linked to revealing action are the means to his achievement.

Cary's successful portrayals of women are those in which his typifying viewpoint recedes behind the powerful individuality of a character who shapes the themes and action of the novel in which she appears. When plot and significance are imposed on character, Cary's schematic world view becomes a restrictive force, transforming character into stereotype. In *A Fearful Joy* an imposed structure and a generalising authorial view deny the all-important individuality of Tabitha Bonser. In contrast, Ella Venn's consciousness not only registers, but *creates* the dilemmas central to the plot of *The Moonlight*, while the juxtaposition of past and present in her memory integrates the novel's historical action and gives it meaning.

The tension between a woman's sexual nature—her role as child-bearer—and her social role is both theme and moving force in *The Moonlight*. In 1951 Cary published an article entitled "The Revolution of the Women"[4] reviewing the changes in women's status from the end of the Victorian era to the 1950s, and labelling both a "burden" and a "responsibility", the new opportunities for independent achievement brought about by social and economic advance. Liberty to choose a career or a family—or both—implied a compulsion to choose, and thus called upon each woman to shape her own life. The article echoed the dilemma of *The Moonlight* which contrasts the women of the Victorian age and the modern to discover both the problems resulting from increased freedom and those aspects of woman's nature which Cary saw as instinctive and beyond change.

In the preface to the Carfax edition of *The Moonlight* Cary cites two sources for the novel, "the story of an elder sister left in charge of a family, who brought them up at the cost of her own happiness . . .", [5] and an earlier "violent reaction against" Tolstoy's *The Kreutzer Sonata*. Tolstoy had concluded in his story that sexual passions, because capable of causing debasement and disharmony, are evil and must be rejected, even at the cost of humanity's extinction. Cary objected to Tolstoy's contempt for humanity and for nature's laws. In response he began "a counter book, which was to be called (as the answer to *The Kreutzer*) The *Moonlight*" (*Moon*, p. 10). A further inspiration for *The Moonlight*, evident in Cary's notes and in the text,[6] is the "idea" informing the works of D.H. Lawrence, and opposed to Tolstoy's "detestable" bias, of a force of life instinctive, enriching, and resisted at peril. This idea captured the minds of a portion of society in the 1920s exemplified by Robin and Amanda in *The Moonlight*, and left its mark on the morality of succeeding generations.

The force of Cary's reaction to Tolstoy and the magnitude of his intended "counter book" are easily judged from this passage in the preface to *The Moonlight*.

> And in the course of the story, the murderess would give the true case for women as a sex, the real dilemma of a girl who is held by nature in so firm a grip; to whom, as it were, nature says, 'You are so necessary to me in my creation of society, that I shall mark you for my own. You shall be set apart like a dynastic clan. You shall have the privilege of the blood and also its pain. If you try to escape into triviality and decadence, you shall be condemned to frustration, for you were born to deal, generation after generation, with great issues, the primal issues of creation, love and birth, the first education. But you shall suffer also, like a dynastic house, the burden of inescapable duty, the constriction of power. and so I seal you with my mark.'
>
> (*Moon*, p. 10)

In his riposte to Tolstoy, entitled "Forgotten Women" (Ms. Cary 172, 269, 270), Cary kept close to the style and the setting of *The Kreutzer Sonata*; a woman in a train compartment confesses to her sister's murder. But the confessional monologue and the close patterning after Tolstoy's story restricted Cary's exploration of the murdered sister's character and failed to accommodate the story of the murderess's daughter, a modern girl like Amanda. The form did not give sufficient scope for Cary's wish to contrast two generations and to explore the social changes which introduce conflict and perplexity into the women's lives.

Cary abandoned this version in a fragmented state. When he returned to the work, he left Tolstoy's model behind. The wider scope of *The Moonlight*, with "a big scene, a contemplative mood, and the classical third person" (*Moon*, p. 11), enabled Cary to juxtapose Ella's rapidly shifting remembered past with Amanda's ever-questioning present so as to bring the book's two plots into meaningful, mutually illuminating relationship.

Ella Venn is the Jamesian centre of consciousness in *The Moonlight*. The narrator who describes the other characters objectively as well as through the eyes of Ella and Amanda, captures the old woman's thoughts and actions. The result is a portrait of Ella which deepens as she gradually perceives the inconsistencies in her own thoughts or words and actions, and those of others. It is a portrait which supplies its own background through Ella's memories and adds shading to its own details as she reacts to the events going on about her. Ella's selective memory composes a plot running parallel to the main plot. Her memories—of nursery prayers, the celebrities who dined at Florence Villa, new ideas in art and education—supply details which make the terms romance, duty and nobility concrete, and enable us to envisage an age.

Ella's imagination questions in retrospect the appearances she once took for reality. Was Rose truly generous, was their father merely weak, was Bessie a good mother? These questions convey the uncertainties, shadings of opinon and belief, and ambivalent feelings towards loved ones which give the book its emotional depth. Finally, Ella's death and the repetition of her experience in Amanda's pregnancy merge past and present in the novel's action. The novel's conclusion follows soon upon Ella's death, preserving the vitality which Ella's character lends to the entire tale.

In a passage from Cary's draft Ella makes the moonlight a trope for the Victorian world view, "Yes, that *is* moonlight—you see only the big things—but you see them clearly".[7] History, morality, passion itself appeared in a moonscape of large black and white shapes, absolutes of dogma, duty, and devotion which had to be preserved with singleminded fidelity simply because they were capable of being undermined by laxity or doubt. Empire, the church, masculine supremacy, a morality of strict convention are elements Cary lists as among the great forms of the age, preserved by devotees fearful to admit a crack in the fabric, lest the structure, and with it confidence in human endeavour, should crumble.

The central form of this civilization was the family. In the Victorian family love created authority, and authority created the sense of duty that held the family and the whole of society in that age together. Cary intended to portray the strength of family ties in the Venn family and, indeed, in Rose he shows the power of love and conscience to sustain authority. Rose's moral authority preserves family ties of affection no less than of discretion, despite the challenges posed by Venn's mistresses, Bessie's initial horror of her husband, and her later flirtations.

159

In Ella and Rose, Cary divides the Victorian character as he had divided the Edwardian in the Wilcher brothers and the childish in the Corners. Rose protects the legal surface of the Victorian moral edifice; Ella, its foundations in feeling. Ella recognises the moral basis of Victorian convention in a respect for human dignity. Love, the emotional side of an instinctive passion, is spiritualised and then codified in practices of religion, government, and family organisation. Ella's loyalty to feeling, the basis of her rebelliousness, evokes the shortcomings of the Victorian moral structure without denying the solidity of its foundations. Ella's relationship with Amanda reveals the profound difference between her own attitude to law and Rose's. Whereas Rose forced Ella to respect convention, Ella feels the need to instil in her daughter a respect for feeling. By urging Amanda to marry Harry Dawbarn, Ella hopes to bring the morality of love to a relationship Amanda regards as an "experiment".

A note for the novel reads, "Victorian was not against sensuality but had an order for it . . ." (Ms. Cary 277, S.14.C). Even Rose is not above compromise in the interests of this order. She tolerates John Venn's liaison with Mrs. Wilmot as long as it can be made to conform to the forms of discretion and family unity. Ella attacks Amanda's boarding school education because to her retrospective vision the regimented school society denied not only the natural order of family life, but any "real tenderness of the heart", even friendship.

Tolstoy's personal horror of lust led him to assert that vicious selfishness motivates women's actions, and to denounce sex as unnatural. Cary (the post-Freudian) believed that "sexual attraction cannot be abolished; it can only be civilised . . ." (Moon, p. 10). From lust civilised were created arts, manners, even friendship. Thus Ella, who admits that her first low frock made her "dreadfully ashamed", also defends the dresses Tolstoy hated. "It was the right thing to wear low dresses—it was only polite . . . Rose would have thought it very rude and—ungenerous of any woman not to make herself as attractive as possible" (Moon, p. 149). Here as in the greater moral issues, convention dignified instinct.

But convention may clash with individual instinct. Ella's

160

actions are dictated by what Cary calls her "creative will". The habit of expressing her will in actions contradictory to her professed intentions reveals the strength of her imaginative impulse over the forms of law or convention. Although Ella's conscience urges loyalty to Rose and the traditions of her upbringing, her will serves the natural passions and her rebellious romanticism. Ella comically embodies Cary's notion that desire and will are the agents of all action and progress. "What confused Ella was the notion, suggested by the mysterious operations of her mind, that people composed a world by thinking it . . ." (*Moon*, p. 286).

Ella wonders at her own ingenuity which appears, in the light of Rose's influence, an evil impulse. "Oh, but—it did happen", she observes of her elopement. "I did run away—I must have plotted—I must have known" (*Moon*, p. 134). Similarly she is horrified to think that she has lost Rose's will on purpose and that her wish for Amanda's fulfilment has designed the girl's seduction. Rose herself acknowledges the power of Ella's creative will. "Tyranny? Ella, it is you who have planned this crazy scheme from the first, and entangled Amanda. How, I don't know, but you have always been so persistent in getting your way" (*Moon*, pp. 102-3).

Cary's notes read, "Ella . . . *gives* way to *law*—and so is caught. She shld have carried it through . . ." (Ms. Cary 277, S.14.C). Having defied convention and Rose in response to nature's laws, Ella succumbs to a self-created law—guilt. Ella's guilt exaggerates her culpability. It is another manifestation of her constant recourse from unhappiness to a created world of fantasy. The old woman's fantasies continue to transform themselves into action. Her wish for Amanda's happiness buys a farm for Harry Dawbarn; horror of her thoughts becomes a confession of a murder that never happened. Finally, identification with her sister's loneliness and an overwhelming sense of guilt for the injustice Rose suffered brings fantasy and action together for the last time as Ella makes the death she had imagined for Rose her own. Ella's guilty capitulations contrast with Amanda's integrity. Amanda refuses to marry Dawbarn without love and to succumb to Robin without purpose. In both cases her action is guided by loyalty to the nature which she cannot deny, but will not degrade.

161

The fertility of Ella's recollections reveals deep sympathy as well as regret. Through Ella's imagination the novel delves Rose's character to find her, too, a wholly female nature, self-sacrificing and loving, but subverted by the processes of sublimation within and misunderstanding from without. Ella's self-revelation discovers that if she is at the mercy of her sensuality, she hates the carelessness of the young people, because for her sex has a near-religious importance derived from the firm law of nature and the power of love.

The flashbacks which occur naturally in Ella's pattern of thought, as impulsive and emotionally organised as her actions, reveal the passage of time as shifting historical states within a context of human consistency. This consistency emerges through repetition of event—in Ella's experience as the mother of an illegitimate child and Amanda's, through similarities between characters, and through Ella's growing ability to see with Rose's viewpoint as she grows older. Ella's lonely inability to communicate her emotions passes into Amanda's consciousness along with the awareness that independence, thus ironically conceived, carries with it an inescapable challenge to initiative. Physical likenesses observed by various characters enhance the impression. Ella, ageing grows more like Rose, and Amanda, as she ages, resembles Ella. Such concrete elements of the action become symbolic of Cary's themes. The lambing scenes at Brook Farm and the harvesting at Florence Villa present the careless inevitability of nature's round of birth and death, to contrast with Amanda's restless questioning of her nature and uncertain future. Amanda's character must be read in the light of other characters in the book. Her imagination shapes a world view based not on experience but on fiction, her psychological and anthropological studies, and a sketchy awareness of that family history which Ellas has lived. It is a measure of her growth that when experience shocks her by its cruelty and confusion, she perceives the human forces underlying scientific generalisations about life, and her studies become subsidiary to a real involvement in that life. Amanda recognises the profundity of life's emotional basis by discovering her inability to assuage Ella's guilt and by accepting the challenge to create a new world for herself and her child. In this perception Amanda differs from her cousin Iris who is content to establish self-sufficiency by avoiding involvement with others, and from Kathy who chooses a sterile life of pleasure with no emotional base. Amanda's perceptions are often flawed, but they grow. Through her eyes Harry's spontaneity, at first attractive and admirable, is revealed as irresponsible; Robin's passionless intellectualism, as sterile and purposeless. Amanda's own determination to complete the task of motherhood as she completes her professional duties reveals her the stronger figure.

Cary's concrete symbols in the novel assume meaning through their alliance with characterisation. The old house, Florence Villa, "in what is called the Italian style, still very unfashionable" (*Moon*, p. 53), is a monument to one of several misplaced romantic impulses in the book. Like the Venn family, its grandeur conceals the commonplace in its construction and the flaws which have crept into its substance. The bedroom which has such an atmosphere of Rose that Ella dare not enter it, the attics which hold relics of a generation's fashion and a family's history make the house both a symbol for an age and the active guardian of its treasures. Most importantly, the house acquires a private symbolism emerging out of the idiosyncratic perceptions of its inhabitants. The furnishings of the house fascinate and terrify Amanda, so strongly do they recreate their time of fashion.

> The red-plush padded chair with its sloping shoulders on which a tattered antimacassar hung like a fichu, seemed to hold out its fat stumpy arms, not with comical welcome, but with an animal sensuality . . . The grey headless Mary Jane in the corner with its absurd tortured waist, its forced-out chest and stomach, became the characteristic form of that for which it stood as representative Victorian woman, a sensual victim and a machine. . . .
>
> (*Moon*, pp. 149-50)

To Amanda, preoccupied by her own womanhood, the moonlit house itself has the look of a woman. Only the contemporary chromium-plated pieces of her own room avoid disquieting suggestiveness.

For Ella the rooms hold ghosts of passions so strong that the house seems to possess her, its owner. Ella bears the house the familiar hatred of one who loves and is dependent, the sentiment she is horrified to feel towards Rose. Finally, Robin Sant's reaction to the Villa is a source of irony; this young man who despises religion and romance regards it with exaggerated admiration as "above fashion . . . like a shrine" (*Moon*, p. 111).

The Pinmouth Fair, too, has symbolic importance. Amanda's physical awakening through her relationship with Harry moves inevitably towards this climactic point. Amanda looks forward to the fair with curiosity and apprehension, Harry with calm expectation, and Ella with excitement; the event is a special one in the book. The words which describe the scene as Amanda and Harry join in the dancing become symbolic of Amanda's feelings and of the action's irresistible progress towards her seduction. They dance "a slow foxtrot to music which wept, which moaned, which suddenly uttered cries of rage" (*Moon*, p. 216). Yet the traditional nature of the scene makes it a fitting setting for the moment when Amanda realises that like Nelly Raft, Mrs. Wicken, Bessie Venn, she is, after all a woman.

The Moonlight Sonata becomes for Ella a symbol for the unutterable passions of her age. For the nieces and nephews who call it "romantic", the sonata evokes feelings of pity and amusement; they respond to it with feigned respect. By drawing Ella's attention to the gulf between her understanding and that of the young people, the sonata comes to symbolise for Ella the loneliness that was Bessie's, and Rose's and now is hers. Rooted thus in Ella's consciousness, and more than a simple alternative to the Kreutzer Sonata, Cary's title becomes a complex symbol of the passions which define women's nature, an age, the fundamental individualism underlying real love as well as loneliness.

The moon itself, whose light so often bathes the scene in the novel, gives the clue to woman's nature, as Cary's notes point out. In Geoffrey Tew's decadent poetry the moon is an image for the woman but inferior to her in brilliance.

> "Oh girl, you beauty's whiter.
> Moon of your breast yet brighter.
> Your swoon more still is
> Than rapture of all lilies."

(*Moon*, p. 70)

Although this "strange and passionate language" thrills Ella with terror, the moon itself terrifies Amanda. Invading the corners of her room, it shows her herself—woman divorced from time and fashion, unprotected woman still, in spite of modernity.

> She threw back the clothes to jump out of bed. But the sight of her own white and plump leg thrust into the moonlight startled her into a new horror—of herself . . . she, too, was woman . . . An animal constructed from top to toe only to continue the species, so that life should not perish from the world.
>
> (*Moon*, p. 150)

Tew's poem compared woman and the moon; Cary identifies them. The connection which creates this symbol for Cary and underlies Amanda's terror is the quality of the moon's light. It is reflected light (Ms. Cary 276, N.114; 277, S.14.C), dependent on its source the sun. Cary compares woman's reason to the cold light of the moon, capable of guiding, but for passion, and warmth, for life, wholly in need of the sun. And in the (not unconventional) symbolism of this book the sun is a man.

Amanda has no real man for a counterpart in the novel. The two men who enter her life at this complicated stage are as much symbols as the sun and moon. Harry Dawbarn, wholly physical, careless of emotional ties, is the sun-man. Intimately involved with the processes of life—the cycle of birth, growth and death at Brook Farm—he brings the warmth of passion to Amanda in spite of herself. Robin Sant, his pale white face and black hair colourless beside the bronze Dawbarn, brings the intellectual side of man to Amanda.[8] He is the ghostly voice of her own hesitation, of the modern spirit which says that women must be independent. In its confused enthusiasm this voice risks destructive exaggeration, for it is Robin who praises the ideas of *The Kreutzer Sonata* and yet leads a life not of continence but of enforced sterility; he has no light to give.

While they expose Amanda's moral dilemma, neither of these characters participates actively in the solution of that dilemma. Their actions are wholly amoral. Lack of ambition and refusal to make choices characterise what Cary's notes call Harry's "deep inertia". His actions are instinctive, spontaneous, and—like the forces of nature with which he is allied—unmotivated by social or personal responsibility. For

Robin, morality is an abstraction. He sees it as a product of the individual psyche rather than of collective responsibility. He, too, succumbs to the inertia which ties him to his unsatisfactory marriage and belies the emotional attachment he professes towards Amanda. The interest of these characters lies in the responses they elicit from Amanda and Ella. Like the other symbols in the novel they are meaningful only as elements in the characterisation of its central figures.

Irony in *The Moonlight* also enhances characterisation by revealing aspects of experience which elude the characters' comprehension but define their predicament. Cary's insistence on the strength of Victorian family ties should have given rise to a portrait of a patriarchal system affirming, in the usual Cary pattern, the need for a male creator in whose service a woman finds fulfilment. But in *The Moonlight* this need is felt through the absence of masculine initiative. Men are conspicuously lacking in all the moments of family crisis. Venn, the fastidious and pleasure-loving Victorian father, abdicates his responsibilities as head of the house in favour of Rose just as he abdicated in favour of his wife in the earlier and more trivial matter of Ella's childhood discipline. James Groom allows himself to be deceived by Bessie, whose imagination masks his failures by creating for him the role of eminent pedagogue. Other men simply run off. Theo absents himself from scenes of family conflict. Geoffrey Tew accepts Ella's unwilling rejection, Ernest Cranage emigrates leaving wife and child behind. The symbolic half-men Robin and Harry leave an overwhelming sense of incompleteness.

Ella's memories, too, reveal ironic discrepancies. Groom, the "great man" of science is tiresome, self-centered and almost cruelly insensitive; Ernest Cranage, though Ella sees him as a delicate, mistreated creature, is in reality weak and dishonest—"a common swindler". In the background hovers the enormous irony, paralleled by Rose's government of her family, that the Victorian England whose morality subjected women's instincts to a rigid convention of masculine dominance was presided over by a woman.

The modern world's ironies increase Amanda's perplexity. For all her education the girl has much to learn about herself. When, urged by Robin to be modern and by Ella to be a woman, she abandons herself to Harry at the fair, her reward from both is astonished disapproval. In the failure of modern open-mindedness or old-fashioned romanticism to approve her action, Cary sees the irony that victimises the emancipated Amanda.

Symbolism participates in the ironies of *The Moonlight*. Beethoven's Sonata is the romantic theme against which Amanda's unromantic sex life develops. The idea of unity in recurrence which characterises the sonata form here shows the young repeating the mistakes of the old. Even Ella involuntarily sees the likeness of her Geoffrey to Robin Sant. The moon itself becomes an ironic symbol as its connotations of chastity provide a lurking contrast for the theme of woman's "special function" and its development in the events of the action.

The persistence of irony preserves *The Moonlight* from tragic finality and rebuffs Tolstoy's pessimism. The book's conclusion has a sombre tone. Amanda's "feeling was one of pity and emptiness . . . It lodged in a vacuum, without object, without will or hope or love . . . a vast still grief" (*Moon*, p. 315). But these are not the last words. A purposeful new Amanda indulges in these feelings of objectless pity and emptiness. The narrator's observations gently mock her thoughts, for her world is not to be long empty, "she was growing big". The vacuum is woman's nature without its completing object of love. Amanda is, after all, Ella's daughter and with the birth of her child Amanda will—following Ella's pattern—discover both the object and the love. Nor is her pity entirely "without will", for "she was not going to let herself off the work only because it was a bore". Amanda has accepted responsibility and even while she denies hope, she stops to ask, "But do miracles happen?"

When irony undercuts idealism and theory in *The Moonlight*, repeated action and impulse in two generations draw a pattern of consistency. Tolstoy's story asked "should the world go on". That the world *does* go on, that the miracle of love is rediscovered by each generation in its own terms is the novel's answer to Tolstoy's question. This, too, reinforced by the repetitive pattern of the novel's sonata-like action, is Cary's answer to Amanda, waiting for her miracle. *The Moonlight*, in exploring woman's nature, affirms once more that liberal world view which is Cary's throughout his works. It emphasises that human nature is a "living thing" in an organic world of chance and growth; it defines freedom as a challenge to responsibility and self-fulfilment, and describes progress from age to age as an aggregate of individual responses to this challenge. Again personal fulfilment emerges as the unselfconscious acceptance of the challenge to create demanded by nature and social relationships in any age.

A Fearful Joy with its fast-moving objective narrative is a striking departure from its "contemplative" and nuance-ridden predecessor. "It is about the *pressure* of change, and its sources in the love (and need) of novelty".[9] Individuals pursuing their emotional or material desires create this presure of progress. Continuity within the episodic structure of a *A Fearful Joy* is discovered in the recurring impulse towards novely. To balance the attraction of novelty Cary poses the restraining power of personal "attachments", by placing at his novel's centre a woman motivated by devotion to her lover and her child. The nature of historical progress is thus revealed as the continual tension in human nature between conflicting desires for adventure and security, multiplied and mirrored on a nationwide scale.

Dick Bonser, Tabitha's lover, epitomises human adventurousness. This con-man joins imagination to creative achievement in the roles he shapes and lives with relish. It is no accident that Bonser, an early devotee of the wireless, is one of the first to apprehend the imaginative appeal of Hitler's demagogery. Blasting forth from the new instrument of mass communication, Hitler's appears to him the voice of change and adventure. Bonser enters and fades from Tabitha's life with the regularity of a basic need and the surprise of an unexpected idea. The periods of Bonser's absence drive Tabitha to other men who offer security and occupation, or to her son John and granddaughter Nancy who seem to need her care. Conservative impulse thus paradoxically forces Tabitha to ally herself with progressive stages of a changing world until, left at last alone, she discovers within herself the power to experience the fearful joy in wilful alliance with life itself.

The quest for novelty and its consequences in historical progress and cultural change are most effectively shown in the novel's portrayal of the revolution in transportation which gathered momentum in the Edwardian years and ramified through the worlds of commerce, recreation and manners. But Cary felt compelled to trace the pursuit of novelty throughout society; he therefore brought the arts, politics, religion and morality within the novel's historical scope, to the detriment of its cohesiveness.

The men in Tabitha's life are the props of the novel's historical structure. When Tabitha becomes mistress to Sturge she enters the art world of the late 'nineties, associating with the aesthetes and impresarios who unite to publish *The Bankside*, a review modelled on the earlier *Yellow Book*. The *Bankside* episode shows the emergence and quick acceptance of decadent art, and its rapid degeneration into the burlesque of the Bunsurge parodies. It encapsulates the Edwardian aesthetic dilemma, paradoxically mingling nostalgia for the romantic past with a frustrated effort to anticipate the forms of an embryonic social revolution.

With Sturge's death, Cary leaves the world of art dangling. Tabitha marries the industrialist James Gollan and exchanges the society of artistic innovators for that of the prophets and profiteers of a technological revolution awaiting only the Great War to establish itself as a way of life. Change here is rapid and far-reaching. Before the reader's eyes the motor car ceases to be a novelty and becomes a fact of life. By the time Bonser impresses John with his sporting Bentley, Gollan is profiting from the motor trade and all have been swept up in his pioneering enthusiasm for the airplane. The war which shocks the nation merely expands Gollan's production. "It was Gollan's special feat of intuition, that of a very simple man without enough political education to weigh secondary causes, to perceive that the war must come soon, and that it would need mechanical transport" (*AFJ*, p. 189). It is a further easy step into the armaments industry.

The transport revolution enables Bonser, too, to profit from timely investments in the rubber industry. More valuably, this involvement equips him to foresee the revolution the motor car beings to popular culture and to cater for it with his roadhouses. In the later portion of the book Cary returns to the transport theme by way of the airman Parkin. The earlier progress of motor transport towards and through the Great War repeats itself in the development of air transport through the Second World War, again followed by the installation of this progress in the commercial sphere. And again the development ramifies in the personal lives of the characters, as Tabitha sees Nancy and Parkin, children of their age, setting out for a new world beyond the reach of one "too old and ill" to fly.

Like the aesthetic movement which moves to the foreground in the *Bankside* episode and then fades from the scene, politics enters the novel fleetingly, through John's conflict with the socialists. Tabitha has seen the Banksiders welcome the rise of the New Liberalism in the early years of the century. Although she feels "the intensification of moral violence" accompanying a sense of revolution in the air, her apolitical natures precludes exploration of the phenomenon. John, another example of the decline of creativeness into conservatism, finds himself drawn into conflict with socialism by his resentment, intellectual rather than political, of a policy which expresses itself in slogans and places emphasis on planning at the expense of individual human considerations.

John's political inclinations are Cary's, and he emerges the sympathetic victim of less intelligent but more committed and wilful forces. Nevertheless, his philosophical detachment denies a full exploration of political policy to the novel. With John's death politics disappears from the action. The great popular revolution which has taken place with the full franchise, the rise of the Labour party, and the advent of the Welfare State, is never fully characterised. The popular voice in Westminster is hushed, perhaps with an intentional touch of irony, behind the restive protests from the ration queues and Parkin's grumblings against "the Government"—the timeless protest of the individual against a disembodied abstract notion.

Cary rounds out his comprehensive historical portrayal in the societies of sportsmen and gamblers, the Edwardian music hall and the civilian war effort through which Bonser moves. Through John he touches on changes in education; through Tabitha, on religion.

The faults of *A Fearful Joy* lie in its historical inclusiveness, in

170

the use of the third person narrator and the present tense, and in a resulting attenuation of character. The present tense in *A Fearful Joy* was to convey "the sense of that driving change, of that world revolution which is so sharply present to our feelings even from hour to hour" (*AFJ*, p.7). Cary had previously enjoyed success with the present tense in the limited, unreflective world of Mister Johnson's adventure. Here in attempting to sustain the sense of immediacy over a vast expanse of time he uncovers one of the limitations of the technique. The sense of successive changing moments must be embodied in significant detail, the accumulation of which is better suited to a shorter span of time. *A Fearful Joy*'s combination of an extended history and a present vision leads to superficiality.

Mister Johnson succeeded because Johnson's preoccupations—immediate and unhistorical—shape the novel. Indeed, his inability to assess his situation in a context wider than the personal was the crux of the novel's denouement. Tabitha, equally naive, remains on the periphery of the novel's action. Each moment, melting into the next, embodies its own consequences in Johnson's story; in Tabitha's, random moments are linked by an historical progress overlaid upon the central character's consciousness and actions. Further, although Tabitha's history embraces interludes of reflection—worry about the future and regrets about the past—such reflection is not reasoned or self-aware. As a result, the narrator, who must explain Tabitha's inner state, intrudes with a perceptiveness alien to her character and to the necessarily imperfect viewpoint of the present moment.

Tabitha's character suffers the generalising effect of her dual function as vehicle for the novel's historical action and for Cary's typical conception of the relationship between creative male and self-forgetful female. Tabitha is typical of Cary's woman characters whose rebelliousness is powerless to direct itself and whose creativeness is called forth in maintaining established relationships. Tabitha's mental state is always characterised by awareness of joy or frustration, but a total unconsciousness of its sources. Cary makes these states evident when he seizes upon an objective representation of emotion or motive. When Tabitha, fleeing Bonser's brutality, is knocked down by a cab, a vision of her hat enables the narrator to evoke the emotional confusion through which hysteria gives way to self-awareness.

> Meanwhile her eyes dwell vaguely on an extraordinary object in the glass opposite her chair: a young woman with blackened eyes and swollen nose, covered with mud and blood, who is making extraordinary faces. But what especially seizes her attention is the woman's hat, a large flowered hat, which has been knocked sideways and smashed . . . and the contrast of its dissipation and the woman's miserable grimaces is for some reason extremely comical.
>
> Tabitha, as she gradually recovers her senses, begins to be aware of this ridiculous aspect of misery; and then perceiving that this woe-begone creature, with blackening eyes, swollen nose plugged with blood-stained cotton wool, torn and muddy clothes and ridiculous hat, is herself, suddenly breaks into laughter.

(*AFJ*, p. 51)

Self-awareness is, however, only fleeting in Tabitha. Most of the time her activity is unreflective, instinctive. Even the fearful joy is not something she seeks, but a gift she receives. Tabitha's passivity extends even to her own sensations. Her sympathy or love for others frightens or excites her; even laughter seizes her; life takes hold of her. Such an essentially passive figure may be a full and engaging character when she serves a sustained inspiration, such as Sara's nest-building urge or Nina Nimmo's subjection to Chester's "grace". Tabitha's inspiration comes sporadically, linked to Bonser's appearances or to the moments when events require her to do battle for John's security, or Nancy's. As a result Tabitha becomes a stereotype caught in a succession of roles and postures.

Tabitha's attitude to religion by which, Cary's notes indicate, he hoped to define her character, requires constant interpretation from without. Throughout her life Tabitha is preoccupied with the forms of religion, incapable of plumbing its substance—a distinction made by the narrator. The profundity of her final spontaneous prayer for life—wholly divorced from the "gentle Jesus" or "Our Father" of her previous preoccupations—too, is the discovery of the narrator who identifies its creative faith with the fearful joy. Tabitha

172

knows only "that she is not going to die that afternoon". Even this union with the vitality of all creation, therefore, occurs to Tabitha and eludes her understanding. Again she is a vehicle for Cary's theme, her character as passive in the hands of its author as it is in its relationship to life.

By using Tabitha to illustrate a generalisation, Cary belies the principle of individualism on which his conceptions of progress and happiness are based. The novel's patterned plot makes Tabitha's spontaneity predictable, and her representative character fails of distinction. As a result, *A Fearful Joy* is more a lively historical travelogue than a convincing exploration of the constitutive relationship between the individual and history.

NOTES

1. Enid Starkie, "Joyce Cary: A Personal Portrait", *Virginia Quarterly Review*, XXXVII, no. 1. (Winter 1961), p. 124.
2. George Moore, *Ave*, p. 216.
3. "Joyce Cary: A Personal Portrait", p. 124.
4. "The Revolution of the Women", *Vogue* (U.S.), CXVII (15 March 1951), pp. 99, 100, 149.
5. Joyce Cary, *The Moonlight*, Carfax ed. (Michael Joseph, 1952), p. 11. Hereafter abbreviated *Moon* and cited in the text.
6. Cary insisted that his "theme" was "*not* D H Las" (Ms. Cary 276, N. 114). Rather he made Lawrence's ideas a part of the experience on which Amanda builds. Nevertheless it is difficult to avoid speculation that *The Moonlight* was written with *The Rainbow* in mind. In that book Lawrence made the moon symbolic of woman's self-centeredness. The book, too, portrayed successive generations of a family. Family crises in *The Rainbow* measure social change but are primarily problems of personal relationships. Such crises in *The Moonlight* use personal relationships to define ideas and conflicts in society at large. Both books pose the problem of the modern woman who has achieved worldly knowledge and self-knowledge, who rejects both gratuitous sensualism and empty convention, and who seeks new terms in which to find fulfilment. At the end of *The Rainbow* Ursula becomes pregnant but has a mystic experience and loses her baby. Amanda at the end of *The Moonlight* will have her baby; if there is to be a mystic experience for her it will be in the child and the love she feels for it.
7. See also Ms. Cary 276, N. 114; 277, S. 14.C.

8. This "division of the male into the physical and the intellectual" is noted by Jack Wolkenfeld, p. 108.
9. Letter from Joyce Cary to Alan C. Collins, quoted by Collins in a letter to Elizabeth F. Lawrence, 8 January 1948, Ms. Cary Adds. I: 69.

7

The Second Trilogy

... the only way in which a human being can make some approach to knowing the whole of a subject, is by hearing what can be said about it by persons of every variety of opinion, and studying all modes in which it can be looked at by every character of mind.

The only part of conduct of any one, for which he is amenable to society is that which concerns others. In the part which merely concerns himself, his independence is, of right, absolute.

J.S. Mill, *On Liberty*

Castle Corner was to have been the beginning of a vast work . . . showing not only the lives of all the characters in the first volume, but the revolutions of history during the period 1880-1935.

(*CC*, p. 5)

[*Prisoner of Grace*] is an odd book but at least I have done what I set out to do—to shew the working of a religio-political imagination in the political world and its reactions with that world.

(Letter to Elizabeth F. Lawrence, 2 January 1952)[1]

Cary's two statements reflect the profound alterations in conception and form which distinguish his early historical work *Castle Corner* from his treatment of the same historical era in the later Nimmo trilogy. "History" is exchanged for politics. Instead of a comprehensive series of lives and events we find a study of one character's ingenuity in dealing with the human, spiritual, and ideological elements in his world, for all three volumes of the second trilogy focus on the politician Chester

175

Nimmo. These fundamental differences almost obscure the many aspects of character and theme in the early work which recur in the trilogy.

The theme of the second trilogy is the ideals of British Liberalism and the downfall of the Liberal party. As in the *Castle Corner* series, Cary wished to illustrate that good government requires practical but humane management and that abstract conceptions—even the most idealistic—cannot alone answer to human needs. Early drafts for the novels of the trilogy contain many passages expressly stating Cary's view of the Liberal case. Chester's attack on authoritarianism was to have opened one version of *Except the Lord*, explicitly connecting the young man's dissillusionment following the experience of the dock strike to the old man's despair.

> I am an old man and they want me to die . . . They say that my policy and that of the government which I served so long, was one of blindness and deceit, I am told that I cheated the people with words while I stole away their substance, that I shut the window on the daylight of truth and opened the gate to the wolves. For it is said liberty is a fraud, freedom is a lie, and the private citizen sand in the wheel. Nothing is good but the state—and nothing wise but a committee of economists. Property is theft except only state property and the state shall own a man's very soul and body from the cradle to the grave.
>
> But I say to you all this is an old tale, it was an old tale when, nearly seventy years ago I was a child and the communists of France had died amongst the ruins of their spite, when I too was young, and bitter, and thought myself betrayed.
>
> (Ms. Cary 128-29)

In another opening Nimmo says he will not act against those who now libel him and threaten even his life.

> I am urged to take action in the courts. That was not our way, in the party. Our way was to trust the people, to lay the truth before them. And I believe that this is a service, the last service that I can do for our beloved country, in the most fearful crisis of her fate. I can make a truth remembered. . . .
>
> (Ms. Cary 128-29)

To enlighten the people is to give them power and thus to make them free. This idea, voiced in *Castle Corner* and in *Power in Men*, links Chester's experience to Cary's principles.[2]

The background of the trilogy is the transition from nineteenth-century to twentieth-century Liberalism. Chester early rejects the attitude which leaves economics to providence just as the Liberal Party in the early 1900s moved away from the Victorian Liberal policy of *laissez-faire* towards social responsibility. The pre-war Liberals recognised the demands of the working class; they responded with the long-awaited Trade Disputes Act of 1906 and the Trade Union Act of 1913, the National Insurance Act of 1911, and they altered the distribution of the tax burden in the budgets of 1907 and 1909. But the beginnings were small, for the Liberals, while anxious to protect individual rights, had no desire to alter the economic structure of the nation nor to make the state any more responsible for the individual than he was seen to be for himself. The nonconformist tradition which provided Liberalism with links to the labour movement also militated against the levelling spirit of socialism, clinging to the spirit of self-help and divine providence.

Nimmo's abandonment of revolutionary socialism for liberalism in *Except the Lord* erupts out of anger at the abstract thinking of the socialists and the brutal disregard for human life and liberty with which they seek their revolutionary ends. In *Prisoner of Grace* Nimmo still denounces poverty and privilege but his aim is to provide, above all, opportunity for men to develop freely. God must work freely through men and this, Nimmo believes, cannot happen when the state works for men.

The psalm that gives the second volume its title and which applies in that book to Nimmo's personal discovery of faith has thus a wider import. Government, like each life, is a house which must be built with the inspiration of—not in spite of—the Lord. This implies that no man or state can be absolute. Conversely, the government which men build must acknowledge a power beyond the human which reflects itself in conscience or reason. It is to this power working in the people that Nimmo attributes the ultimate success of the London dockers' strike, "won not with cannon but by the conscience of a nation, the active soul of a people".

The failure of Liberalism, its eclipse by the Labour Party as the voice of the working people, arose in part from the unwillingness of an economically oppressed people to await the benevolence of providence. A Labour Party pamphlet of 1929 criticised Lloyd George for not taking immediate steps in the manner of a providing Joseph when the depression first threatened. He ignored, the pamphlet says, "the necessity of taking steps to counteract his errors, both by emergency measures for the provision of employment and by permanent steps for the reorganisation of the British industrial system".[3] This failure is adumbrated by Nimmo's history, from his decisive response to the needs of starving miners in the '80s to his ambivalent attitude in the General Strike, when sympathy with the people is undermined by the conviction that "the country is slipping into . . . a revolution it doesn't even want. That nothing can save it now but a national government of all parties . . . For this is war . . . for the soul of England—the very heart of liberal Europe".[4]

In Chester's defeat and his response to it Cary captures the ironies of the Liberal downfall. The Liberal Party which "carried the nation" by its social reforms "into the modern age"[5] is engulfed by the socialist spirit of that age. The disillusionment which overtakes Nimmo at the end of *Prisoner of Grace* and colours the tone of *Except the Lord* is characteristic not only of Liberal reaction to party failure, but of a revulsion on the part of many Liberals—who saw Hitler's Germany and Stalin's Russia in the offing—against contemporary expressions of the popular will. This distrust of popular power and an attendant failure of faith in the constructive power of freedom distorted the liberalism of many party supporters. Chester fails to see that the continuing discontent of "men who owe us unemployment insurance" is the same revolution he joined in his youth and to which he devoted his career. Nimmo, who advanced that career and promoted radical change through his persuasive rhetoric and effective policies, accuses his young critics of being "under a spell of words . . . the power of sorcerers . . ." (*ETL*, p. 274).

The sum of Nimmo's revelations in *Except the Lord* and Nina's in *Prisoner of Grace* points out the inevitability of change, the wisdom of flexibility. The spirit of compromise with which Nimmo approaches the striking factions, even the Communists, in *Not Honour More* is as weak as Liberalism's own position at the time, but it stands sharply in contrast to uncompromising Fascism. Stirrings of Fascism in Britain between the wars were

178

evoked by nationalism, economic uncertainty, fear of Communism and admiration for Mussolini's rise to power. Jim Latter exemplifies in the trilogy's domestic scene, the Fascist mentality. Although avowedly uninterested in Fascism,[6] Jim fulfils Cary's view of the Fascist, lacking imagination and respect for life, reacting against intelligence and acting on passionate impulse. In addition he fits the substantiated stereotype of the British Fascist, being of middle class and an ex-army officer.[7] Jim thus completes the trilogy's historical portrayal of the world in which Liberalism as a policy grew and died.

The trilogy developed in two stages. In *Prisoner of Grace* Cary devised a complex plot to balance the activities of an eventful political era against the tensions of a turbulent domestic experience. Nina Latter, formerly Lady Nimmo, narrates *Prisoner of Grace*. Her account of her marriage to Chester tells the story of his political career and the peculiar "atmosphere" surrounding the charismatic radical.

Only after *Prisoner of Grace* was completed did Cary realise—with an access of enthusiasm—that its scheme was pregnant with the materials for "a new kind of trilogy". In the story of Nimmo's grace Cary found his opportunity at last to draw the link between politics and fundamental religion in a further "memoir". *Except the Lord* is Chester's own narrative, the first volume of his memoirs. The book tells of Chester's introduction to political action as a trade union organiser and of his religious upbringing in a nonconformist home. It tells of his loss and rediscovery of faith and the personal and family crises that marked these revolutions.

Not Honour More is the violent apologia of the soldier and murderer Jim Latter, Nina's cousin, seducer, and ultimately husband. In this third member of the Latter-Nimmo-Nina triangle Cary discovered the vehicle for completion of the trilogy's historical and domestic dramas and for its final comment on the relationships of personal liberty and responsibility, pragmatism and morality. Just as Nina's memoir, punctuated by its parenthetical qualifications, reveals her own personality while she talks of Nimmo, so Jim's sharp, slangy, none too refined prose attack on Nimmo and the political "wangle" exposes its narrator's irrational and essentially self-deceived character.

The picture of a household engaged in a flurry of defensive memoir-writing which concludes *Prisoner of Grace* provides Cary with the means to control an elaborate historical portrayal. From the Palm Cottage *ménage à trois* issue all three narratives, supposedly composed within roughly a year of each other.

Each of the three narratives focusses on a key historical period or event. *Prisoner of Grace*, covering the years 1900 to 1924, forms the core of the series. It portrays the years in which social Liberalism captured the hopes and the votes of the British people and reached its zenith under Asquith and Lloyd George, before party strife and economic disaster destroyed it. These are the years of Nimmo's career as a leading Liberal politician and of his marriage. The two sides of his life interact throughout the novel to illustrate Cary's premise that "politics is the art of human relations, an aspect of all life".

Except the Lord returns to Nimmo's childhood among cottagers to show the politician before the days of power. Covering the years between about 1860 and 1879, its historical focus is on the early efforts of the labour movement in agricultural unionism and the dockers' strikes of the 1870s. The historical and domestic aspects of this novel meet in Cary's portrayal of a powerful evangelism which shaped lives and politics at the same time.

Not Honour More completes the triad by portraying Chester in 1926, after the height of his political career. Again, to balance *Except the Lord*, the focal historical event is a strike, the General Strike of May 1926. This event disrupts the precarious peace of the Nimmo-Nina-Latter triangle established at the end of *Prisoner of Grace*. Jim, thrown into the turmoil of peacekeeping as a special constable, sees events in the Maufe trial vindicate his hatred of political compromise and discovers political deception corrupting his homelife as well. Jim's outraged conservatism, more a state of mind than a political stance, embroils him not only in conflict with Nimmo's conciliatory attitude towards the Communists, but also in confused dealings with Fascist sympathisers.

The two strikes in *Except the Lord* and *Not Honour More* point to the major change in government of the period—its progressive orientation towards the working class. The strikes delineate the causes and duration of the Liberal ascendancy. The labour unrest of the late 1800s and the accompanying growth of the trade union movement brought about a resurgence of the Liberal Party with its creed of social responsibility. In turn, the General Strike, although it failed to obtain its immediate aims, marked the entry of the common man into the arena of active political participation at a time when the Parliamentary Labour Party had replaced the Liberals as the workers' voice in Parliament.[8] These two events round out Nimmo's personal history as well. In the dock strike Chester's youthful revolutionary enthusiasms meet disillusionment and his mature pro-labour and anti-socialist position solidifies. The General Strike sees Chester amidst the ruins of his party still loyal to its spirit, resisting the socialists but seeking a Tory overthrow in a centre party of the old guard.

As important to the Nimmo trilogy as its dramatisation of Liberal Party history are the liberal principles weighed by its action and reflected in its structure. *Except the Lord*, the central volume, defines Nimmo's—and Cary's—liberalism. It emphasises the necessity for principle to be tested and proved valid by experience. The experience presented asserts the supreme value of liberty and tolerance as principles of political action. In this priority lies the key to Cary's attitude towards the characters of the trilogy, for commitment to the principles of liberty and responsibility define Chester's strength, Nina's weakness, and Jim's absolute failure.

A description of Liberal toleration which illuminates Cary's theme and his method in the Nimmo trilogy may be found in Hobhouse's *Liberalism*.

> The Liberal does not meet opinions which he conceives to be false with toleration, as though they did not matter. He meets them with justice, and exacts for them a fair hearing as though they mattered just as much as his own. He is always ready to put his own convictions to the proof, not because he doubts them, but because he believes in them. For, both as to that which he holds for true and as to that which he holds for false, he believes that one final test applies. Let error have free play, and one of two things will happen. Either as it develops, as its implications and consequences become clear, some elements of truth will appear within it. They will separate themselves out; they will go to

enrich the stock of human ideas; they will add something to the truth which he himself mistakenly took as final; they will serve to explain the root of the error; for error itself is generally a truth misconceived, and it is only when it is explained that it is finally and satisfactorily confuted. Or, in the alternative, no element of truth will appear.[9]

Cary himself exacts for the narrative of each of his characters a "fair hearing". As their comments on each other, their own stories and their actions reveal the nature of each character, error sorts itself out from truth, not without being found to harbour the peripheral "elements of truth" of which Hobhouse spoke. *Except the Lord* illustrates the Liberal ideal of the man who, by experience, discovers the nature of truth and error and independently distinguishes between the two. To the dismay and consternation of many of his critics, Cary carries the Liberal method of argument, as described by Hobhouse, through the trilogy's final volume by refusing to condemn Jim Latter explicitly. Latter's narrative as it develops is self-incriminating in terms of the principles of love, humanity, and respect for liberty illustrated elsewhere in the trilogy.

Latter's error is that he fails to appreciate the need for compromise in life and politics. Hence he condemns Chester's politics and Nina's emotional agility out of hand. He fails to distinguish between genuine honour or genuine love and the sham excuses for selfishness and self-deception he offers under their names. Jim's selfishness emerges in his first seduction of Nina, and self-deception culminates in the jealous rage which causes her death. To have condemned Jim simply, through the mouth of Nina or Chester, for his resistance to change and compromise, his inflexibility, his selfishness, would not have been enough, for Cary had already established the subjectivity of the other two narratives. Jim's demonstration in word and deed of his personal failings places him in relation to the others and makes it possible for the reader to form the desired assessment of the trilogy's whole scene.

At no stage in his mature life did Cary's political position alter significantly. Like the novels of the Nimmo trilogy, his later essays dealing with politics are glances back at the liberal tradition and its role in shaping British democracy.[10] He continued to reject authoritarianism in government and to welcome progress. Although Cary's political principles were akin to Nimmo's, his belief in progress precluded any wish to turn back the tide of history to the conditions under which they reached their ascendancy. Cary accepted the evolutionary character of British political development; hence, his fiction is not polemical. The effectiveness of his political trilogy lies in its skilful analysis of a crucial stage of political evolution, in characterisation, and in its application in fiction of the liberal principal of permitting a truth to emerge through juxtaposition of opposing viewpoints.

Prisoner of Grace

The roots of *Prisoner of Grace* lie in Cary's earliest historical portrayals, *Castle Corner* and its sequels. Nimmo's political career nearly duplicates that outlined there for Porfitt. Both characters bring to politics a desire for social justice and an evangelistic zeal, and both reconcile principle with political pragmatism. Nimmo, like Porfitt, chooses for his wife the daughter of a landed Liberal family who, though naturally passive and sensuous, responds to her husband's idealism. *Prisoner of Grace*, like the projected "Over the Top", depicts a marriage held together by forces of will and instinct stronger than the impulse of love. Tom Nimmo is like Cleeve Corner's son Dick, a war-hero and a post-war casualty.

In Jim Latter, Cock Jarvis is resurrected. The boy brought up by relatives, with a passionate love of the family home, and the enthusiastic young soldier impatient with the Government recall the Cocky of *Castle Corner*. Jim's behaviour in Africa is again reminiscent of Cock Jarvis, this time the Jarvis of the unpublished novel. Jarvis-like, Jim fights the Government on behalf of his natives—that is, in an attempt to preserve them from civilization—and earns not promotion, but an ever-worsening position in Africa.

Latter is, however, less stable and less heroic than Jarvis. Cary deprived this character of the religious principles, personal introspection, and peculiar generosity which complicated Jarvis and made him sympathetic. He pushed Jim's African experience into the background of *Prisoner of Grace*

183

and *Not Honour More* in the interests of structure, and in doing so ensured that the attractive qualities of the Nigerian Service men he knew, and of such heroes as Chinese Gordon, whose dynamism enlivened Jarvis's characterisation, did not colour Jim's portrayal.

While Jarvis, in *Castle Corner*, quarrelled with his superiors out of loyalty to Ireland, Latter inexplicably grows impatient with the army and leaves it on a sudden impulse, "he told me nothing about his sudden determination to leave the army, except that he had always disliked the colonel, who was, he said, a 'half-breedun'" (*PG*, p. 78). Cocky joined the political service in order to return to the African territory which he once conquered, but Jim is sent to Africa by a family anxious to see him settled in a steady job far from the occasions of his financial and romantic follies.

Intervening works, most significantly the unfinished trilogy "The Captive and Free", evolved the shape of *Prisoner of Grace* and its sequels. "The Captive and Free"[11] was a title first applied to a fiction of 1934-36 which explored the rise of socialism in Britain and the influence of extreme religion on the confused youth of the nation between-the-wars. One version offered a clear precursor of *Except the Lord*'s Georgina Nimmo, in the character of a plain girl called Georgy Mann who sacrifices herself to the care of an elderly father and a spoiled sister.

Cary transferred the title, the sisters, and the historical preoccupations of these drafts to a projected series of novels which he worked on intermittently from 1944 to 1952. The theme of captivity and freedom develops in two contexts: economics and the female character. In a Galsworthian manner Cary explores the influence of money on the values of society and on individual lives. To further measure the individual character against the social role, he contrasts the ways different women seek the real freedom of fulfilment.

The paradoxical identity of captivity and freedom in the story anticipates the Nimmo trilogy's concept of "grace".

> The Free are Captive of human limitations but *understand* the whole position . . . this is the *exercise* of imagination . . . Freedom is *power to act*, i.e. to love with wisdom . . . The battle for freedom is battle for power in oneself . . . Captive of necessity, luck, fear,

jealousy, spite. Free in *creation*, love, joy and wisdom.

(Ms. Cary 281, N.92)

A further note makes explicit the nature of grace as confidence in inspiration: "Grace. A *feeling* of God" (Ms. Cary 282, S.17.C).

The self-revealing narrative was part of Cary's scheme from the start. Initially, Cary planned two novels narrated from the viewpoints of sisters—plain, passionate Hannah, and beautiful, passive Leila who prefigured Nina Nimmo. In 1949 he adopted the trilogy scheme, plotting three volumes called "The Captive and the Free", "Easy Money", and "Bow Down to Heaven".

In structure and in characters the work increasingly resembled the Nimmo trilogy. Emphasis shifted from the sisters to a love triangle: Hannah, her husband Drummer (who, like Nimmo, starts his career as a clerk, furthers it by marriage, and earns a peerage), and her lover Major Gye (a military aristocrat like Jim Latter) are involved in shifting marital configurations similar to those of the later work. The original of Aunt Latter, too, is to be found in these drafts, in the governess Millie Barfoot who organises her world with great efficiency in response to an aim or object of faith, but who falls apart, neglecting appearance and conduct, when such impetus is lacking.

Like the later trilogy, "The Captive and Free" was organised around significant historical events—the late-Victorian capitalist imperialism, the slump of 1924, the General Strike (which Cary called the "culmination of general push for money running into facts of poverty"), and the collapse of the gold standard in 1930.

Nina Nimmo's defensive narrative, rebutting the revelations "soon to appear about that great man who was once my husband, attacking his character and my own" (*PG*, p. 9), was anticipated in drafts for "Easy Money" where Cary proposed a narrative by Drummer's mistress repudiating the scandal which has ruined them.

New Beginning. '49. Coo Pilcher tells the story. sensible, sensual, plausible. I can't blame him. I couldn't blame him . . . She *must be sensible*, well educated to describe Drum's ambitions and to give her own views . . . I'm not blaming anyone—but I think people should know.

(Ms. Cary 282, S.17.D)

The theme of political morality, too, was linked to a story primarily concerned with the nature of a woman's happiness in a further draft, called "Juno" or "The Homely Nurse", which thus forms a bridge between "The Captive and Free" and *Prisoner of Grace*.[12]

Cary abandoned "The Captive and Free"; his preoccupation with woman's nature found expression in *A Fearful Joy* and *The Moonlight*. Uppermost in his mind when he began *Prisoner of Grace* was his desire of long standing to write a book about a politician and the politics of the Liberal decline. The woman's story now found its most sophisticated form as the vehicle for exposing the nature of politics as "the art of human relations", and for exploring the character of Cary's archetypal politician.

Cary's primary occupation in the early drafts of *Prisoner of Grace* was the search for Nina's proper narrative "form". He sought a narrative method which could reveal at once Nina's nature, Chester's character, and what Cary called "the political experience". He struggled to devise an opening situation encapsulating the tensions in the personal life of the characters and setting the scene for the book's political action. Cary recalled, in a radio talk given in 1957, that he had recognised in the marriage, envisaged for "the Captive and Free", between an "ambitious young man" and a "clever girl",

> a good situation for my political novel. The ambitious young man will be my politician, the clever girl shall tell the story. What's more, since she does not love him and is pushed into marriage with him by Aunt X, she will have on her hands a political job, in handling a husband so different from herself in ideas, in character, and in taste.[13]

Initially, the first person narrative proved unsuccessful. Early versions, including the one called "Turkish House", which placed emphasis on the girl's childhood, and another with the Blakean title "Another London Then I Saw", emphasising Nina's changing attitude to her surroundings and experiences under Chester's vitalising influence, focussed too much on Nina's thoughts and not enough on Chester and the political scene.

Cary recognised the lack of depth and drama in these early

narratives. Nina's wiliness and her evasiveness, her own "political" character did not emerge.

> In 1st person/difficulty—description of Nina/and a certain trickiness—i.e. Nina has to describe the others and *record the dialogue*—she has to make it all up and put it in form. She has to say 'I said so-and-so' and *make herself appear* as if dodging an issue.
>
> (Ms. Cary 288, S.20.J)

In the preface to the Carfax edition of *Prisoner of Grace* Cary says that at this point he abandoned the first person narrative.

> I began again in the third person and found that the scene at the railway station would not come through. In despair I tried the false first, I gave Aunt Latter a brother, a retired civil servant devoted to Nina, and made him tell the story. He ran away with the book and ruined it, everything was falsified and cheapened, the acuteness of the observer only emphasised his lack of real understanding. . . .
>
> (*PG*, pp. 7-8)

In fact Cary worked on the novel for a full year before the failings of its narrative and substance became clear to him. His experiment with alternative narrators was brief, for, as he rightly observed, the story quickly lost what vitality it had when removed from Nina's consciousness. Aunt Latter's brother knew far too much about Nina's inner thoughts to be credible, and his presence in all the major scenes was extremely awkward and improbable. Other approaches to the first person— including the retrospective narrative of an elderly, impoverished Nina, and a diary, too, failed.

Finally, in the second year of the novel's genesis, Cary revised Nina's narrative and introduced a few "brackets", to contain her qualified judgments. Here was the solution, a characteristic "form" for Nina. "When I tried the brackets", he says in his preface, "they did make Nina a credible witness. They enabled her, even in the first person, to reveal her own quality of mind" (*PG*, p.8).

The brackets were extremely important in establishing Nina's identity. In *Herself Surprised* Sara Monday translated all her impulses and perceptions into vibrant homely metaphor, which conveyed her unreflective and highly personal apprehension of her world. ". . . air as warm as new milk and still as water in a goldfish bowl". But, Cary noted, "*Nina is not another Sara*" (Ms. Cary 287, N.145). The verbal device which conveyed immediacy and sensuousness in Sara's case did not suit Nina's sophistication. Hence her speech contains few characteristic images. The only noteworthy symbols associated with her narrative, apart from the ironic use of political jargon, are the types of comparisons she chooses to make—sailing images to describe political situations or references to novels or paintings to describe her domestic life and surroundings. Such direct comparisons, along with Nina's reminiscences about her love of boats, the water, the peace and security of Palm Cottage, and the inviting worlds of fiction, at once supply details of her background and clarify the escapist side of her nature. Lacking a characteristic idiom, Nina has instead a characteristic style. Her qualified statements reveal, as Cary intended, that she "is essentially a woman who can understand another's point of view" (*PG*, p. 8). This power makes Nina shrewd, if often passive: "Then Nimmo wrung my hand (he was too clever to kiss me) and darted away, and I asked (not bothering to say that I wouldn't marry him) if he knew about my condition" (*PG*, p. 24). The brackets which reveal Nina's shrewdness contain the intimate detail of manner and motive which brings alive the weaknesses and attractions of Nimmo's striking character.

> I would catch an expression . . . when he walked across the floor to pull the bell (Chester was a great bell-ringer in hotels—he was always rather fierce with men-servants) a look at once resolute, but also confident and joyful (Chester had a lot of expression—like lions—in his legs and back and the way he carried himself). . . .
>
> (*PG*, p. 103

Through the brackets Nina can show that while Chester's moral force—his grace—overwhelms her, she understands the role of expediency and compromise in any moral or political situation. Thus Nina's narrative itself explains her skill as a manager of people, a politician in her own right. Sara Monday's intuitions and her means of expression were one; Nina's story is like a political speech, the finished product of much exploration and evaluation of motive, alternative, practicality. Her brackets are the backroom talk behind the public performance. Finally the brackets reveal the inseparability of the various sides of Nina's life—the politician, the hostess, the wife and mother.

> It was in the second year of the war . . . while I was powdering with great care (Chester hated a sign of powder) I was still in a quiet panic about Tom, still worrying about Jim, who had not written for two months, still praying that the dinner would be eatable (we were beginning to have "servant trouble"), and still raging against the shop that had not sent my new shoes.
>
> (*PG*, p. 271-72)

Another of Nina's distinctive modes of expression, understatement, defines her nature and her role relative to Chester. Understatement, especially about such serious matters as the delicate situation caused by her illegitimate babies and the tragedy of her son Tom's death, is the voice of Nina's passivity. Her understatement about Chester's seeming-hypocritical actions both parallels the facility with which Nimmo could, in the practice of politics, reconcile himself to compromising situations and demonstrates Nina's aware acceptance—a political compromise on her part—of her husband's motives. Of the Contract scandal Nina says, ". . . it would have been *quite misleading* for Chester to have told the whole story of Banks Rams. It might have produced a *great injustice*, that is, the ruin of Chester's career" (*PG*, p. 214).

The technique enhanced the structure of the novel when the need for the final events to happen with seeming inevitability, through the mysterious effects of grace, led Cary to replace several chapters devoted to Nina's divorce with two paragraphs of Nina's shrewd, understated observation. A rapid succession of events was necessary to show Chester's sudden eclipse on the political front, and so Nina's succinct account characteristically juxtaposes the public Chester and the private, political motive and principle.

> And since Chester had just been defeated again, in the last great disaster of '24, there was no longer any political reason why I should not be divorced. Indeed, Chester himself (over the heads of his political advisers) proposed it. He wrote reminding me that he had always thought it wrong, in principle, to hold any human soul to a "legal"bond, against spiritual conviction. And he wished me all happiness in my new "responsibilities".

It was a truly great-minded letter and it was passed round in a cyclostyle copy among Chester's friends and supporters. Chester always said that he did not know how it got out; and perhaps this is true. He was a man who had long ceased to know what did not suit him. But since it had become public (as he explained to me later), he was sure I would agree that it had better have official publication, with proper comment, in his forthcoming memoirs.

(*PG*, p. 360)

The divorce, thus anti-climactically treated, becomes a passing event in a personal situation which it fails to alter. The vital situation is the Nina-Chester-Jim triangle, and to this relationship Nina's divorce brings little alteration, for its bases are not legal ties but the irresistible attractions of love and grace.

In Nimmo's grace Cary found the means to join the idea of a woman's happiness in devotion to her man, with the idea of the power a forgiving—hence, liberating—nature could exercise. Nina's narrative makes clear the paradox of her happiness. She can discuss Chester's hypocrisy and describe her own feelings of despair, anger, or mirth without denying the fact of her happiness and its dependence on Chester. Grace reveals to her the truth of her happiness.

And the moment I *said* this, I felt all that Aunt had said about Chester's special position and his goodness to myself . . . And so, far from life being "impossible" that night, it was all at once surprisingly happy (though still with rather a special tense kind of happiness).

(*PG*, pp. 46-7)

Because she appreciates the power of imagination in art, Nina recognises Chester's creative genius in politics; her abundant human sympathy responds to the substance of his principles. Thus Chester's electoral triumph makes Nina "truly" glad and the marital reconciliation that follows is an acknowledgment of this success.

I opened my mouth to say something about my "position", but Chester (he knew I was beaten before I knew it myself) had already put his arm round my waist and I knew with real "certainty" that what was "impossible" for me was taking the risk of his being wasted.

(*PG*, p. 113)

190

Nina's malleability likens her to those upon whose political suggestibility Chester plays, "I think I was probably capable of anything because I had begun to suspect that I could reconcile myself to anything" (*PG*, p. 25). Her innocent duplicity rivals Chester's own craft.

Humour plays continually around the events in *Prisoner of Grace*, delivering its own insights and supporting Cary's optimistic attitude. The humour which signals sanity, balance, and open-mindedness sounds in the works of humanist writers from More and Shakespeare to Byron, Dickens and Henry James. Though by no means the prerogative of any political ideology, humour has often provided writers of optimistic, melioristic tendencies with a vehicle for the constructive self-criticism which belittles exaggerated egotism, exposes hypocrisy, and asserts a confidence in change. The humour of ridicule—often a conservative weapon for enforcing conformity—is not the predominant note in this tradition; the humour of sympathy is its lifeline. The ability to discover humour in the midst of error, pain, or fear is often itself a sign of a healthy, optimistic purview.

Cary exploits humour in *Prisoner of Grace* to assert the narrator's sanity and to guide the reader's response to potentially painful situations. Nina has a keen sense of the incongruous. The irony which is frequently present in her understatement is a powerful critical weapon and a source of rich comedy. For example, she sums up Chester's dexterity in rationalising his involvement in the Western Development electricity firm with the telling but glancing observations that none of Chester's chapel friends could object "to a syndicate which intended to make electricity and which had for its motto . . . 'Let there be light,'" and that he had joined the firm in order to save himself from bankruptcy and his career and causes from ruin, "and not because, as some of his critics said (including Aunt), that he thought he was going into business with God" (*PG*, p. 140).

Nina has a keen sense of the incongruous. Cary gave Nina this awareness, her "*humorous* grasp of the *position*" (Ms. Cary 288, S.20.C), to deepen her bondage to Chester and to balance the novel's complicated plot. Nimmo's fear of being made to look petty or ridiculous creates a continuing task of vigilance for

Nina. She foresees the danger in circumstances which could mock Chester's dignity, and it becomes part of her sustaining role to protect him from that danger. In a complicated plot which shows basic human reactions in an abnormal and exaggerated "political" situation, Nina's comic sense maintains proportion by revealing the ridiculous in seemingly normal situations.

Cary was a master of the grotesque. Many episodes of *The Horse's Mouth* make this plain, as do scenes in *Prisoner of Grace* itself. None is more effective than the description of Nina's sudden awareness of the alterations time, politics, and the shock of war have worked on Chester:

> But just then an unexpected silence made me look across the foot of the bed and I was surprised by an extraordinary shadow on the wall of what looked like a witch with an immense chin and nose and goggles and her thin hair blowing up in a draught. I thought, "What a caricature!" and looked at Chester on the rug in front of the just-lit fire (even in May we hade a fire for him)—Chester in his baggy pyjamas stooping down and peering through his big new reading goggles at a newspaper beside a table light, which was shining through his white hair onto his shiny skull and throwing deep shadows under his big eyebrows (so that the eyes were in dark caves) and under his nose (which certainly stuck out more as his cheeks had grown thin) and his under lip (so that the famous "fighting jaw" seemed to be thrust even further forward); and suddenly, in front of my eyes, a kind of transformation scene took place . . . the Chester I had known for more than twenty years grew suddenly dim and melted into the worried haggard fierce old man, who then stood before me like an apparition.
>
> (*PG*, p. 310)

The grotesque enables Cary to include and control physical violence in the novel. Physical violence in *The Horse's Mouth* although abundant, affected mainly the indestructable Jimson, preserved from harm by his "presence of imagination". The early drafts of *Prisoner of Grace* contained frequent scenes of violence: of slum lodgings where wives and husbands beat each other in the streets, of Nina brutally and vulgarly mistreated at Chester's pro-Boer meetings, of Chester himself beating Nina. Cary realised that this physical brutality was unsuitable to the novel whose thematic impact depends on Nina's growing awareness of the intellectual and moral brutalisation which human relationships can effect.

Characteristically, therefore, the scenes of violence which Cary retained are stylized and coloured by the comic grotesque. He impersonalises the violence of the pro-Boer meeting by making Nina step back and view her own actions as an outsider:

> And, what is extraordinary, I, too (as I was told afterwards, for I have no recollection of it, and in fact for a long time I wouldn't believe it), was shrieking "Cowards!"—and even "Kill them!". . .

Nina's characteristic understatement, the afterthought details of her brackets, and her disproportionate awareness of minor discomforts also reduce the violence. The prickliness of the soldier's overcoat makes more of an impression on her than her more severe injuries.

> The end of it was simply that nearly all my clothes were torn off, somebody smacked my face so hard that both my eyes were blackened, and after a confused foolish struggle I found myself (I have no idea how) wrapped in a very prickly overcoat with metal buttons (it was a soldier's coat). . . .
>
> (*PG*, p. 57)

In the episode of Nina's second "suicide" Chester defeats Nina by preventing her from leaping from an upper storey window and escaping from their shared life. Chester's own comic defeat, however, diminishes Nina's.

> But just then Chester's pyjamas (he had taken to them at last when he had begun to visit generals—but he did not manage them very well) began to slip down and he grabbed at them with such an offended look (as if they had tried to "betray" him) that I had a horrible impulse to laugh.
>
> (*PG*, p. 308-9)

The grotesque in *Prisoner of Grace* mitigates the harshness of Cary's portrayal of the hardening effect which the politics of simple human relationships can have on those working to preserve those relationships. It also confirms Nina's discovery that tragedies have an undercurrent of humour, of the ridiculous, which recurrently wells up to show that "an 'impossible' situation was not only possible—it was quite absurdly simple" (*PG*, p. 309).

Cary's use of myth, like the use of humour, extends the implications of *Prisoner of Grace*. The myth of the Fall further illuminates the paradox of Chester's grace. Analogies both with Adam and with Satan describe Chester's character and his relationship with Nina. Once again the challenge of necessity, which Cary sees as a Blakean "fall into freedom", evokes creativeness. Many heroes of the romantic-humanist tradition respond to this challenge and achieve or envisage new heights of human development. Such a man is Chester who approaches his world with a purpose of change and plays politics with its every aspect—love, religion, government. But in such heroes—Faustus and Byron's Cain, Prometheus and Blake's Miltonic Satan—the heroic and the diabolical are close-linked. Cary casts Nimmo the politician in the role of Satan, history's first politician, master of spell-binding appeal. One is reminded of Chester's own fascination with Milton's Satan in *Except the Lord*. Nina states that "getting into love" with Jim was "like a fall" (*PG*, p. 82), but this is merely a romantic notion, "what they mean by falling in love". Chester, however, makes Nina the archetypal Eve. Aunt Latter's new lodgings become a virtual Eden in *Prisoner of Grace* as the man whom both Jim and Aunt Latter call a "little snake" (*PG*, p. 38, 152) becomes a marvellous satanic figure.

Aunt Latter's characterisation of the politicians's diabolical cunning sets the scene,

> . . . I tell you he's a devil—and a fool, too, They're all alike, these climbers—creepers and bullies. They don't trust anybody. They have only one idea for a friend or a wife—an imbecile like Bootham, who licks their feet, and a slave woman who trembles at a word. You see if he doesn't start on you now—sneaking and hissing and winding himself round you and crushing you into pulp—just female pulp. . . .
>
> (*PG*, p. 152)

And while Nina feels "surrounded with treachery" the devilish image becomes real, ". . . Chester walked in, with a large basket of fruit, and greeted us in the most unembarrassed manner" (*PG*, p. 153). The fruit-bearing appearance of Aunt Latter's metaphorical Satan soon tempts even that formidable lady into a reconciliation and subsequently Chester's sly flattery, "(but still with that touch of malice)" (*PG*, p. 156), once again makes Nina his slave.

But Chester is both tempter and husband; Nina's falls in a post-lapsarian world are not from grace but into grace, not transgressions but "conversions". Conversion is Nina's word for Chester's captivating displays of imaginative power and force of will which reveal the nature of his creative genius and the meaning of her own life. Nina is an Eve in relationship to Chester's Adam. Her initial fall to Jim leads to a more profound relationship with Chester, itself a constant challenge to imagination. Repeated falls and reconciliations demand new responses and bring new "grace". Myth thus helps to illuminate the necessity of Nina's peculiar situation both during her marriage to Chester when, as mother of Jim's children she continues to serve Chester's career as his wife, and in the final Palm Cottage "retirement" when she cannot turn Chester out "For I should know that I was committing a mean crime against something bigger than love". The notion here embodied adds a further dimension to the concept of "grace", adumbrating in comic fashion the liberal idea that men respond to inner standards and promptings, variously called conscience or duty, and that these personal sanctions alone give the laws by which men live.

When Nina leaves Chester she preserves her happiness by preserving the "situation" which has complicated their lives throughout.

> The tension is like a perpetual crisis . . . But what is strange is that I have never had so much happiness because Jim has never before been so much in love . . .
>
> But how could I make him understand that it is because that happiness is so precious to me I dare not turn Chester out . . .
>
> I should despise myself, which is, I suppose, what Chester means when he says that such and such a "poor devil" is "damned". And I am terrified of "damnation", for it would destroy my happiness and all the joy of my life, and Jim can only shoot me dead.
>
> (*PG*, p. 402)

Chester's politics are those of compromise and coalition;

through them he boldly keeps his career and his principles afloat. Nina's tactics are the same; by serving all parties, she contrives to make all parties serve her happiness.

Nina's character was the product of a long evolution. Chester Nimmo's characterisation was greatly facilitated by Cary's use of David Lloyd George as an historical model. The Prime Minister's biography provides the framework for Nimmo's career from his religious boyhood, through his initial national success as a forceful opposition orator in the Boer War controversy, into Parliament and the higher levels of government. As Lloyd George became President of the Board of Trade in 1905, Chester in that year becomes Under-Secretary for Mines. He is promoted to Asquith's Liberal Cabinet in 1908, the year Lloyd George became Chancellor of the Exchequer. In Asquith's 1915 Coalition Government Chester is offered the Ministry of Production, paralleling Lloyd George's move to the Ministry of Munitions, and finally Chester becomes a member of Lloyd George's own War Cabinet. The disastrous election of 1922, brought about by the withdrawal of Conservative support for Lloyd George's Coalition, occasioned the resignation of the Prime Minister and is, in the novel, the hour of Nimmo's defeat and political downfall. In the end, both cottager's sons become Peers.

Lloyd George's characteristic turns of phrase increase Nimmo's vitality. Like Lloyd George, Chester invests his political speeches with the evangelical flavour and Biblical overtones instilled by his religious upbringing. Nimmo's unexpected decision to support the war finds expression in words strikingly like those with which Lloyd George made clear his readiness for war leadership. Compare the two:

> There is no man in this room who has always regarded the prospect of engaging in a great war with greater reluctance and with greater repugnance than I have done throughout the whole of my political life . . . Why is our honour as a country involved in this war? Because in the first instance, we are bound by honourable obligations to defend the independence, the liberty, the integrity, of a small neighbour that has always lived peaceably . . . to defend Belgium and her integrity.

. . .

That is what we are fighting—that claim to predominancy of a material, hard civilisation, a civilisation which if it once rules and sways the world, liberty goes, democracy vanishes. And unless Britain and her sons come to the rescue it will be a dark day for humanity.
(Speech delivered 19 September 1914 at the Queen's Hall, London)[14]

Chester "confessed to being deeply mislead" and to never having believed it possible for any civilized people to be guilty of so dastardly a crime (the invasion of Belgium) against the very basis of civilized religious liberty, which was the sanctity of the pledged word. And so, with a reluctance which those who knew him and his record could understand, he had been compelled, as an act of conscience, to support the cause of truth, which was also that of peace and freedom, against oppression which he could only describe as devilish.

(PG, p. 267-68)

Chester's attitude towards Jim re-enacts the personal incompatibility between Lloyd George and his wartime Commander in chief, Field Marshall Sir Douglas Haig. Chester sums up Jim as "A political idiot" (*NHM*, p. 215) and Lloyd George's description of Haig reflects the same impatience,

Haig could not hold his own in conference with soldiers or statesmen who could explain their ideas clearly and fluently. He therefore distrusted them and preferred men who had no ideas to set in competition with his own. He liked conventional officers with a soldierly deportment. A solder who fulfilled the description of "an officer and a gentleman" fulfilled his requirements.[15]

It is interesting to note that even "grace", that peculiarly Nimmo word and concept was not alien to Lloyd George's tongue. Lucy Masterman quotes Lloyd George as saying of an unsuccessful acquaintance,

"You know there is a good deal in the old doctrine of 'finding grace'. Though Chaplin started out with everything in his favour—money, descent, position, and not at all a bad brain—yet he frittered it all away and never found grace."[16]

Nimmo is, however, no mere shadow of Lloyd George. Other politicians as diverse as Ramsay Macdonald, "ruined", as some said by "civilization", and Aneurin Bevan, implacable enemy of deprivation, coloured Nimmo's portrait. Even though Chester behaves like Lloyd George in the General Strike, his words that "this is war. War for the soul of England" (*NHM*, p. 166), recall Asquith who called the strike "a war against society".[17] In order to illustrate Cary's general theme, Nimmo had to be not a specific politician but a typical one. "Chester", said Cary,

> is only a lively democratic politician. Have they forgotten Gladstone Disraeli Bright, Acland, Chamberlain, Lloyd George and even Churchill—he has changed his *party* pretty often. The question is simply what is right for the given political context.[18]

Cary defines Chester's character through the same episodes that trace the novel's historical progress. The politician's selection of poverty as an unassailable cause, his support for Lloyd George's land bill and the fight against the Lords in 1909 reflect the Liberal response to the revolutionary upheavals in domestic politics during this crucial period. Chester early espouses the cause of education and later cools towards this and prohibition, recreating the Liberal experience of the early 1900s.[19] A blend of fictional and real events provides the tones of intrigue and decisiveness which characterised government at the top around the war years and reflected the passion, bravery and confusion of the nation at large in the time of upheaval. The secret meeting between certain Ministers and the Committee of Imperial Defence threatens Chester as a member of the peace faction; Lloyd George's great munitions drive produces the fictional "Brome affair" which will have repercussions in *Not Honour More*; the shadowy discussions prior to the break-up of Asquith's Government and the confusing and ultimately destructive demands of the "khaki election" create tension in the Nimmo home.

Chester's role as a Liberal politician immediately suggests some of the paradoxes of his nature and occupation. Chester is a man of religious impulse who deals with worldly problems, a man committed to liberty whose task and genius lie in the management of men. His is the practical work of turning principles into policy and policy into practice. In the political arena the real acts as a ruthless sculptor's tool on the ideal.

198

Nimmo's "great betrayal" of the pacifist cause, his business dealings, so out of character with his early anti-capitalist stance, his abandonment of grass-roots Liberalism for the coalition government illustrate the paradoxes of the British political scene in the early 1900s when pacifists waged war and liaisons between parties were often stronger than internal party links.

To illustrate the inevitability of such compromises and to define effective government as the creative management of people, Cary places Chester in an extraordinary domestic situation which acts as a trope for the political scene.

> Only point of *strange plot* to shew NATURE of REAL GRASP of position which continually FADES. UNLESS RENEWED by grace of imaginative love, and sympathy (i.e. need of continuous imaginative and ARTISTIC effort simply to maintain a faith, not only in marriage but politics because world fundamentally Feeling). . . .
>
> (Ms. Cary 288, S.20.C)

Nimmo's assumed role as father to Jim Latter's children and Nina's devoted loyalty to the man she never loves demonstrate compromise and creativeness. Nina's narrative explains their workings through the novel's central paradox, the inspiring and imprisoning "grace". Grace is most simply confidence that one's aims and actions are inspired, the belief that the purpose one had imaginatively grasped is a valid one. Chester understands grace through the sentiment of the psalm, "Except the Lord build the house, their labour is but lost that build it". God's presence must be felt in every undertaking if it is to be worthy and, conversely, there is no limit to the possibilities of change or innovation in policy or action when the inspiration of grace is present. Change is part of Chester's faith, "Send us the life of the *soul* which is to be born again every moment into a new world of life and love . . . The forgiveness of God is in the life of the soul, the everlasting fountain of His grace, renewed every moment" (*PG*, p. 45-6). Chester's political genius and the sign of his grace lie in his ability to captivate others and to enlist their aid, advice and enthusiasm so that they make his schemes their own. The man able to silence a hostile crowd with his rhetoric and win his audience to tears and applause by his evident sincerity, holds his wife in a similarly powerful spell.

> The truth is that a man like Chester, just because he had such a lot of imagination, such power of putting himself in other people's places and minds, was *nearly always sincere* . . . Chester needed always to believe what he took up, he *needed to be sincere*, for if he had any doubts he could not "put himself over" with effect. Sincerity (as he well knew) was the secret of his power as a speaker; all those sudden "virtuoso" changes of voice, and similes and inspired gestures were the direct result (as, I suppose, in most great preachers and saints) of a "burning" conviction.
>
> (*PG*, p. 230)

Thus Cary provides, through the objective fact of Chester's dramatic oratorical skill—a fact validated in the narrative of *Except the Lord*—an explanation of Nina's helplessness to oppose or draw away from him. In turn, Nina's narrative shows the effectiveness of Chester's skilful persuasion on the person nearest him and thus convinces us of the politician's charisma.

Sex makes Nina a participant in Chester's inspiration which is "bigger than love". Nimmo, compelled by a Puritanical streak to elevate sex to the level of the miraculous in order to justify its enjoyment, must consider his union with Nina blessed, sex itself a continual "revelation". A sensuous person, Nina gladly accepts her duty to provide the physical refreshement which remains for Chester an earthly manifestation of the renewing power of "grace".

Principle and expediency are inseparable in Chester's politics. His pro-Boer speeches were "his great chance—a turning point in his life" (*PG*, p. 52). His pacifism is both a Christian impulse and a way to the top when "the whole country is waiting for a lead" (*PG*, p. 250), and his entry into the War Cabinet which "may be my duty" is accompanied by the realisation (Lloyd George's own astute observation) that "this is going to be a new kind of war—and it's going on for a long time. All this fuss will be forgotten in six weeks" (*PG*, p. 267).

The successful impulse, the "fair gamble", link with Chester's belief in "the immense *truth* of the Christian idea" because, as Nina explains, "what he meant by truth was the *practical truth*, something that *worked*" (*PG*, p. 223). Chester can reconcile this practical idea with principle because he believes that his intuitions are the work of God, that his enterprise is blessed.

That Chester is a man of inspiration and of action, an "artist in politics", leads Cary to question challengingly the impact of the creator's exercise of liberty on that of others. Cary's concept of the creator who uses people the way an artist uses his brushes or his clay is not unique. Lloyd George has been called "an artist expressing himself through the political medium",[20] and Cary himself is one of many commentators who have pointed to the thwarted painter behind the hideous masterpeice of Nazi Germany. For these people the creative impulse is the primary impulse. A critic said of Lloyd George, "Essentially, he was not a Nationalist, or a Radical, or even a reformer . . . He was a governor of men; one of those who is fitted to direct the lives and energies of his fellows".[21]

When people are the artist's medium each is tapped to the extent that he can serve the politician's schemes. While the artist, typified by Gulley Jimson in *The Horse's Mouth*, remains independent in order to create, the politician is in danger of estranging himself so that he can manipulate: "I hardened my heart" (*ETL*, p. 257). The concessions demanded by commitment to political ends are dramatically mirrored in the Nimmo home. Aunt Latter and Tom Nimmo register both the compelling power of grace and the damage wrought to their characters by an enforced sacrifice of individual impulse to Chester's career.

Here, where Cary confronts the problem of conflicting freedoms, the novel most challengingly places before the reader the trilogy's recurrent theme of the discrepancy between means and ends. Chester is not directly responsible for Aunt Latter's deterioration or for Tom's death, but indirectly both are bound up with his career and personality, and the reader rightly questions whether Nimmo's successful career and the achievement of many of his political aims justify such sacrifices. If Cary defends this career, is the novel fundamentally immoral? Here, as so often in the trilogy, Cary presents a situation which, viewed carefully from various angles, offers both a criticism of Nimmo and a further exploration of liberal principles.

Here Nimmo fails most severely in terms of his liberal values: he stifles the growth and infringes the personal liberty of others. Once we have recognised and disapproved in Nimmo the failure of these principles, we have been made to subscribe to their validity. But Cary dramatises in these characters themselves specific aspects of his liberal beliefs. In Aunt Latter the self-respect essential to the rational exercise of liberty is undermined. The results are egotism and intolerance. Aunt Latter shares Nina's respect for Chester and her love for Jim, while resisting the shared fulfilment of compromise through which Nina finds happiness. (She is, however, instrumental in promoting Nina's compromises; she keeps Nina mindful of her responsibilities by repeatedly pointing out her potential influence on Chester's important career). Lacking self-confidence, Aunt Latter asserts herself through interference, and cultivates an anti-democratic conservatism based on snobbery and scorn. Her inability to place confidence in others or to accept their failings along with their virtues signals her lack of "grace" and augments her frustration. These evident deficiencies also point to a kinship not only familial but moral between Aunt Latter and her favourite nephew Jim. Aunt Latter's presence, along with Chester, Jim, and Nina at Palm Cottage underlines the novel's final situation as the epitome of political compromise.

> . . . they come together again at end manage well prisoners of grace Nina has to go to Chester but Chester has to accept Jimmy because Nina wants him from the very guilt that Chester has taught her and Aunt L. has become dependent on Nina.
> They are past small differences.
>
> (Ms. Cary 288, S.20.A)

In Tom Nimmo a failure of moral education leads to incomprehension, frustration and despair. Chester's much-indulged son enjoys a life of few restrictions, but what Chester fails to provide for him is best expressed in his own requirement, in *Except the Lord*: "freedom which is room to grow". Tom's tragedy springs from his failure to understand Chester's inspiration. The child cannot comprehend compromise between moral principle and practical means. Chester's principles create standards for Tom which belittle the boy's efforts and provoke his revolt against Chester's politic manipulations of truth.

Whereas Chester in *Except the Lord* learns to accept the

principles which guide his father despite that man's evident failures, Tom reacts against Chester and his principles. Gifted like Chester in appealing to an audience, but unable to compass his religious fervour, Tom escapes from Chester's principles to the burlesque stage. He uses Chester's talent, not to convert but to amuse, not to convince but to mock. His art, lacking in moral content, is harmless but also meaningless, and therefore fails to satisfy him. Ultimately grace destroys Tom. Because he cannot turn his back on his own standards, he turns away from life. His inability to dissemble his disappointment in failure provides a further contrast to Jim's "honour", itself a disguise for jealousy, hatred, and selfishness.

Tom's presence in the novel enhances Cary's historical portrayal, for he provides a link between the Nimmo household and the apolitical world. Through Tom, Cary captures the spirit of the music halls, the emergence of social drama, the curious pre-war euphoria which lasted even into the early days of fighting, and the gay, flippant time of disorientation which followed the war. Nina's evocation of the Oxford scene captures what Cary called in an essay "that extraordinary calmness with which we faced a war that was actually the end of our liberal civilization".[22]

> In those days there was beneath everything a sense (in spite of the "wicked" Liberal Government) of security and peace. I don't mean that no one expected the war—everyone said that war was likely. That confidence, in fact, which we all shared was something very mysterious; it was, I suppose, simply a feeling that life would always be worth living, and the peace which seemed to rest on the fields and the lovely town, and to sound from the water plopping under the punts, and to shine placidly on all the different rivers when you looked from bridges, was not really there at all. . . .
>
> (*PG*, p. 246)

When the calm of pre-war days gives way to the shock of war and the subsequent heightening of pace and lowering of morals it is, ironically, Tom who is able to find a place in the new order and to make his way. While Chester's political world crumbles, Tom finds momentary success in the new night clubs, "even respectable papers mentioned him as the brilliant Mr. Tom Nimmo . . ." (*PG*, p. 339). A parallel may be drawn between

Tom's failure through inability to communicate with his German audiences and Chester's failure once his policies cease to strike a common note with the voice of the people.

A final irony in the book's complex plot makes Chester himself the object of political and domestic management. Chester occupies a central position of knowledge, influence and power in the nation's politics. His needs and activities are acknowledged to dictate the family routine. His actual role, however, is more complicated and less authoritative.

From earliest days Chester is under the influence of the "chapel" people, notably his friend Edward Goold. His aims and theirs coincide and he is hardly aware of the strength of their power to direct his activities. Only when he has achieved political success does he find that they are not willing to accord him the independence his practical methods require. In small things they dictate his social behaviour, keeping a critical eye on the way he dresses, the people he entertains, and the amusements her permits himself. With tragic consequences they interfere with his family life. Goold forces Chester into the fatal remarks which destroy Tom's faith in his stepfather's integrity.

Nor are Chester's political moves made without their prompting. His move to pacifism follows upon prayer with the Tarbiton faithful and a consequent "revelation. I owe an eternal debt of gratitude to Ted for making me understand the force and truth of local feeling—a truly Christian feeling" (*PG*, p. 231). The truth of local feeling has already been made plain through Nina:

> ... for the Radical Council threatened to withdraw its support and look for another candidate, "who will truly represent our Christian people, and lift his voice against the bloody-minded men who seek war in Europe".
>
> (*PG*, p. 222)

Chester defies the chapel radicals and joins the War Cabinet only in response to pressure from the Prime Minister himself.

But Chester is a prisoner of more than constituents and party. He is most fundamentally a prisoner of those principles which inspire him. Chester's Liberalism, as *Except the Lord* shows us, is born out of a radical impulse which rejects the constraints of socialism. The rise of the Liberal Party confirms Chester's belief that his cause is blessed and the Party's downfall shatters that sustaining faith. Because Nimmo has believed in the social reforms of his Government he cannot understand "the wickedness of the people. 'Those questions—and the hisses at the factory—from men who owe us unemployment insurance'" (*PG*, p. 327). The sense that his cause is no longer sanctioned deprives Chester of the imaginative power through which he has shaped his life to his desires, and occasions a momentary lapse of "grace". Only the constructive impulse to give the Cause a new expression in his memoirs, restores grace, and with it vitality. When Chester's vitality—of mind and body, albeit in a fashion more comical than spiritual—returns, so does Nina, again to "manage" Nimmo.

The agent of grace is as much bound as its prisoner. Nimmo must insist on Nina's trustworthiness, lest "grace" be revealed a sham, and when Nina plays freely on this trust, Chester is bound, by his public life, to gloss over her deceptions and, privately, to forgive her.

Nimmo is similarly trapped into becoming a prisoner to Bootham and Sally. The protective guard which the two mount over him in wartime—against opponents, petitioners, and Nina—becomes a restrictive wardenship to Nimmo in defeat. Ostensibly assisting his memoirs (and, incidentally, preparing their own) they keep him under constant watch, and reserve the right to permit or forbid his every action. His public image prevents Nimmo from rebelling against this "loyalty" and "devotion", and only when Bootham's tenacity as a spy is at last rewarded with an unexpected glimpse of Chester's sexual antics, is the pair routed and Chester's liberty restored. But Chester remains a prisoner to his need for Nina and the novel's tense close balances this bondage with Nina's own renewed surrender to Nimmo's power. Of this extraordinary domestic compromise, Cary's notes comment, "they have been *pushed* into discovery that it will work and provide a civilized happiness" (Ms. Cary 287, N. 145). The link between politics and human relations is clear.

The continuing discovery of nations and peoples is twofold. It is the discovery made by Nina, and by Georgina in *Except the*

Lord, that humane management is achieved not through service to absolute ideals but through sympathy. And it is Nimmo's discovery "that in the change of situation due to life and imagination, the dogma or principle . . . becomes out of date" (Ms. Cary 287, N.145), and new imaginative creations are required. Like domestic happiness, government depends on day to day changes in course, critical re-interpretation, in order to pursue an ostensibly consistent course towards the ideals on which it is founded.

Nimmo sees the world outstrip his ideas just as he once piloted a move away from old dogma. Nimmo's final bewilderment at the failure of the people to appreciate the good intentions of Liberalism is no more dramatic than Lloyd George's own. The man who so effectively read the signs of the people's needs and shaped his party's policies to anticipate their demands, unconsciously enunciated that party's later failure in this striking appeal,

> Liberalism has a definite task which it is essential to the national interests that it should accomplish effectively. *It cannot do so without convincing the electorate of the need*, and the truth that Liberalism alone can supply that need.[23]

With the people, in 1924, clamouring for more immediate needs, Lloyd George's offer of "liberty" bore the fatal ring of abstraction.

Except the Lord

"Left-wing politics", wrote Cary to Cass Canfield in December 1952, ". . . has very deep roots in Protestant religion, an influence still powerfully at work. It is strange to me that the critics did not see it working in the Prisoner of Grace. The new book will give them something new to think about in providing a new angle on the Prisoner".[24] Cary summed up the "angle" for Elizabeth Lawrence, "Nimmo is *attacking* all ideologies on the ground that liberal ideals of tolerance and freedom are rooted in our religious history and that State-systems of socialism which deny private rights are the enemies of religion and God himself".[25] Nimmo's memoir was to provide the background for such sentiments and the record of Nimmo's own steps towards their appreciation and acceptance.

The book's final chapter, added at the proof stage, underlines this intention. Nimmo links the lesson of Georgina's love and her pride to the aims and achievements of his political life. "'Here,' I said, 'the story began and here it shall begin again, in the things I lived with this forgotten one, in the young cruelty of the world, in the making of our souls'" (*ETL*, p. 287).

Cary opens with only a brief reference to Nimmo's present situation.

> Yesterday, an old man nearing my end, I stood by the grave of a noble woman, one of the three noblest I have ever known, my mother, my sister, my wife. If I draw back now the curtain from my family life, sacred to memory, I do so only to honour the dead, and in the conviction that my story throws light upon the crisis that so fearfully shakes our whole civilization.
>
> (*ETL*, p. 5)

This opening prepares the way for Nimmo's defence of Liberalism and instructs the reader to view the advent of British socialism which is the culmination of *Prisoner of Grace* and *Not Honour More*'s starting point, in the light of his memoir.

Except the Lord makes the trilogy's central statement about the ideals of British Liberalism while portraying the forces which transformed the Liberal Party in the period between Gladstone's eclipse and the 1906 revival. The novel's plot illustrates the origins of the New Liberalism which aimed at social reform and drew working class support.

Gladstone had made freedom the Liberal watchword. He had championed small nations against great oppressors. Glastonian Liberalism had introduced the secret ballot in 1872 and extended the franchise to agricultural workers in 1884. Political stirrings from the rural section of the community thus found a new outlet and radicalism became the voice not of reforming aristocrats, but of the people on the land and in the villages.

Education similarly penetrated all localities when the Education Act of 1870 compelled attendance and set up local school boards. Disputes between Church and Dissent which accompanied the passage of the Education Act were reflected in political alignment. Nonconformists supported the Liberal

Party, the descendant of that Whig party founded by Protestant dissenters in the early 1800s.

Nonconformity shared a common evangelistic spirit with the mid-Victorian leaders of every creed, including the High Church Gladstone, and found practical common ground in support of Gladstone's Newcastle Programme, which included prohibition and Church disestablishment in Wales and Scotland. By 1875 the wealthier classes, their reforming zeal sated, drifted towards Conservatism. The new alliance of working and middle class within the Liberal party was fostered and cemented by nonconformity.

Latter day Liberalism had seen the weakness of that compromise between political ideology and religious belief which had translated Mill's humanist view of the relationship between progress and individual liberty into a belief in automatic progress under providence. By adopting social reform and assisting the small man against the oppressor, the New Liberalism acknowledged men's power to alter their world constructively. But faith in providence had, paradoxically, cemented individualism as the cornerstone of Liberal principle. Individualism fulfilled the essentially Protestant idea of the need for each man to consult his own conscience and interpret God's law. This individualism survived in the New Liberalism wherein the Protestant spirit of independent judgment joined with faith in human reason as a guide to action. The result was a new concept of responsible government. Still the appeal was to God, to truth or the dignity of human nature, rather than to the "brood of slogans" which Nimmo sees as a cover for irresponsible or inhuman actions (*ETL*, p. 274). L.T. Hobhouse describes the faith which underlay Chester's "grace".

> Liberalism applies the wisdom of Gamaliel in no spirit of indifference, but in the full conviction of the potency of truth. If this thing be of man, *i.e.* if it is not rooted in actual verity, it will come to nought. If it be of God, let us take care that we be not found fighting against God.

The division, which Hobhouse, for one, drew, haunted Liberals of Nimmo's generation.

The true opposition is between the control that cramps the

personal life and the spiritual order, and the control that is aimed at securing the external and material conditions of their free and unimpeded development.[26]

Socialism, while promising the second, seemed to the Liberal too anxious to exercise the former type of control.

"Liberalism is by name the party of freedom", Cary wrote in a notebook of the late 1930s;

> and socialism is not. Just as Liberalism, talking of freedom, secured much justice by the way; so socialism, talking of social justice, secures freedom by the way . . . It lays no emphasis upon freedom, and it is accustomed to speak of freedom as something of little importance beside justice or merely beside efficiency, health.
>
> (Ms. Cary 267, N.59)

Liberalism thus rejected socialist planning which, however well-meaning, presumed to treat justice as a force within human control and freedom as an illusion. Chester Nimmo's history, in paralleling this rejection, unfolds a triumph of the Liberal ideal.

In *Except the Lord* the socialists' demands for justice are mocked by the horrors of a dockers' strike perpetuated through terrorism and destruction. Balanced against this failure is the "strange" victory of the London dockers ten years later, when "money and encouragement poured in from every side, from all classes", because the "country saw the justice of the dockers' case . . ." (*ETL*, p. 275). Justice, Nimmo points out, was here achieved through humanity's innate reason and conscience, not through socialist force or plan. Thus Nimmo stands by his Liberalism which acknowledges a higher law and defends human individualism, and which acquiesces in the sentiment of psalm 127: "Except the Lord build the house, their labour is but lost that build it; /Except the Lord keep the city, the watchman waketh but in vain".

Cary's intent was not to write a religious work, but to unfold what he described in a note as "THE WHOLE LIBERAL ANGLE AND ITS RELIGIOUS BASIS" (Ms. Cary 289, N.154). Novelists of the previous century, from George Eliot to Mark Rutherford had exploited the associations of religion and politics in rural or nonconformist enclaves.

209

Cary's picture of the twentieth-century Liberal party thus begins with Chester Nimmo's childhood in the nonconformist rural community. Here, where middle class dissenters had long sought liberty, the lower classes, exposed to the possibility, were now restless for freedom. Chester Nimmo's discovery that freedom lies in power represents the experience of these groups. With education came enfranchisement; with the vote came the power to elect sympathetic governors, and hence the power to dictate to their governors; with the introduction of the Parliamentary stipend members of the lower-middle or even working classes, could themselves represent their fellows. Power in turn brought greater freedom through social reform.

The late nineteenth and early twentieth century Liberal and socialist camps harboured many radicals of dissenting background and religious upbringing, like Nimmo. Lloyd George preached as a boy and led his nonconformist school-fellows in a strike against repeating the catechism of the Established Church; [27] Keir Hardie's success in winning members of the working class away from Liberalism to socialism has been attributed to his stirring use of the nonconformist idiom. This idiom colours Nimmo's style throughout.

Chester's infatuation with the militant labour movement in *Except the Lord* grows out of religious principle mingled with real experience of social injustice. Religion itself bore a militant aspect in the Nimmo household. Chester's father, "at once soldier and prophet", defends his right to preach with the conviction that a solider shows in battle, and accepts injustice in the unquestioning way a soldier accepts orders from above. His wife's death is "the work of Providence" and he warns his daughter, "You did not earn yourself, Georgy, and you would have no right to cry if you were crooked" (*ETL*, p. 39).

Nimmo's father belongs to the Victorian Christian soldiery led by such men as the aged preacher Leddra who enjoins the starving tin miners to refrain from violence, and whose weapon in economic warfare is charity. This creed at once sharpens conscience and stirs rebellion in the Nimmo children.

When faith in their father's God diminishes, Chester's seeking conscience and raw awareness of men's sufferings draw him to the anarchical humanist Lanza. Lanza's appeal predictably moves the young Nimmo, as it combines the dramatic skill of the spell-binding orator with rejection of the same God that Nimmo has rejected. Lanza champions humanity against law which—in its natural and man-made forms—has repeatedly offended Chester. But the speculativeness of this anarchic thought drives Chester towards those whose methods are direct and whose objects are more immediate.

After his own failure to establish an agricultural workers' union in the Tarbiton area, Chester meets the Marxist union leader Pring and becomes directly involved as his "chief aide-de-camp" in the disastrous Lilmouth dock strike. Pring impresses Chester initially by providing "authority and policy", conveyed in the politician's arresting manner which suggests at once power and personal concern. Thus, just as Chester learned the power and technique of oratory through his childhood experiences of religion, he imbibes the manners of political diplomacy along with the socialism he is later to reject. That Pring "loved power too much and men not at all" is the discovery which wrenches Chester's sympathies from the militants. It prepares the way for his rediscovery of religion— the belief that all human emotions and endeavours are manifestations of God—and his subsequent espousal of the policies of Liberalism. These the old and dying Nimmo defines thus, "tolerance which is room to learn, freedom which is room to grow, private rights and private property which are the only defence against public wrong and public breach of trust" (*ETL*, p. 276).

Cary's research for *Except the Lord* yielded the exact physical and sociological detail which gave a firm basis in realism to the simple, personal style of Nimmo's memoir. To supply background for the character of Chester Nimmo's father, an adventist preacher, Cary turned to numerous books and essays on Seventh Day Adventists.[28] The religious attitudes of the west country adventist and naturalist Philip Henry Gosse and the characteristic blend of science and religion in his expression contributed to the portrait of Preacher Nimmo.[29] Edmund Gosse's sensitive memoir *Father and Son* no doubt contributed to Cary's portrayal of Nimmo's nonconformist childhood. Chester's Biblical language in *Except the Lord* resembles Gosse's in such phrases as "whereupon my Father lifted up his voice in prayer".[30]

211

Background details for Chester's involvement in agricultural unions and the dockers' strikes came from Sidney Webb's *History of Trade Unionism*, Sir Hubert Llewellyn Smith's *The Story of the Dockers' Strike* and *New Survey of London Life and Labour*, and various other books and periodicals. Benjamin Tillett, one of the leaders of the London dock strike, suggests the Nimmo of *Except the Lord*, "Of slight and delicate physique, but of a restless and energetic temperament, with indomitable pluck and a strong vein of ambition . . .".[31] A west country youth like Nimmo, Tillett first made his mark in an early abortive strike of a month's duration at Tilbury docks. Like Chester, he grew seriously ill from exposure during the strike and witnessed the distress and disorganisation which befell the union once the labourers, lacking support from the community at large, lost heart.

Webb's *History of Trade Unionism*, in addition to providing statistics, described in detail the importance of the union secretary in organising a strike, a description which virtually outlines Chester Nimmo's activities as a union official and the progress which led him towards a career in politics.[32]

Nimmo writes his memoir to evoke those liberal values which seem threatened by the rise of British socialism. Cary chose to protect the sincerity of the old and disillusioned politician's memoir by preserving the immersion of Nimmo's mind in the ambience of the childhood and youth in which those values were acquired. The dramatic impact of childhood events on Chester is registered through the child's objective vision.

> Disaster, for us children, came without warning, quietly as the fall of a leaf. One morning we were told that we were to move, the stock to be sold, the auctioneer was already in the yard.
>
> A hay-cart was waiting for us—within the hour we were creaking away on the rough track. Richard and Georgina stood up to look over the tall side of the cart at the last of Highfallow . . . The day was fine, the pale November sun shone on the boards, gulls were crying overhead, I had the consciousness, delightful to a child, of being on a journey . . .
>
> What amazement fell upon me to find myself in a mean cottage, one narrow slice out of a terrace in Back Lane, Shagbrook, with only a muddy road in front and a muddier yard behind. For days I wandered in a trance, which was too bewildered to be misery.
>
> (*ETL*, p. 11-12)

From Gosse, as, possibly, from Dickens of *Great Expectations* and David Copperfield, Cary absorbed the dramatic immediacy of a childish lapse into the present tense to recall a scene. Compare, for example, the following passages; the first Gosse, the second Nimmo:

> Out of the darkness of my infancy there comes only one flash of memory. I am seated alone, in my baby-chair, at a dinner-table set for several people. Somebody brings in a leg of mutton, puts it down close to me, and goes out. I am again alone, gazing at two low windows, wide open upon a garden. suddenly noiselessly, a large, long animal (obviously a greyhound) appears at one window-sill, slips into the room, seizes the leg of mutton and slips out again.[33]
>
> I recall with great vividness another scene. My father is going to market—five or our blackfaced sheep are penned between two gates and I am flattered to think that I am guarding them while my father harnesses the mare.
>
> Suddenly a huge red man appears from the hill—he speaks to my father, argues, begins to wave his great fists.
>
> (*ETL*, p. 6)

This immediacy lends an air of conviction to the memoir which seeks to recapture not only past experience, but the growing sense of the particular values which it is Nimmo's aim—and Cary's—to defend.

Simplicity, sympathy, and realism mark Nimmo's memoir. The structure of *Except the Lord* polarizes around the figures of Chester and his sister Georgina. Other characters assume significance through their influence on one or both of these figures. Georgina herself demonstrates for Chester the creative force of "a heart that could not know despair because it forgot itself in the duty of its love" (*ETL*, p. 287). The most important characters after Chester and Georgina are, of course, the other members of the Nimmo family. Preacher Nimmo offers the first of a series of ideological influences on Chester. The death of their beloved mother, Ruth's marriage, Richard's academic success and his subsequent London failure provide a succession of domestic revelations which Chester turns into political lessons and which Georgina, characteristically, interprets as the signs of necessity.

A further group of characters appears individually and

213

successively as outside influences on the young Chester, each one laying a slightly larger and more direct role in determining the boy's actions. These are Leddra, Lanza, the Dollings, and Pring. Finally, an outer ring of characters define the world the Nimmos live in. Mrs. Coyte and her son Fred, the shopkeeper G. and his son Edward, Doan, Will Wilson, Cran, and Nina Woodville make up this group.

It is interesting to note that missing from this study of nonconformist religion is the element of the grotesque which often characterised Cary's portraits of dissenting preachers. Puggy Brown, the ex-butcher, in *To Be a Pilgrim* is a fine example:

> His short squat figure stood black against the crimson sign of the "Wilcher Arms," hanging behind him. Its gilt lettering, sparkling in the sun, made a kind of glory round his head and shoulders; the shoulders of a giant, or a dwarf; and the face of a prize fighter, pug nose, jutting brows, thick swollen lips, roaring over all the noise of bullocks and sheep.
>
> (*TBP*, p. 20)

Preedy, the eccentric faith-healer of the posthumously published novel *The Captive and the Free* is a grotesque foil for the inconsistencies of those he converts, and another self-styled preacher in the first "Captive and Free" walks about with religious slogans painted on his long mackintosh.

Cary avoided the grotesque in descriptions of Nimmo's father and the book's other dissenting preachers, for such descriptions would diminish their stature as influences on the impressionable young Nimmo. The crippled Leddra, portrayed in early drafts as almost inhuman in appearance, thus emerges simply as "an old man and infirm" (*ETL*, p. 66), a venerable if inadequate fighter for charity and mercy in time of economic strife.

Nor is there humour in the second abortive advent vigil when Nimmo's father leads his little band out into a dawn rainy and cold "like a dirty rag" (*ETL*, p. 120). The failure does not, like Preedy's final open air address in *The Captive and the Free*, mock the preacher's embarrassing inadequacy in the face of contrary nature. Preedy's rout, when the rain falls and his listeners scatter, is a personal defeat, and Cary invests it with comedy.

A shadow slowly deepened over the group; a new cloud was coming up. A sudden cold gust blew from the Park. A drop of rain fell. It mildly disconcerted the preacher . . .

The rain suddenly thickened into a downpour, and the crowd began to melt. Preedy began to shout at the top of his voice, 'Let me tell you what I did—'

But already the whole gathering had run off except for three figures at the back . . .

Prince came up with a taxi and Preedy began to get in. Suddenly he stopped and looked at the sky. 'There's the sun again—'

'I'm afraid that's only a gleam.' Marris took one arm and the girl the other to help him into the car. The rain was growing more violent. He submitted to them.[34]

The failure of the second coming in *Except the Lord* is, however, not a setback like the failure of the sun, but a disaster. Preacher Nimmo wisely does not attempt to detain his followers.

> 'I would not have any man stay here in the wet who does not believe that my Lord will come. For if he stay without faith, then the rain could harm him. And you, Fred, have your earache, you Edward, have your weak chest.'
>
> (*ETL*, p. 121)

And though Mr. Nimmo attributes the failure to lack of faith in the congregation, loss of faith in the Nimmo children is the episode's sadly ironic consequence.

> But Richard understood me, 'Afraid of that poor old God who can't even stop Ruth from coughing or keep mother Weaver out of the workhouse—I'd be ashamed. Why, if He was real, I should have to hate Him.'
>
> (*ETL*, p. 122)

The whole episode underlines the helplessness of the depressed faithful. To the child such episodes are not grotesque but fearful and moving. Placing himself, through Nimmo's memory, inside the child that Nimmo was, Cary leaves aside the later Nimmo's cynicism, seen in *Prisoner of Grace*, and subdues his own comic vision, to make the memoir wholly characteristic and forceful.

Another key to this forcefulness lies in the amount of brutality portrayed in this simple memoir. Scenes of physical violence in

The Horse's Mouth, Charley is My Darling, A Fearful Joy and others belong to a grotesque genre where physical pain is less than the pain of injustice.

Brutality in *Except the Lord* is not grotesque or exaggerated; it is dramatically understated, presented in terms of bare, matter-of-fact realism. Georgina's brutalisation by the shopkeeper G. at the age of eleven is accepted even by her brother.

> At that time, you must understand, even half a century ago, the world was a much rougher place than it is to-day. There were many places where no woman could go unprotected, and almost every woman, except among the most sheltered class, was accustomed to incidents which would now be thought fit for a police court . . . So Georgina's silence as a child of eleven about what happened in the shop was respected and approved. . . .
>
> (*ETL*, p. 55-6)

The incident is one of a stream of violent scenes; Georgina beaten by the Battwell girls, Chester set upon and beaten by Doan and Kimber, Georgina attacked by Fred Coyte, Richard broken by London, Chester hardened by his role in the strike, strikers themselves beaten by their fellows with cool and horrible efficiency.

Brutality throughout *Except the Lord* is a fact of life. Moments of extreme violence are understated, because in the whole spectrum their effect is no more dramatic than the continuous demoralising and devastating effects of a poverty-striken life manifest in illness, injustice, ignorance, and pervading hopelessness. The striking development in the novel is no single violent scene, but the lesson Chester carries away despite such scenes—his father's and Georgina's lesson—of the value of the individual, the presence of God, the nature of love.

Chester's own experience focusses these lessons. His personal dishonesty and callousness exemplify the moral destruction that poverty, accompanied by spiritual deprivation, could work on its sufferers. His participation in brutality shows the power of an abstract goal to destroy charity and humanity. He is implicated in the assault on an innocent striker and subsequently in the self-abasing resort to a self-protecting lie. Chester's most profound errors are thus an infringement of personal liberty and of truth. Nimmo's recognition of these wrongs provokes his crucial recoil from socialism and his return to his father's belief in truth and to the liberal belief in man's dignity and his right of individual liberty.

Not Honour More

Not Honour More was designed and written to complete Cary's tripartite dramatisation of the downfall of the New Liberalism and to confirm his evocation of Liberalism as a set of principles and a mode of conduct. *Not Honour More* is the least independent of the three volumes. It relies on the events of *Prisoner of Grace* to clarify its setting and plot. It requires the theme of *Except the Lord* to explain Nimmo's compromises in the General Strike and his fight for an outmoded Liberalism, and also to clarify Cary's attitude to Jim Latter's final resort to murder. Nevertheless, the novel preserves its own integrity in the vitality of Latter's monologue and in Cary's realistic portrayal of the mood and events of the General Strike.

Searching for the terms in which to put Jim's apology, Cary began with "Jim's point of view. She is a flirt and infinitely false." Jim's own virtue is not ambiguous in these notes and hence, Nina emerges as unquestionably corrupt. Cary felt uneasy with this development, as a note dated "Sept. 52" suggests, "Note all this suggests simply a study of the false. but the book is *study of Jim* as honest man among the crooks and time servers" (Ms. Cary 289, N.154). Gradually Cary saw that if the trilogy's theme of the nature of liberalism were to be sustained, the inflexible, conservative, violent Latter could not be portrayed as a hero and allowed to condemn the other characters out of hand. Nina's "emotional anarchism", as Cary described her inconsistency, and Chester's deviousness in the pursuit of a political or ideological goal had been freely revealed. Certainly Nina had not been wrong in noting inconsistencies in Jim's character.

Further, Jim had an essential role to play in the trilogy's historical scheme. His misguided but sincere assessment of the direction in which his country was moving and the steps necessary for its salvation provided a plausible explanation for the emergence of Fascist sympathies in democratic Britain.

Jim's actions had to illustrate Cary's assessment of the character of those who responded to Fascism, as revealed in a note, ". . . the mob mind . . . blind instinctive selfishness defeating its own ends" (Ms. Cary 267, N. 59).

Jim's character as an egoistic military conservative ultimately yielded up its own flaw. To a soldier and a gentleman honour would be the principal virtue. But in terms of the trilogy's concurrence in the ideal of personal liberty, the "honour" which leads Jim to murder could only be seen as a self-deceiving mask for liberty's criminal violation. Cary chose well in making honour Jim's watchword, as love had been Nina's and freedom Chester's. The quality implies the strength of men of Jim Latter's type at the same time that it uncovers the flaw in Jim the individual. This dual effect developed as the book took shape.

Cary felt great sympathy for the ideals of honour and service which Jim claimed to hold. He had expressed the hope that his sons would inherit from him "the traditions of service, and duty—the honourable traditions of their class. . ."[35] The idea of duty took Cary himself to Hay's Wharf to load pigs' carcasses on the S.S. Smolensk[36] in the General Strike. A personal link, therefore, existed in Cary's psyche between the theme and chief event of this novel. Although he had, in 1918, defended the rights of workers to strike in wartime,[37] and in 1919 had naively described himself as "a bit of a socialist",[38] the impulse to serve when needed seems, in 1926, to have overriden political considerations for Cary. The split between sympathy with the workers and an ideal of duty which marked Cary's attitude to the General Strike was dramatised in *Not Honour More* in the opposed characters of Nimmo and Latter. Nimmo points to the dangers of the strike, "the country is slipping into revolution, a revolution it doesn't even want" (*NHM*, p. 166), but maintains overt support for the strikers' cause. The view of those who saw the nation's order and safety as the first consideration, and the workers as tools of extremist agitators is vividly embodied in Jim Latter, for whom the strike put "the whole country into danger" (*NHM*, p. 127). Cary could epitomise those who saw rabid Communism behind every picket in Latter's characterisation. He could even mock his own tendency to react with a blend of militarism and paternalism by permitting Latter to compare the strike to the African situation.

> The lunatic fringe. The minority that makes all the trouble in the world, swindles, robberies, murders, and revolutions . . . But I'd seen such crowds before, in Africa. I knew they were ready for anything. They'd been shaken up . . . They were all saying to themselves, 'Something's going on. This strike we've heard of is really a big thing. It's stopped our market bus.'
>
> I'd seen a crowd like that in Africa and just as quiet, quieter, turn into a dangerous mob in about two minutes . . . The same in England and Africa. Only the African is a little quicker to get crazy and then goes off with a bigger bang.
>
> (NHM, pp. 112-13)

The Maufe Case brings the fictional treatment of the General Strike to its climax and creates clearly divergent positions for Nimmo and Latter. But the definition of Jim's character depends on his being a constant witness to events public and domestic—the strike, the activities of the various political factions, Nina's unfaithfulness, Nimmo's attempted comeback. Through his comments on these events he paints a portrait of himself which receives its final colouring only in the last moment when disillusioned with legal justice and overwhelmed by jealousy, he accomplishes in the name of honour his wife's "execution".

To expose the deficiencies in Jim's character was Cary's chief task in characterisation. His notes emphasised the need to underline the insubstantiality of Latter's vaunted honour.

> Jim's honour. Point out only artificial. Highest honour to sacrifice oneself. Afraid of public opinion—of what people will say. This 'honour' is artificial, trivial, it is *really cowardice*. Have another reasoner elsewhere to put this point . . . Raise whole question of *honour as duty to service*. Opposite to grab . . .
>
> (Ms. Cary 134-35)

Cary did not employ another reasoner to describe the quality of Jim's honour. His dislike of such figures, expressed in the *Castle Corner* preface, no doubt encouraged him to make Jim his own betrayer.

Jim's concern for public opinion—or, in his words, truth— emerges immediately. Like Nina he hopes his narrative will correct wrong impressions; like Nimmo he hopes to explain the

219

true motive for his actions. But Jim's confession, self-vindicating and absolute in its condemnation of others, contrasts with Nimmo's confession of the great personal error which led him to an understanding of freedom, and with Nina's description of the relative nature of truth, particularly in personal dealings. From the start Jim protests too much that his motives are pure, just, and impartial. The language that Cary called "officialese" of the opening,

> This is my statement, so help me God, as I hope to be hung. My name is Latter, James Vandeleur, late Captain 21st Hussars and District Officer Nigerian Political Service, retired, resident at Palm Cottage near Tarbiton, Devonshire, England, with wife and one child; also a visitor, Lord Nimmo, who occupied one room on ground floor.
>
> (*NHM*, p. 5)

soon gives way to the subjective statement which throughout is the vehicle for Jim's barely contained hysteria.

> I should like to state here and I can call witnesses to prove I had always objected to Lord Nimmo's presence in my house as I considered him a faker and hypocrite. Neither was this a new idea with me due to personal feeling, as has been charged, as I can prove from my book *The Lugas and British African Policy. The Great Betrayal*.
>
> I wrote this book ten years ago when I was hounded out of the African Service for trying to protect my people, the Lugas, from the government policy of what they called civilization but is really materialism and general European degeneracy.
>
> (*NHM*, p. 8)

Jim's characteristic style of defensive statement continually marks his concern for himself and for the impression others receive: "It's charged against me from the first I acted too hastily. I say each time I saved serious trouble" (*NHM*, p. 112); "It's not true we got hold of this vital witness on information" (*NHM*, p. 196); "It is not true I placed myself on the bank for this purpose. Nor is it true I returned early from shooting because of any suspicion . . ." (*NHM*, p. 7); and finally,

> Look at the way the papers have handled this thing. As a sex murder. As a common adultery case . . . the men who write the papers and make them up in the office, don't believe in anything

but materialism, big business, jabberwocks and power-grabbers, they can't see the simplest facts; they take all this mass of lies and grab for something you can't do anything about.

(*NHM*, p. 221-23)

Jim's first attempt on Nimmo's life elicits the same plea to the press as the last, "If you cut out Nimmo's act against my wife, people will think I acted from jealousy and had no good reason" (*NHM*, p.28). In the end an additional reason has been provided by the Maufe case, "a great crime had been committed and how could we just pass it over" (*NHM*, p. 221). But again the address to public opinion belies the claim to personal honour. "I killed her for an example because it was necessary . . . I told him why I'd had to kill my wife, as an honourable man, and why I was glad of publicity" (*NHM*, p. 222), ". . . it wasn't a murder I did. It was an execution" (*NHM*, p. 223).

Jim's language in *Not Honour More* echoes Cock Jarvis's: "The trouble with a government," says Cocky,

> is that it's made up of office wallahs who live in a perpetual funk of something or other and to save their own and each other's skins they'd sell their mothers.[39]

Jim, too, despises government and time servers, "all lies and dirt and grab and the gimmes ready to sell their mothers for loot—monkey-hill at scratch time" (*NHM*, p. 84). But Jarvis's fits of angry sarcasm—like Jim's usually aimed at "official justice"—are invariably mitigated by his appealing swagger or, when aimed at persons, by regret. Latter's narrative has a constant hysterical tone. Jarvis reproves himself for using forgiveness to gain advantage, and can, at least, laugh at the irony when told that his unfaithful wife is tormented by conscience because he is "*kind*". But Jim Latter never admits forgiveness as a possible course of action. When Nina, who deceived Chester in response to Jim's love, in turn deceives Jim in response to Chester's "grace", Jim's reaction is remote from Cocky's sad laughter or Nimmo's politic tolerance: he tries to kill Nimmo. Whereas Jarvis's suicide is the desperate action of a man who wants to do good but cannot, Jim's final act— murder—is the inevitable expression of his vindictiveness and cowardly self-deception.

It is of interest to compare Latter to Rudbeck in *Mister Johnson*. At the end of that novel Rudbeck, too, carries out an execution. The death of Clerk Johnson is required by law, but Rudbeck, at his own risk, tempers that law with humanity. Cary leaves the reader with the understanding that while he has a great deal more to learn, about himself and the world, Rudbeck is on the right track. Jim Latter, by taking it upon himself to fulfil a law which admits no mercies, like the Othello he crudely parodies, is on the wrong track.

Jim Latter's style has all the vibrancy of Gulley Jimson's with none of its sane humour. Latter's talk is often clever but it is rarely funny. His slang is brisk and facile. "Young pups on the dash or old soldiers on the dole" (*NHM*, p. 73), and he constantly employs images of bestiality, excrement, disease, and decay: "A whoreshop for syphilites—everything goes beause you'll all get it ..." (*NHM*, p. 67), ". . . Elizabethan linenfold oak made out of chewed paper painted olde shitte colour" (*NHM*, p. 73), "monkey-hill at scratch time" (*NHM*, p. 84). It is important that Jim's jokes should be facile, for the insight which gives rise to true comedy embraces sympathy and self-comprehension. Jim's lack of humour, along with his haunting fear of appearing a figure of ridicule to the public isolate him from sympathy with others. This isolation bulks the ego which first sees itself as above the law and then makes itself the executor of a law of its own.

By showing Latter's hatred for the "cleverness" of the "talky boys", the democratic politicians, his condescending attitude towards the working classes, and his love of military trappings in his role as head of the local special constabulary, Cary draws a portrait of the sort of Englishman upon whom the later Fascist groups in Britain exercised an appeal. Cary exaggerated little in creating for Latter a style blending slang and emphatic statement, reflecting an hysterical quality of mind in erratic grammatical construction, and displaying egoism in insistent defensiveness which gives way to libellous attack. The style is that of Carlyle's reactionary *Latter Day Pamphlets*. Amusingly Jim's style is prophetic of that of statements made long after the novel's writing by the dashing leader of the British Fascists, Sir Oswald Mosley.

A broken home certainly did not result in my becoming a mother's boy, deep as was my devotion to her. The wiseacres of psychological science may ascribe to this background some political tendencies in my later life which they dislike, but after a considerable study of the subject I am convinced they are talking nonsense . . . Yet every sob-sister in the popular press feels she is competent in a breathless little article of slipshod appraisal and spiteful disapprobation to analyse the alleged complexes of every giant or dwarf who traverses the world scene.[40]

Language is a strikingly efficient, economical mode of characterisation in *Not Honour More*. The military jargon and race course slang which pepper Latter's speech constantly recall his background and interests. Chester and Nina achieve autonomy within Jim's self-preoccupied narrative through their own words. The Nimmo of the first two volumes is recalled in the language of the third Shagbrook address, and Nina's letter to Jim reflects the blending of fact and opinion, tactfulness and shrewd observations that characterised her own narrative.

An important aspect of Jim Latter's self-deception is his sentimentality. Disenchanted with the society around him, he falsely idealises his primitive Luga blacks. He defends the Cavalier Lovelace's poem which gives *Not Honour More* its ironic title[41] as "The most beautiful and true of all poems" (*NHM*, p. 126), yet perverts its sentiment into grisly execution, "I say I never loved this sweet woman so much as now when I knew she had to die . . . Because there was no truth or justice anywhere any more . . ." (*NHM*, pp. 220-23).

Jim's sentimentality explains his blend of professed Liberalism and actual hatred of change. His Liberalism is conservative in origin, a Whig family tradition carried on. "You know very well I belong to one of the oldest Liberal families in the West and have always been for the people, against all oppression" (*NHM*, p. 30). Despite his claim that "as a Liberal I had always been against starvation wages anywhere," the General Strike terrifies Latter because "It will finish old England . . ." (*NHM*, p. 30). In comments such as these Jim's narrative reveals the tragic inconsistency at the heart of the man's frustration. A Whig and a sentimentalist by nature, he is an anachronism in the cynical postwar Britain which has already once elected a socialist government.

223

There is in Latter's narrative, too, a reflection of a frustration wider than the personal one. Cary noted the growing disillusionment reflected in the politics of the time, "end of optimism and return towards *violence* . . . *totalitarianism* . . . international plan enforced—*a new imperialism* . . ." (Ms. Cary 291, S.21.A). Although Latter rejects both forms of totalitarianism currently being offered to the world, State Communism and Fascism, his own response to events is to distrust the leaders and members of the democracy, to resent change in the established order at home, and to participate in violence.

Jim's pessimistic belief that "truth and honour" had been destroyed in an England sinking morally and culturally into degeneracy contrasts with Nimmo's renewed optimism. The novel contains, in Sally, Jim's daughter, a further comment on the aimless frustration which gripped the nation. Sally is devoted to her stepfather, Nimmo, loves Jim, and is married to Nimmo's former secretary, Bootham. Close to Nimmo's infirmity and inconsistency, Sally grows disillusioned with his Liberal principles, and impatient with Bootham's even more pragmatic and uninspired politics. She becomes fascinated by the right-wing radical Brightman. Jim condemns this tendency towards Fascism in Sally with his usual hatred for all left or right-wing radical movements which he lumps together, "common or garden plan-merchants like Brightman, Pincomb and the rest" (*NHM*, p. 146).

Sally's interest in Fascism reveals the attraction the movement held for those whose sympathy for the working class was combined with sentimental nationalism and a desire for efficiency through regimentation. Her shock at Brightman's virulent attack, first verbal, then physical, on Latter, once again conveys the strains of Cary's theme of liberalism.

> The whole affair was a considerable surprise to the young lady. She was quite red in the face. She said it was an outrage. She hadn't known such things could happen in England. And Brightman was not the man she took him for. He was a bad man who had deserted Liberal principles.
>
> (*NHM*, pp. 186-87)

Liberal principles: the experience which teaches respect for human liberty and personal dignity crops up once again, and Sally falls back on the terms of her stepfather and husband to condemn the outrage. And, in the line again drawn between the irresponsibly violent and those with respect for others, the novel's comment on Latter's ultimate act is further prepared.

Early in his career Cary confessed to his wife,

> I can't make a lovely lady in distress without revealing that she is a human being with human weaknesses. I can't manage a hero at all, and I am quite unable to produce a villain, a wicked parent, a cruel mamma, or a cunning uncle.[42]

His sympathy for Jim Latter's dilemma made Latter's hard-hitting, lively monologue one of Cary's most striking essays in characterisation. Admiration for the author's virtuosity in *Not Honour More* is easily transferred to the "villain" himself. This, I think, causes some critics to overlook Jim's inadequacy. Robert Bloom states that "Jim's capacity for pity and his sense of Chester's self-deception are evidence of humanity and intelligence".[43] But such pity as Jim shows is part of his own self-deception. He pities Nimmo only when he himself has the upper hand. Significantly, the passage Bloom takes for his example of Latter's pity, is that where Jim is in the classic position of advantage, having caught Nimmo in his wife's bed:

> I saw the real Nimmo, a miserable old wreck fairly coming to bits with his own putrescence. A canting mummy who talked of liberty and believed in swindling the people. A living lie who'd ended by lying himself into looking-glass land. And from that moment I began to be sorry for the old crook, thrown out on his neck.
>
> (*NHM*, p. 164)

Elsewhere he pities Nina only to avoid acknowledging her willing complicity in Nimmo's schemes.

Jim's failure is the same failure condemned throughout the trilogy—in Pring and in Nimmo's withdrawal from human sympathy after his electoral downfall. In caring less for people than for "honour," he worships an abstraction.

Jim's uncompromisingness and his idealism are measured against Chester's pragmatic compromises in the book's central political event. Cary brings the atmosphere of the General Strike to life by following a selected group of characters through the series of incidents leading up to the climactic Maufe trial.

The trial, which precipitates Jim Latter's crime, also exposes the varied reactions in the community to the strike itself. These reactions recall the evident needs and incipient threats which lay at the heart of the General Strike.[44]

Once again the trial calls attention to the questionable morality of practical politics as practised by Chester Nimmo. Nimmo's effort to avoid conflict with the Left is an attempt by the democrat to stave off potentially destructive revolution. It is also the desperate bid of the politician to rescue his own Liberalism from a death of neglect by both the nation's vocal radical elements and its powerful Conservative rulers.

In the connivance over Maufe's conviction the trilogy's repeated question of means and ends re-emerges. Maufe's guilt of the violent attack on the Communist leader, Pincomb, is never proved in the novel. Nor is his innocence. But there is no doubt that his conviction was accomplished more neatly that it might have been had the accusation lacked the support of Nimmo's headquarters. Nimmo's connivance in bringing Maufe to trial (with the expectation of conviction) is aimed at forestalling Communist claims of victimization and public indignation at the powers of the special constables. This is the compromise which, throughout, Nimmo hopes will avert revolution, prevent violence, and revive support for progress on the Liberal pattern through the efforts of a united Left.

> 'Very lucky I moved so promptly in the Maufe case. It had the best effect on relations here. I saw some of the Labour leaders last night at their H.Q. and I was asked if it was our intention to bring Maufe to trial. They were most comically divided between regrets that they've lost the chance of a real grievance and relief that they won't be forced to back up the Communists . . .'

(*NHM*, p. 217)

Prisoner of Grace and *Except the Lord* made it clear that while ends in politics most often dictate means, the means should not be ultimately inimical to the ends. Politic deceit was justified in Nina's narrative; inhumane disregard for personal liberty was rejected in *Except the Lord*. In this third volume, Jim Latter, the apolitical figure caught up in the political life of the Nimmos, finds himself in what is clearly a political dilemma. His jealousy is not without foundation; yet because he refuses to acknowledge this impulse he cannot take the available legal steps to remedy the situation. Just as Chester dressed his unscrupulous ambition, in *Except the Lord*, in the ideal glow of the promise of radical socialism, and in the name of that ideal committed crimes gainst human liberty, Jim calls his jealousy a sense of honour and in the name of that honour kills his wife. *Except the Lord* has already told us that only a false end dictates such means and that no ideal can justify a violent crime against another's person. It is no accident that Cary, in bringing the picture of Liberalism to a close introduces the idea of Fascism, even mentioning Nazism, in this volume. The trilogy's implicit condemnation of Jim Latter's action becomes a condemnation of Fascism. The practitioners of that ideology, too, showed total disregard for the human right to sanctity of person and for liberty's basis, life itself.

Critical preoccupation with the location of truth in the Nimmo trilogy belittles the brilliant irony of Cary's treatment of truth throughout. Truth motivates the writing of all three narratives. Nina writes because "revelations" are to appear about herself and Chester, and she wants to set the truth against these "stories". Nimmo writes to free the truth of his beliefs from the "spell of words". Latter intends his "statement . . . to have the truth the whole truth and nothing but the truth, so help me God" (*NHM*, p. 27), because the newspaper treatment of his story "cut out the only important bit, the heart of it, the truth" (*NHM*, p. 223). Needless to point out, each of these versions presents a different "truth", none of which can be utterly denied.

Nor are these the only versions current of the Nimmo story. The revelations Nina fears are Sally and Bootham's "'true' story of Chester Nimmo". Aunt Latter, too, is writing her memoirs which, says Nina, "among the half-dozen or so now being written round Chester and his career, may well be the most damaging of all" (*PG*, p. 390). She also refers to the continual assessment of Chester's actions by the press, historians, and biographers. The press is Jim Latter's target, for "they weren't selling truth. They were selling the paper. And the men who write the papers and make them up in the office . . .

can't see the simplest facts . . ." (*NHM*, p. 223). Neither Nina, Chester, nor Jim believes that facts alone guarantee truth.

These characters find that the truth of experience, in addition to that of the written word, can often be called into question. Tom's burlesque of Chester embodies enough of the old statesman's behaviour to upset Nina, and later Chester's own thin and cracking voice as he re-delivers old speeches has the grotesque quality of a caricature. Whether the feeling of peace, or the fact of war, is more real perplexes Nina in Oxford. Goold accuses Chester of hypocrisy, of deserting the people and of gaining the world and losing his soul. But in the course of his own career he gains a manor house with servants, a car, and a knighthood, and casually justifies these extravagances, "the house was 'more convenient', the carriage was 'an economy' . . ." (*PG*, p. 218).

Even Jim Latter practises the politic deception. Nina recalls the saving effect of his feigned confidence during a near-disastrous sailing episode. Nina then compares Nimmo's ability to convince himself and others of his sincere intentions with Jim's.

> No one would dream of calling Jim a hypocrite for pretending to himself and me, in the middle of a violent storm, that we were doing something reasonable and possible. And no one has any right to call Chester, who had ten times more imagination than Jim, a hypocrite for pretending in the middle of a political storm (which went on all his life; he was never "in harbour"—there is no such thing in politics) that he had always meant this or that when, in fact he had only taken note of it as a "way out".
>
> (*PG*, p. 230)[45]

A truth, in Cary's view, can only be known in the context of a real experience.

The ambiguities of *Prisoner of Grace* display the impossibility of discovering an objective truth. From here Cary proceeds to carve out of the confusion his own idea of the nature of truth as subject to reason and love. Chester's childhood memories reveal the importance truth held for the Nimmo children. In the words of Preacher Nimmo, while there is truth in the soul salvation is possible, but "if we deceive ourselves then we have the lie in our soul". Yet a politic lie brings Georgina greater understanding of her father and, with it, deeper devotion to him and all the

228

family. "But from this time he became to her a person who, like ourselves, sometimes needed to be handled, managed, who could not be trusted to know his own advantage" (*ETL*, p. 52). To this responsibility Georgina sacrifices health and happiness, but it saves her from despair by teaching her love.

Similarly, Nimmo says that Nina gave him "the perpetual knowledge of a truth that is truth's very substance, the faith of the heart . . ." (*ETL*, p. 214). While this remark, dictated to Nina and couched in Chester's suspect rhetoric, may have an ironic sound, it nevertheless witnesses to Nina's consistency in service if not in veracity itself. And this consistency which brings about the final Palm Cottage "situation" is of the same nature as Nimmo's consistency in politics. Though he seems to abuse truth in his practice, Nimmo remains loyal to the aims and the fortunes of his party.

Chester understands "how people work"; his imagination grasps their most impulsive workings. This gives him power over Nina who looks for consistency in others in order to accommodate them. She readily sympathises with Tom's predictable follies or with Aunt Latter's characteristic meddling, while Chester's greatest successes enrage her, dependent as they often are on inconsistency and self-deception. Nina learns to accommodate Chester's impulsive nature as she learns to accept the possibility of "impossible" situations. In other words, she learns the inevitability of change and with it the relativity of truth. Nina's discovery repeats Georgina's and Chester's own; in apprehending the relativity of truth the heart is open to sympathy and tolerance, out of which grow love. The opposite to this understanding is Jim Latter's unbending and abstract truth which admits only stark alternatives—right or wrong, love or hate, life or death.

Truth as a moral element in each novel is, by Cary's design, limited by the prejudices and personality of the character who tells the story. The trilogy's multiple viewpoint exposes the relative nature of truth. Theme and morality are expressed through character because for Cary they had to be inherent in the dramatic situation itself, just as truth had to be located in a real experience.

Cary augments the verisimilitude of the trilogy by using the objective truth of the progress of historical events. By weaving this truth into the lives and actions of his characters he creates a character for history itself. Liberalism teaches respect for human liberty—more specifically for the freedom of humans to fulfil themselves emotionally, intellectually, and physically in the secure possession of life itself. Liberalism as a political force in Britain has declined, but not without bequeathing many of its attitudes to its successors on both left and right. Cary's trilogy captures this victory-in-defeat. Its theme and Cary's technique uphold and illustrate the principles of Liberalism at the same time that the novels portray vividly and memorably the stages and causes of the Liberal downfall. For Cary the value of human life was supreme. In affirming this truth he and Nimmo unite to make the trilogy a statement as well as a picture of Liberalism.

NOTES

1. Ms. Cary Adds. III:1.
2. In early drafts of *Except the Lord* Nimmo indicts the Fabians for assuming an elitist authoritarian attitude and therefore denying liberty to a people regarded as inferior in wisdom.
3. "How to Conquer Unemployment", Labour Party Pamphlet (London, 1929), p. 7.
4. Joyce Cary, *Not Honour More*, Carfax ed. (Michael Joseph, 1955), p. 166. Hereafter abbreviated *NHM* and cited in the text.
5. Alfred Gollin, *Proconsul in Politics* (Anthony Blond, 1964), p. 385.
6. This was not an unusual attitude at the time. Prior to the General Strike, many of the organisations which proved precursors to Mosley's 1932 British Union of Fascists did not openly describe themselves as Fascist. The term connoted foreign influence, and even the British Fascists altered their name soon after their founding in May 1923, from British Fascisti in order to eschew foreign associations. Among other groups, the paramilitary Ulster Volunteers, later lauded by the Fascists, had a purely local concern. The anti-Communist and nationalistic British Empire Union and National Citizens' union considered themselves pre-Fascist and greeted the rise of Fascism with casual acquiescence, but essential aloofness. Robert Benewick, *Political Violence and Public Order* (Allen Lane the Penguin Press, 1969), p. 24-42.
7. Among the leaders of the pre-1926 British Fascists were many retired military officers and the later British Union of Fascists was led by men principally "solidly middle class", many of whom "had not only done military service but had been officers". Benewick, pp. 32, 127.
8. By acknowledging the general trend towards socialism in the structure of the trilogy, Cary avoided having to portray members of the working class.

This was a task of which Cary was incapable, as the failure of the *Castle Corner* sequels suggests. Although his notes for "Green Jerusalem" read, "wanted in this book. Action in . . . English lower class", he never attempted to sketch scenes of working class life. Ms. Cary 263, N.54.

9. *Liberalism*, pp. 116-17.

10. See, for example, "The Foundation of Liberalism", *The Spectator*, 17 March 1939, p. 450; "Proposals for Peace—III", *Nation*, 10 January 1953, p. 28; "Is the World Getting Anywhere?" *Vogue* (U.S.), CXXIII (15 March 1954), pp. 68-71; "L'influence britannique dans la révolution libérale", trans. M. Bouvier, *Comprendre*, nos. 13-14 (June 1955), pp. 45-51; "Faith in Liberty", *Time and Tide*, XXXVI, no. 29 (16 July 1955), pp. 933-34; "Political and Personal Morality", *Saturday Review*, 31 December 1955, pp. 5, 6, 31, 32; "Britain is Strong in Herself", *New York Times Magazine*, 22 April 1956, pp, 12, 32, 33; "Joyce Cary's Last Look at his Worlds", *Vogue* (U.S.), CXXX (15 August 1957), pp. 96-7, 150-51, 153; "Peace and Liberty", Ms. Cary 243.

11. I have used the form "The Captive and Free", usually abbreviated C and F by Cary in his notes, to distinguish this work from the later novel *The Captive and the Free*, published posthumously by Mrs. Winifred Davin in 1958.

12. One section of Cary's notes refers to Juno's story as "The Turkish House", a title Cary later tentatively gave to *Prisoner of Grace* (Ms. Cary 113-15). "Juno" is also a source for *A Fearful Joy* and *The Moonlight* (Ms. Cary 173-74, 281, 282).

13. "Unfinished Novels", broadcast 2 February 1957. Text in Ms. Cary 249, p. 7. Cary's description in this talk is somewhat misleading. He conflates the several stages outlined above in the development of *Prisoner of Grace*, and his recollection of the way Nina's "political job" leapt into his mind and the plot fell together gains instantaneousness and facility from hindsight.

14. David Lloyd George, "Through Terror to Triumph" (Liberal Publications Department, 1914), pp. 3, 13.

15. David Lloyd George, *War Memoirs*, II (Odhams Press, [n.d.]), p. 2017. Cary Collection of Printed Books, B.393.

16. Lucy Masterman, *C.F.G. Masterman A Biography* (Nicholson and Watson, 1939), p. 143.

17. Trevor Wilson, *The Downfall of the Liberal Party*, 1914-1935 (Collins, 1966), p. 339.

18. Letter to Dorothy Erskine Muir, 21 September 1952, Ms. Cary Adds. IV: 179. Cary had not only historical figures as exemplars; he was a careful reader of the novels of Disraeli, Trollope, and other writers of "political" fiction.

19. The Liberal revival of 1906 owed much to reaction on the part of nonconformists to the Conservative Education Acts of 1902-3 which compelled support of Church Schools through the rates. Many nonconformists who had drifted away in the 1880s and 1890s returned to Liberalism in protest against the Acts. Paul Thompson, *Socialists, Liberals and Labour* (Routledge and Kegan Paul, 1967), p. 168.

20. E.T. Raymond, *Mr. Lloyd George: A Biography* (W. Collins, [1922]), p. 105.

21. *Proconsul in Politics*, p. 386.
22. "Joyce Cary's Last Look at His Worlds", *Selected Essays*, p. 242.
23. "Liberalism and Liberty", p. 10. Italics supplied.
24. 30 December 1952, Ms. Cary Adds. III: 112.
25. 25 May 1953, Ms. Cary Adds. III: 137.
26. *Liberalism*, p. 147.
27. *Mr. Lloyd George*, pp. 13, 17.
28. Listed among Cary's research materials are *Church Manual*, 1940; *Catalogue of Seventhday Baptist publications in America and Great Britain*, 1893; *Catalogue of Seventh-day Baptists in Europe and America*, 1910; "The seventh-day-man in his vanity of his Jewish sabbath, and presumptuous contempt of gospel rest, together with the sabbath-day error", 1724; *Seventh Day Baptist Year Book*, 1922; James Black, "The Oddity of the Seventh Day Adventist", *New Forms of the Old Faith*, 1948; "Seventh-day adventism", *Encyclopaedia Britannica*.
29. Cary annotated his copy of Edmund Gosse's biography of his father, *The Life of Philip Henry Gosse* (Kegan Paul, Trench, Trubner, 1890). Cary Collection of Printed Books, B.122.
30. Edmund Gosse, *Father and Son* (William Heinemann, 1907), p. 61.
31. Hubert Llewellyn Smith and Vaughan Nash, *The Story of the Dockers' Strike* (T. Fisher Unwin, 1889), p. 31.
32. Sidney and Beatrice Webb, *The History of Trade Unionism*, revised ed., extended to 1920 (Longmans, Green, 1920), pp. 458-61.
33. *Father and Son*, p. 18.
34. Joyce Cary, *The Captive and The Free*, Carfax ed. (Michael Joseph, 1963), pp. 298-300.
35. Letter to Mrs. Cary, 30 May 1919. Ms. Cary 309.
36. Letters to Mrs. Cary, 11 May 1926, from S.S. Beltara and S.S. Smolensk. Ms. Cary 311.
37. Letter to Mrs. Cary, 14 November 1918. Ms Cary 308.
38. Letter to Mrs. Cary, 16 March 1919. Ms. Cary 309.
39. *Cock Jarvis*, p. 24.
40. Sir Oswald Mosley, *My Life* (Thomas Nelson and Sons, 1968), pp. 21-2.
41. Richard Lovelace, "To Lucasta, Going to the Warres," *The Poems of Richard Lovelace*, ed. C.H. Wilkinson (Oxford, Clarendon Press, 1930, reprinted 1953), p. 18. (The concluding lines are "I could not love thee (Deare) so much,/Lov'd I not Honour more.") Cary's use of the poem is especially ironic in light of events in *Prisoner of Grace*. The poem begins, "Tell me not (Sweet) I am unkinde,/That from the Nunnerie/Of thy chaste breast, and quiet minde,/To Warre and Armes I flie." In *Prisoner of Grace* Jim flies back to his regiment in the middle of his leave, upon learning that Nina is pregnant. His ally, Aunt Latter, sums up the nature of his honour, "You know perfectly well that Jim can't marry you. No subaltern in the 14th is allowed to marry . You don't want to force him out of the regiment" (*PG*, p. 21). The irony is intensified when Jim suddenly and inexplicably leaves the army, without apparent concern for the precious honour.
42. Letter to Mrs. Cary, 30 September 1919. Ms Cary 310.

43. *The Indeterminate World: A Study of the Novels of Joyce Cary* (Philadelphia, University of Pennsylvania Press, 1962), p. 187.
44. To construct Jim's role in the General Strike Cary consulted W. Arbuthnot Lane of the Metropolitan Special Constabulary who had himself been a special at the time. Letter to Cary from W. Arbuthnot Lane, 14 September 1954, Ms. Cary 289, N.154.
45. The image of politics as a storm was probably suggested to Cary by a passage he annotated in Lord Rosebery's *Miscellanies* which begins, "There is never a calm on the political ocean. . . ." *Miscellanies Literary and Historical*, II (Hodder and Stoughton, 1921), p. 213, Cary Collection of Printed Books, B.168.

Selected Bibliography

JOYCE CARY:
LIST OF WORKS CITED

Collection of The Papers of Joyce Cary in the Bodleian Library, Oxford.
Cary Collection of Printed Books in the Bodleian Library, Oxford.

Novels

Aissa Saved, Carfax ed. (Michael Joseph, 1952, first published 1932).

An American Visitor, Carfax ed. (Michael Joseph, 1952, first published 1933).

The African Witch, Carfax ed. (Michael Joseph, 1951, first published 1936).

Castle Corner, Carfax ed. (Michael Joseph, 1952, first published 1938).

Mister Johnson, Carfax ed. (Michael Joseph, 1952, first published 1939).

Charley is My Darling, Carfax ed. (Michael Joseph, 1951, first published 1940).

A House of Children, Carfax ed. (Michael Joseph, 1951, first published 1941).

Herself Surprised, Carfax ed. (Michael Joseph, 1951, first published 1941).

To Be a Pilgrim, Carfax ed. (Michael Joseph, 1951, first published 1942).

The Horse's Mouth, ed. Andrew Wright, authorised ed. (George Rainbird in assoc. with Michael Joseph, 1957, first published 1944, Carfax ed., 1951).

The Moonlight, Carfax ed. (Michael Joseph, 1952, first published 1946).

A Fearful Joy, Carfax ed. (Michael Joseph, 1952, first published 1949).

Prisoner of Grace, Carfax ed. (Michael Joseph, 1954, first published 1952).

Except the Lord (Michael Joseph, 1953).

Not Honour More, Carfax ed. (Michael Joseph, 1966, first published 1955).

The Captive and the Free, ed. Winifred Davin, Carfax ed. (Michael Joseph, 1963, first published 1959).

Cock Jarvis, ed. A.G. Bishop (Michael Joseph, 1974).

Non-Fiction

Art and Reality (Cambridge, Cambridge University Press, 1958).

Britain and West Africa (Longmans, Green, 1946).

'Britain is Strong in Herself', *New York Times Magazine*, 22 April 1956, pp. 12, 32, 33.

The Case for African Freedom (Secker and Warburg, 1941).

"Faith in Liberty", *Time and Tide*, XXXVI, no. 29 (16 July 1955), pp. 933-34.

"The Foundation of Liberalism", *The Spectator*, 17 March 1939, p. 450.

"Is the World Getting Anywhere?" *Vogue* (U.S.), CXXIII (15 March 1954), pp. 68-71, published as "The Idea of Progress", *The Cornhill*, no. 1000 (Summer 1954), pp. 331-37.

"Notes sur l'Art et la Liberté ", trans. A. Prudhommeaux, *Preuves*, XLII (August 1954), pp. 28-32.

"The Novelist at Work: A Conversation Between Joyce Cary and Lord David Cecil", *Adam International Review*, XVIII, Nos. 212-13 (November-December 1950), pp. 15-25.

"The Old Strife at Plant's", *Harper's Magazine*, CCI (August 1950), pp. 80-96; printed with illustrations by the author at the New Bodleian, Oxford, 1956.

Power in Men (Nicholson and Watson, 1939).

Process of Real Freedom (Michael Joseph, 1943).

"Proposals for Peace—III", *Nation*, 10 January 1953, p. 28.

"The Revolution of the Women", *Vogue* (U.S.), CXXVI (15 March 1951), pp. 99, 100, 149, Selected Essays, ed. A.G. Bishop (Michael Joseph, 1976).

Verse by Arthur Cary (Edinburgh, Robert Grant, 1908).

Other Sources:

I. Selected Works Consulted from Cary Collection of Printed Books

Asquith, Margot, *The Autobiography of Margot Asquith* (Thornton Butterworth, 1920). Cary B.94.

Barker, Ernest, *Political Thought in England From Herbert Spencer to the Present Day* (Williams and Norgate, 1915, repr. 1924). Cary B.363

Baudelaire, Charles, *Les Fleurs du Mal*, ed. Enid Starkie (Oxford, Blackwell, 1942). Cary B.204.

Berger, P., *William Blake Poet and Mystic*, trans. Daniel H. Conner (Chapman and Hall, 1914). Cary C. 105.

The Holy Bible, (Eyre and Spottiswoode, [n.d.]). Cary B.368.

Blake, William, *Poems and Prophecies*, ed. Max Plowman (Everyman's Library, J.M. Dent, 1927, repr. 1942), Cary B.98.

Cezanne, Paul, *Letters*, ed. John Rewald, 2nd ed. (Oxford, Bruno Cassirer,1944). Cary B,371.

Charles, C.H., *Love Letters of Great Men and Women* (Stanley Paul, 1924). Cary B.106.

Cripps, Sir Stafford, *Democracy Up-to-Date* (George Allen and Unwin, 1939). Cary C.1364.

Darwin, Charles, *The Expression of the Emotions in Man and Animals*, rev. and abr. by Surgeon-Rear-Admiral C.M. Beadnell (Watts, 1934). Cary B.310.

Disraeli, Benjamin, *Coningsby* (Everyman's Library, Dent, [n.d.]). Cary B.113.

Disraeli, Benjamin, *Endymion*, 3 vols. (Longmans, Green, 1880). Cary B.114, B.115, B.116.

Disraeli, Benjamin, *The Letters of Disraeli to Lady Bradford and Lady Chesterfield*, ed. the Marquis of Zetland, 2 vols. (Ernest Benn, 1929), Cary B.117, B.118.

Disraeli, Benjamn, *Lord Beaconsfield's Letters: 1830-1852*, ed. Ralph Disraeli (John Murray, 1887). Cary B.119.

Dostoevsky, Fyodor, *Crime and Punishment*, trans. Constance Garnett (William Heinemann, 1914, repr. 1917). Cary B.208; trans. Jessie Coulson (Oxford University Press, 1953). Cary B.209.

Dostoevsky, Fyodor, *The Brothers Karamazov*, trans. Constance Garnett (William Heinemann, 1912, repr. 1930). Cary B. 207.

Gosse, Edmund, *The Life of Philip Henry Gosse* (Kegan Paul, Trench, Trübner, 1890). Cary B.122.

Hankey, Donald, *A Student in Arms* (Andrew Melrose, 1916). Cary C.322.

Huxley, Aldous, *Point Counter Point* (Chatto and Windus, 1930). Cary C.367.

Keynes, John Maynard, *The End of Laissez-Faire* (Hogarth Press, 1926). Cary B.389.

Lawrence, D.H., *Kangaroo* (Martin Secker, 1923). Cary B.146.

Lloyd, Lord of Dolobran, "Leadership in Democracy", Walker Trust Lectures on Leadership No. VII (Oxford University Press, 1939). Cary B.391.

Lloyd George, David, *War Memoirs of David Lloyd George*, new ed., 2 vols. (Odhams Press, [1938]). Cary B.392, B.393.

Locke, John, *An Essay Concerning Human Understanding* (J.F. Dove, 1828). Cary B.326.

Maeterlinck, Maurice, *The Life of the Bee*, trans. Alfred Sutro (George Allen, 1901, repr. 1908). Cary B. 232.

Maeterlinck, Maurice, *The Life of the White ant*, trans. Alfred Sutro (George Allen and Unwin, 1927). Cary B.397.

Mansfield, Katherine, *Journal of Katherine Mansfield*, ed. J. Middleton Murry (Constable, 1927). Cary C.449; definitive ed. (Constable, 1954). Cary C.448.

Mansfield, Katherine, *Katherine Mansfield's Letters to John Middleton Murry 1913-22*, ed. J. Middleton Murry (Constable, 1951). Cary B.151.

Mill, John Stuart, *On Liberty*, 3rd ed. (Longman, Roberts and Green, 1864). Cary B.401; The Scott Library ed. (Walter Scott, [1901]), Cary B.402.

Moore, George, *Confessions of a Young Man* (William Heinemann, 1917). Cary B.155.

Moore, George, *Hail and Farewell!: Ave*, 2nd ed. (William Heinemann, 1914, reprinted 1921 [first printed 1911]). Cary C. 486.

Moore, George, *Hail and Farewell!: Salve* (William Heinemann, 1920 [first published 1912]). Cary C.487.

Moore, George, *Hail and Farewell!: Vale* (William Heinemann, 1920 [first published 1914]). Cary C.488.

Moore, George, *Impressions and Opinions* (T. Werner Laurie, 1914). Cary B.156.

Moore, George, *Memoirs of my Dead Life*, limited ed. no. 189 (William Heinemann, 1921). Cary C.491.

Morley, John, Viscount, *On Compromise* (Watts, [1933]). Cary B. 404.

Private No. 940, "On the Remainder of our Front —" (Harrison, 1917). Cary B.162.

Proust, Marcel, *A La Recherche du Temps Perdu*, 15 vols., *Le Temps Retrouvé*, XIV, XV (Paris Editions de la Nouvelle Revue Francaise, 1949 [first published 1927]). Cary C.953, C.954.

Proust, Marcel, *Du Côté de Chez Swann*, 2 vols. (Paris, Editions de la Nouvelle Revue Francaise, 1922 [first published 1919]). Cary C.961, C.962.

Proust, Marcel, *Letters of Marcel Proust*, trans. Mina Curtiss (Chatto and Windus, 1950). Cary B.237.

Proust, Marcel, *Remembrance of Things Past*
Swann's Way, trans. C.K. Scott Moncrieff, Phoenix Library ed. II (Chatto and Windus, 1929 [first published in English, 1922]). Cary C.964.

Within a Budding Grove, trans. C.K. Scott Moncrieff, Phoenix Library ed. I (Chatto and Windus, 1924). Cary C.965; II, Phoenix Library ed. (Chatto and Windus, 1929 [first published in English, 1924]). Cary C.966.

The Guermantes Way, trans. C.K. Scott Moncrieff, Phoenix Library ed., 2 vols. (Chatto and Windus, 1930 [first published in English, 1925]). Cary B.240, B.241.

Cities of the Plain, trans. C.K. Scott Moncrieff, Phoenix Library ed., 2 vols. (Chatto and Windus, 1936 [first published in English, 1929]). Cary B.238, B.239.

The Captive, trans. C.K. Scott Moncrieff, Uniform ed., 2 vols. (Chatto and Windus, 1941 [first published in English, 1929]). Cary B.242, B.243.

The Sweet Cheat Gone, trans. C.K. Scott Moncrieff, Uniform ed., Chatto and Windus, 1941 [first published in English, 1930]). Cary B.244.

Time Regained, trans. Stephen Hudson, Phoenix Library ed. (Chatto and Windus, 1941 [first published in English 1931]). Cary B.245.

Rhythm, nos. 1, 1 (2nd impr.), 2, 4-14 (1911-13). Cary C.549/1, 1*, 2, 4-14.

Rosebery, Lord, *Miscellanies Literary and Historical*, 2 vols. (Hodder and Stoughton, 1921). Cary B.167, B.168.

Shaw, Bernard et al., *Fabian Essays in Socialism*, 5th ed. (Fabian Society and George Allen and Unwin, 1931). Cary C.1458.

Spencer, Herbert, *Essays: Scientific, Political, and Speculative*, III (William and Norgate, 1875). Cary B.418.

Stocks, J.L. [and] Gilbert Ryle, *John Locke Tercentenary Addresses* (Oxford University Press, 1933). Cary B.327.

Strachey, Lytton, *Eminent Victorians* (Chatto and Windus, 1918). Cary B. 171.

Taylor, Jeremy, *Holy Dying* (Halifax, Milner and Sowerby, 1852). Cary B. 177.

Tolstaya, Gratinya Sofia Andreevna, *The Countess Tolstoy's Later Diary 1891-1897*, trans. Alexander Werth (Victor Gollancz, 1929). Cary B.287.

Tolstaya, Gratinya Sofia Andreevna, *The Diary of Tolstoy's Wife: 1860-1891*, trans. Alexander Werth (Victor Gollancz, 1928). Cary B.286.

Tolstoy, Leo, *The Kreutzer Sonata and Other Stories*, ed. Aylmer Maude, The World's Classics (Oxford University Press, 1924, reprinted 1926 [first published 1899]). Cary B.283.

Wesley, John, *John Wesley's Journal*, abr. by Percy Livingstone Parker (Isbister, 1903). Cary B.187.

II. Selected Works Consulted

Adam International Review, XVIII, nos. 212-13 (November-December 1950).

Adams, Hazard, "Blake and Gulley Jimson: English Symbolists", *Critique*, III (Spring-Fall 1959), pp. 3-14.

Adams, Hazard, "Joyce Cary's Three Speakers", *Modern Fiction Studies*, V, no. 2 (Summer 1959), pp. 108-20.

Aldred, Guy, *Essays in Revolt*, 2 vols. (Glasgow, The Strickland Press, 1940).

Allen, Walter, *Joyce Cary*, Writers and their Work: No. 41 (Longmans, Green, rev. ed., 1954).

Bailey, W. Milne, *Trade Unions and the State* (George Allen and Unwin, 1934).

Beebe, Maurice, James Lee, and Sam Henderson, "Criticism of Joyce Cary: A Selected Checklist", *Modern Fiction Studies*, IX, no. 3 (Autumn 1963), pp. 284-88.

Behrs, C.A., *Recollections of Count Leo Tolstoy, together with A Letter to the Women of France on the Kreutzer Sonata*, trans. Charles Edward Turner (William Heinemann, 1893).

237

Benewick, Robert, *Political Violence and Public Order* (Allen Lane The Penguin Press, 1969).

Bergson, Henri, *Laughter: An Essay on the Meaning of the Comic*, trans. Cloudesley Brereton and Fred Rothwell (Macmillan, 1911).

Bergson, Henri, *Matter and Memory*, trans. Nancy Margaret Paul and W. Scott Palmer (Swan Sonnenschein and Co., 1911).

Black, James, *New Forms of the Old Faith* (Thomas Nelson, 1948).

Blake, William, *The Complete Writings of William Blake*, ed. Geoffrey Keynes (Oxford University Press, 1966).

Blease, W. Lyon, *A Short History of English Liberalism* (T. Fisher Unwin, 1913).

Bloom, Robert, *The Indeterminate World: A Study of the Novels of Joyce Cary* (Philadelphia, University of Pennsylvania Press, 1962).

Booth, Wayne, *The Rhetoric of Fiction* (Chicago, University of Chicago Press, 1961).

Bradbury, Malcolm, *Eating People is Wrong*, re-issued with new Introduction (Secker and Warburg, 1976).

Brodrick, The Hon. George C., *Liberal Principles* (The Liberal Central Association, 1877).

Bullock, Alan and Maurice Shock, eds., *The Liberal Tradition from Fox to Keynes* (Adam and Charles Black, 1956).

Bunyan, John, *The Pilgrim's Progress*, ed. James Blanton Wharey, 2nd ed., revised by Roger Sharrock (Oxford, The Clarendon Press, 1960).

Carlyle, Thomas, *Critical and Miscellaneous Essays*, 5 vols. (Chapman and Hall, 1899).

Cecil, Robert, *Life in Edwardian England* (B.T. Batsford, 1969).

Cohen, Nathan, "A Conversation with Joyce Cary", *The Tamarack Review*, no.3 (Spring 1957), pp. 5-15.

Cole, G.D.H., *British Working Class Politics 1832-Working Class Movement 1789-1927*, complete ed. (George Allen and Unwin, 1932).

Cole, G.D.H. *British Working Class Politics 1832-1914* (George Routledge, 1941).

Collis, Louise, *A Private View of Stanely Spencer* (Heinemann, 1972).

Collis, Maurice, *Stanley Spencer: A Biography* (Harvill Press, 1962).

Craig, David, "Idea and Imagination: A Study of Joyce Cary", *Fox* [c. 1954], pp. 3-10.

Crook, Wilfred Harris, *The General Strike* (Chapel Hill, The University of North Carolina Press, 1931).

Fisher, Barbara, "Joyce Cary's Published Writings", *The Bodleian Library Record*, VII, no. 4 (April 1970), pp. 213-28.

Foot, Michael, *Aneurin Bevan: A Biography, Volume One: 1897-1945* (MacGibbon and Kee, 1962).

Foster, Malcolm, "Fell of the Lion, Fleece of the sheep", *Modern Fiction Studies*, IX, no. 3 (Autumn 1963), pp. 257-62.

Foster, Malcom, *Joyce Cary: A Biography* (Boston, Houghton Mifflin, 1968).

Gilbert, Martin, ed., *Lloyd George* (New Jersey, Prentice-Hall, [1968]).

Gollin, Alfred, *Proconsul in Politics: A Study of Lord Milner in Opposition and Power* (Anthony Blond, 1964).

Gosse, Edmund, *Father and Son* (William Heinemann, 1907).

Hamilton, Kenneth, "Boon or Thorn? Joyce Cary and Samuel Beckett on Human Life", *Dalhousie Review*, XXXVIII (Winter 1959), pp. 433-42.

Hardy, Barbara, "Form in Joyce Cary's Novels", *Essays in Criticism*, IV (1954), pp. 180-90.

Harrison, Fairfax, *The Devon Carys*, 2 vols. (New York, The DeVinne Press, 1920).

Hobhouse, L.T., *Liberalism* (Williams and Norgate, 1911).

Hoffman, Charles G., "The Genesis and Development of Joyce Cary's First Trilogy", *PMLA*, LXXVIII (September 1963). pp. 431-39.

Hoffman, Charles G., *Joyce Cary: The Comedy of Freedom* (Pittsburgh, The University of Pittsburgh Press, 1964).

Hoffman, Charles G., "'They Want to Be Happy": Joyce Cary's Unfinished *Castle Corner Series*", *Modern Fiction Studies*, IX, no. 3 (Autumn 1963), pp. 217-25.

"How to Conquer Unemployment", Labour Party Pamphlet (London, 1929).

Howe, Irving, *Politics and the Novel* (New York, Horizon Press Books, 1957).

Hughes, Richard, "Joyce Cary", *The Spectator*, 18 December 1953, pp. 738-39.

Hutt, Allen, *The Post-War History of the British Working Class* (Victor Gollancz, 1937).

Hynes, Samuel, *The Edwardian Turn of Mind* (Princeton, Princeton University Press, 1968).

Johnson, Pamela Hansford, "Three Novelists and the Drawing of Character: C.P. Snow,

Joyce Cary, and Ivy Compton-Burnett", *Essays and Studies*, N.S. III (1950), pp. 82-99.

Karl, Frederick R., "Joyce Cary: The Moralist as Novelist", *A Reader's Guide to the Contemporary English Novel* (Thames and Hudson, 1963).

Kerr, Elizabeth M., "Joyce Cary's Second Trilogy", *University of Toronto Quarterly*, XXIX, no. 3 (April 1960), pp. 310-25.

Kettle, Arnold, *An Introduction to the English Novel*, 2 vols. (Hutchinson's University Library, 1951).

Killam, G.D., *Africa in English Fiction, 1874-1939* (Ibadan, Ibadan University Press, 1968).

King, Carlyle, "Joyce Cary and the Creative Imagination", *The Tamarack Review*, no. 10 (Winter 1959), pp. 39-51.

Larsen, Golden L., *The Dark Descent: Social Change and Moral Responsibility in the Novels of Joyce Cary* (Michael Joseph, 1965).

Lea, F.A., *The Life of John Middleton Murry* (Methuen, 1959).

Lloyd George, David, "Liberalism and Liberty", a speech to the London Liberal Federation at the National Liberal Club, London, 12 May 1924. Liberal Publication Department.

Lloyd George, David, "Through Terror to Triumph", Speech delivered 19 September 1914 at the Queen's Hall, London (Liberal Publication Department, 1914).

Lovelace, Richard, *The Poems of Richard Lovelace*, ed. C.H. Wilkinson (Oxford, Clarendon Press, 1930, reprinted 1953).

Mahood, M.M., *Joyce Cary's Africa* (Methuen, 1964).

Masterman, C.F.G., *The Condition of England* (Metheun, 1909).

Masterman, C.F.G., *The New Liberalism* (Leonard Parsons, 1920).

Masterman, C.F.G., *In Peril of Change: Essays written in time of tranquillity* (T. Fisher Unwin, 1905).

Masterman, Lucy, *C.F.G. Masterman: A Biography* (Nicholson and Watson, 1939).

Meredith, George, *An Essay on Comedy and the Uses of the Comic Spirit*, *New Quarterly Magazine*, VIII (January-July 1877), pp. 1-40.

Mill, John Stuart, *Autobiography*, ed. J. Stillinger (Oxford University Press, 1971).

Mill, John Stuart, *Three Essays: On Liberty, Representative Government, The Subjection of Women* (Oxford University Press, 1975).

Mill, John Stuart, *Utilitarianism, On Liberty, Considerations of Representative Government* (Everyman, 1910).

Mitchell, Giles, *The Art Theme in Joyce Cary's First Trilogy* (The Hague, Mouton, 1971).

Mitchell, Giles, "Joyce Cary's *Prisoner of Grace*", *Modern Fiction Studies*, IX, no. 3 (Autumn 1963), pp. 263-75.

Modern Fiction Studies, IX, no. 3 (Autumn 1963). Joyce Cary special number.

Monas, Sidney, "What to Do with a Drunken Sailor", *Hudson Review*, III (Autumn 1950), pp. 466-74.

Morley, John, *On Compromise*, new ed. (Macmillan, 1923).

Mosley, Sir Oswald, *My Life* (Thomas Nelson, 1968).

Murry, John Middleton, *Between Two Worlds: An Autobiography* (Jonathan Cape, 1935).

Murry, John Middleton, "Coming to London", *The London Magazine*, III, no. 7 (July 1956), pp. 30-7.

Murry, John Middleton, *William Blake* (Jonathan Cape, 1933).

The New Age, VII, no. 2 (12 May 1910), pp. 25-7.

Obumselu, B., "The Theme of Creativity in Joyce Cary's Novels", D. Phil. thesis, Oxford University, 1966.

O'Connor, William Van, *Joyce Cary*, Columbia Essays in Modern Writers, no. 16 (New York, Columbia University Press, 1966).

Quigley, J., *Leandro Ramon Garrido: His Life and Art* (Duckworth, 1913).

Raymond, E.T., *Mr. Lloyd George: A Biography* (W. Collins, [1922]).

Reid, Andrew, ed., *Why I am a Liberal* (Cassel, 1885).

Runciman, The Rt. Hon. Walter, M.P., *Liberalism As I See It* (Ernest Benn, 1927).

Ryan, Marjorie, "An Interpretation of Joyce Cary's *The Horse's Mouth*", *Critique*, II (Spring-Summer 1958), pp. 29-38.

Smith, Hubert Llewellyn and Vaughan Nash, *The Story of the Dockers' Strike* (T. Fisher Unwin, 1889).

Spencer, Gilbert, *Stanley Spencer* (Victor Gollancz, 1961).

Stanley Spencer 1891-1959, intr. Elizabeth Rothenstein, British Painters Series (Beaverbrook Newspapers, 1962).

Starkie, Enid, *A Lady's Child* (Faber and Faber, 1941).

Starkie, Enid, "Joyce Cary: A Personal

Portrait", *Virginia Quarterly Review*, XXXVII, no. 1 (Winter 1961), pp. 110-34.

Stevenson, Lionel, "Joyce Cary and the Anglo-Irish Tradition", *Modern Fiction Studies*, IX, no. 3 (Autumn 1963), pp. 210-16.

Stockholder, Fred, "The Triple Vision in Joyce Cary's First Trilogy", *Modern Fiction Studies*, IX, no. 3 (Autumn 1963), pp. 231-44.

Tawney, R.H., *Religion and the Rise of Capitalism* (John Murray, 1926).

Thompson, Paul, *Socialists, Liberals and Labour: The Struggle for London 1885-1914* (Routledge and Kegan Paul, 1967).

Thornton, A.P., *The Imperial Idea and its Enemies: A Study in British Power* (Macmillan, 1959).

Vincent, J.R., *The Formation of the British Liberal Party, 1857-1868*, 2nd ed. (Hassocks, The Harvester Press, 1976).

Webb, Sidney and Beatrice, *The History of Trade Unionism*, revised ed. (Longmans, Green, 1920).

Wilson, Trevor, *The Downfall of the Liberal Party, 1914-1935* (Collins, 1966).

Wolkenfeld, Jack, *Joyce Cary: The Developing Style* (New York, New York University Press, 1968).

Woodcock, George, "Citizens of Babel: A Study of Joyce Cary", *Queens Quarterly*, LXIII (Summer 1956), pp. 236-46.

Wright, Andrew, *Joyce Cary: A Preface to his Novels* (Chatto and Windus, 1958).

Index